SPITFIRES
AND
POLISHED METAL

SPITFIRES
AND
POLISHED METAL
Restoring the Classic Fighter

Researched and written by
Graham Moss

Photography by
Barry McKee

MBI Publishing Company

This edition first published in 1999 by MBI Publishing Company,
729 Prospect Avenue, PO Box 1, Osceola, WI 54020-0001 USA.

© 1999 Graham Moss and Barry McKee

Previously published by Airlife Publishing Ltd, Shrewsbury, England.

MBI Publishing Company books are also available at discounts in
bulk quantity for industrial or sales-promotional use. For details
write to Special Sales Manager at Motorbooks International Wholesalers & Distributors,
729 Prospect Avenue, PO Box 1, Osceola, WI 54020-0001 USA.

Library of Congress Cataloging-in-Publication Data available

ISBN 0-7603-0741-5

Printed in Hong Kong

(OPPOSITE): Mk XVIe TD248 provides the backdrop in this group shot. In the middle of the front row is wartime Spitfire test pilot Alex Henshaw. On his immediate left is Clive Denney, Tim Routsis and Air Vice-Marshal Sir John Allison.

Foreword

When asked to write this foreword, I willingly agreed, having visited Audley End on a number of occasions. Not only did I find this little grass airfield had a rustic charm all of its own but that opening the large hangar doors revealed an aeronautical engineer's delight. It exuded a businesslike, professional atmosphere amidst an array of vintage engines, airframes and parts that were slowly but surely being restored to their former glory. There was no doubt in my mind that this small team made up of Tim Routsis, Ian Warren and Clive Denney were not only experts in their own field but also loved the work in which they were engaged. In saying that, I could never overlook Linda Denney, whom I suspect worked harder than anyone to keep the whole show so immaculately clean.

This is not a book for the frivolous or lighthearted, nor does it concern flying of any consequence. It is a very well-researched compilation of all the various marks of Spitfires and narrated in a manner that will not overburden the reader with obscure technicalities. It also contains data that I have not seen before, particularly details of the terrible misuse of the RAF Entrance Gate Spitfires, that turned out to be the means by which Historic Flying first got off the ground. There is also an up-to-date record of all the different marks of Spitfires in the world which are either fully restored and flying or are in the process of being restored. To me, however, the most valuable part of this excellent book is the easy, readable style in which detailed descriptions are given for the 'whys and wherefores' of each particular alteration. The Spitfire's absolute necessity in those traumatic years of war is also described.

Although I was deeply involved, from start to finish, with this dramatic saga, I became more absorbed as I perused each chapter. Barry McKee and Graham Moss are to be congratulated on a fine piece of work that I am quite sure will be welcomed wholeheartedly by that loyal group of Spitfire devotees concerned with its remarkable history.

It is now over fifty-two years since I flight-tested my last fighting aircraft – a Seafire 16. This was the climax to six years of strenuous, always demanding and at times, dangerous association with the incomparable Spitfire. Because it is known that I flew more of this unique machine and its variations than anyone, I am expected to quote facts and figures without hesitation. Nothing could be further from the truth. With the passage of so much time, the mind can play many tricks and I, for one, am delighted to have such a reliable reference, rather than having to 'wade' through many almost illegible logbooks and other well-thumbed technical publications.

Alex Henshaw

FOOTNOTE:
Alex Henshaw was invited to test fly Supermarine Spitfires on the outbreak of World War II. After six months at Eastleigh he was appointed Chief Test Pilot at the huge Spitfire and Lancaster works at Castle Bromwich, near Birmingham. During over five years of war, 37,000 test-flight sorties were carried out.

He won his first accolade when he was awarded the Siddeley Trophy as a boy in the 1933 King's Cup Race, and in 1938 won this event at the fastest speed ever recorded. The next year he broke all records to Cape Town and back. This record not only stands today as a solo flight but is also arguably the most outstanding solo flight in the history of aviation. He was awarded the Britannia Trophy for this feat and an MBE for his role as test pilot. He received his most recent award last year when HRH The Duke of Edinburgh gave him the Jeffrey Quill Medallion on behalf of the British Air League.

Preface
by Barry McKee

The photographic work for this book commenced in late 1991 and was complete by the middle of 1997. It was a unique opportunity to document the process of rebuilding a substantial number of Spitfire airframes to flying condition . . . in colour, a luxury not afforded to the wartime factory photographer.

To produce a book that comprehensively covered the subject I had to have commitment at managerial level and co-operation from the engineers on the shop floor. I had an abundance of both throughout the project. On a number of occasions Tim Routsis threw me the building keys and said, "Lock up when you're through Barry, I'm off to Duxford." Mark Parr and Martin Henocq were always willing to help, pointing out areas of the process that were important for inclusion. All of the HFL engineers, without exception, assisted where they could for the duration of the project. We had a commonality of purpose, to produce a book which accurately reflected their superb workmanship.

Once the photographic side was well underway it was time to discuss the written content. Feedback from the Directors and Engineers concurred in two areas. The book produced had to be informative and accurate in detail. To achieve this meant that the people at Historic Flying had to take an active role with regard to selecting the photographs which were most representative of the total process, and advising on the accuracy of the written input in both the text and the photograph captions. Eight of the engineers selected the photographs to be used, whilst another three gave constructive input with regard to their captioning. Both Tim Routsis and Clive Denney gave generously of their time and gave authoritative interviews on the process aspect. Terry Lawless has produced splendid schematic drawings. Graham Moss joined me in 1997 and wrote up the chapters on the aircrafts' histories, structural aspects and the design variations between the different marks of aircraft. Charlie Brown gave informative material on testing the completed machines whilst Tim and Clive's pieces on their first flights were for me a thing of joy to read.

Each and every visit to this facility was as rewarding as the first. I was very privileged to be allowed the freedom of access given and can only hope that through the lens of the camera, and with the written input from all concerned that you, the reader, will be as fascinated as I was with the rebuilding work undertaken at this facility.

No book of this type could be possible without the support of a large number of people in the industry. To all those who contributed I extend my thanks – but deserving of particular note are Stephen Grey, Guy Black, Angus Spencer-Nairn and Martin Sargeant.

In parting I would like to give sincere thanks to two people who gave me the encouragement required to start . . . and finish this project . . . Ernie Taylor and Danny Morris of The Fighter Collection, Duxford.

CONTENTS

1
Historic Flying –
The Company and Their Spitfires

Historic Flying in November 1991 during one of the company's busiest periods. Top Left: RW382, the first Spitfire to be completed by the company in July 1991 . Bottom left: Rudy Frasca's former Indian Air Force Spitfire XVIII TP280. Centre: Former Israeli Defence Force high-back Spitfire Mk IX serial TE566 recovered from Israel in 1960 by Rob Lamplough. On the extreme right are three more aircraft awaiting rebuild: Mk XIV (former Belgian Air Force), Mk V, and high-back Mk XVI.

In early 1988, few people could have foreseen the impact discussions then underway between Tim Routsis and the U.K. Ministry of Defence, would have on the world's airworthy warbird population. Even Tim Routsis, on his own admission, had no idea what the long-term future of his envisaged project was going to be. His personal ambition was simple – he wanted to fly a Spitfire. In fulfilling his ambition, which he achieved on 7 August 1991 from Duxford airfield, he created a restoration facility at Audley End which rebuilt rather more than the number of Spitfires initially projected.

By providing the Ministry of Defence with twelve fibreglass Spitfire and Hurricane look-alikes for the gates of a number of Royal Air Force Stations around the U.K., Tim was, albeit indirectly, the catalyst for the decision by the M.o.D. to withdraw all historic airframes and put them into storage at R.A.F. St Athan and Shawbury for use as trading material by the Royal Air Force Museum at Hendon. This meant many would end up in private hands where they would be restored to flying condition. During the rescue process, Historic Flying was formed by Tim Routsis, Clive Denney and Ian Warren to rebuild the other gate guards to a fully operational condition.

Both Clive Denney and Ian Warren were already in business part-time, contributing significantly towards the warbird industry. Clive's Vintage Fabrics was a going concern, set up and run with his wife Linda. Ian Warren was, and thankfully still is, a gifted sheet-metal and systems engineer. The

(ABOVE): The Historic Flying Team pose with Eddie Coventry, the then owner of TD248. Left to right are: Dave Coe, John Loweth, Linda Denney, Martin Henocq, Laurie Tremble, Clive Denney, Bruce Gordon, Eddie Coventry, Dennis Jones, Tim Routsis, Phil Parrish, Ian Warren, Hugh Smith, Mark Parr, Paul Mercer.

first Spitfire to undergo restoration, a bubble-canopied Mk XVIe serial RW382 had already been removed from the gate at R.A.F. Uxbridge and was at the Vintage Fabrics workshops at Rayne where it was being dismantled at the time that the company was formed. Plans were then made for its restoration to airworthy status. This first aircraft was to serve almost as a template for the rebuild programme of other airframes, and served as a learning tool for the successful rebuild of those machines that were to follow.

Doug Arnold of Warbirds of Great Britain, then based at Blackbushe, had been the first individual to suggest a trade of former gate guard aeroplanes to the Ministry of Defence in return for supplying aircraft on the Royal Air Force Museum's 'wish' list. This was to be a most important factor in the contract later signed by the M.o.D. and Tim Routsis, for it set an important precedent which Tim was able to build on.

Tim had stated that the provenance of the aircraft was one of the most significant factors in the selection of the airframes he was to obtain from the Ministry, along with, of course, the state of the airframes themselves and their suitability for restoration. At the time, there was a growing trend, particularly in the U.K., for potential Spitfire owners to locate and purchase maker's plates or very small sections of Spitfire centre fuselage and literally build aircraft around that, a practice Tim personally disliked.

The five Spitfires short-listed by Tim, after extensive examination of all the aircraft by the Historic Flying Team were subsequently offered by the Ministry of Defence. These included a Mk Vb which had seen action in Polish hands during the Second World War, and four Mk XVI machines including the high-back Spitfire XVI, serial TB252, which saw operational flying in 1945 with the Free French Air Force.

The first aircraft to be considered for restoration was also the first to be removed from its R.A.F. location. Serial RW382, it was a Mk XVIe which had guarded the gate at R.A.F. Uxbridge since 4 April 1973, and was the second gate guard to be assessed for restoration by the team. Spitfire F.22 PK664 at R.A.F. Binbrook had been the first – and very nearly the last, as the condition of the aeroplane was so poor that Tim had been tempted to abandon the whole project at that point. The condition of RW382 was substantially better and encouraged them to continue. Assessment showed corrosion was slight, the only major components missing from the aircraft at the time being the two fuel tanks.

Spitfire RW382 was initially ordered from Vickers-Supermarine (Castle Bromwich) Ltd as part of the fifteenth order for contract B981687/39/C.23, dated 20 January 1944 and specifying 700 Spitfire F.21 aircraft. The order was cancelled in August the same year and subsequently partially reinstated as an order for forty Mk IXs. To confuse the issue further, the aircraft were built as Mk XVIs, between June and July 1945. RW382 was delivered to No.6 Maintenance Unit (M.U.) at R.A.F. Brize Norton on 20 July. It had been allocated the Castle Bromwich construction number CBAF-IX-4640 during construction and was completed as a LF.XVIe, complete with an American built Packard Merlin 266 engine.

Brize Norton, near Oxford, was to be her home for the next twenty-one months; RW382 was not allocated to a squadron until 1 April 1947, when 604 (County of Middlesex) Squadron Auxiliary Air Force took the aircraft on strength.

The squadron had been reformed barely a year before. It was flying only Mk XVI Spitfires at the time, although the war years had seen it flying operationally with Blenheims, Beaufighters and, more recently, with Mosquitos when it formed part of 2nd T.A.F. supporting D-Day operations, both in the UK and Normandy. In early 1947, the squadron was operating from R.A.F. Hendon, although two years later, on 28 March 1949, it moved to North Weald. Vampire F.3s began replacing the Spitfires from November 1949, though RW382, which had been coded as NG-C, lasted until 14 April 1950 when it was flown to 33 M.U. R.A.F. Lyneham and placed in storage.

On 12 June 1951 RW382 was posted to No.3 Civilian Anti-Aircraft Co-operation Unit (C.A.A.C.U.) at Exeter airport and allocated the code letter 'A'. RW382 resided here only briefly, moving to the Fighter Command Control and Reporting School at Middle Wallop on 17 October, adopting the codes 3L-Q. No.45 M.U. at R.A.F. Kinloss took her on charge for two weeks in the summer of 1953 before, on 28 July, she moved to 29 M.U. at R.A.F. High Ercall. The aircraft was declared to be non-effective stock on 14 December 1954 but she remained in storage at High Ercall until 28 November 1955, when she was allocated to 609 (County of West Riding) Sqn R.Aux.A.F. at R.A.F. Church Fenton as a ground instructional airframe.

Later allocated the ground instructional serial 7245M for this purpose and displayed at the station wearing the 3L-Q codes (and the back-to-front serial M7245), 1959 saw a move to R.A.F. Leconfield for further gate guard and display duties. During her stay at Leconfield, she acquired the serial RW729 and 610 (County of Chester) Sqn markings DW-X – ironic as 610 Sqn neither flew Mk XVIe Spitfires nor was ever based at Leconfield or Church Fenton. When she was dispatched to Henlow in 1967 for a role in the film *Battle of Britain*, she still wore the serial RW729 but was painted in the 234 Sqn codes AZ-B.

After some cosmetic work to make the low-back shape of the Mk XVIe look rather more like the earlier mark of Spitfire, RW382 graced the set of the *Battle of Britain* wearing three spurious serials – N3314, N3316 and N3320 – and four sets of squadron codes – AI-G, DO-L, DO-M and EI-G. RW382 saw use as a static aircraft, being used for set dressing throughout the filming, and did not return to R.A.F. Leconfield until 5 December 1969 taking up a position on the gate again. Ravages of film work had obviously taken their toll on the aircraft over the three years spent at Henlow with the *Battle of Britain* team. Eventually, RW382 was moved to 5 M.U. at R.A.F. Kemble on 19 May 1970 for refurbishment. She returned to Leconfield on 6 July after less than two months of work and wearing green/dark earth camouflage paint with 1940-style roundels.

Still wearing these colours, she was taken by road to R.A.F. Uxbridge, arriving on 4 April 1973 where she was displayed in a flying pose on a pylon close to the main gate, visible from both inside and outside the station. Allocated the instructional serial 8075M, which she was never to wear at

(ABOVE): RW382 showing how the aircraft appears prior to the cowling fitting process and flight testing.

Uxbridge, it is reported that she bore the codes Q-31 at some point during the early part of her fifteen-year stay there. Codes NG-C – the 604 Squadron codes she once wore operationally – were restored to her and the serial RW382 was reapplied.

It was in this state that Tim Routsis and Clive Denney discovered her in 1988. Internal corrosion had been limited by liberal use of lanolin and the aircraft appeared to be in comparatively good health. The canopy was crazed well beyond further use but nothing major had been stolen or added to the airframe – apart from some jury wiring which would have made the engine runnable for the *Battle of Britain* film. RW382 was removed on 26 August 1988 and moved to Clive Denney's Vintage Fabrics workshop to begin the painstaking restoration which would see her fly again on 3 July 1991 from the small airfield at Audley End.

The aircraft was purchased by David Tallichet's Military Aircraft Restoration Corp., based in California, in early 1989. The arrangement was that Historic Flying should rebuild the aircraft on Tallichet's behalf – and operate it in the U.K. for a short time following rebuild.

The tail cone and undercarriage doors were rebuilt first with Ian Warren undertaking most of the work, including the start of building the necessary fuselage and wing jigs. The engine was dispatched to Vintage V-12s in California for a complete zero-time rebuild. After dismantling the airframe, the fuselage was jigged and stripped during 1989, while the following year the wings began to near completion. The Merlin had been fitted to the airframe and was run for the first time on 12 February 1991 with the finishing touches made and the cowls fitted shortly after.

Following registration as G-XVIA to Historic Flying Ltd, her first flight, in the hands of Sir John Allison, was to take place from the small Audley End airfield on 3 July 1991 – something less than three years from the liberation of the aircraft from her pole at R.A.F. Uxbridge – under a permit to test from the Civil Aviation Authority.

Her first public showing was at Duxford's Classic Fighter Display on 14 July 1991, following a week of intensive testing. Although she did not fly at Classic Fighter, interest in this newly rebuilt aircraft was considerable. She did get to display at Duxford's Autumn Air Day on 13 October – formation passes with Bf 109G Black 6 proved to be a real crowd pleaser.

Mid-1993 saw David Tallichet dispose of the main body of his significant Warbird collection. RW382 was sold to Bernie Jackson, being crated and dispatched from Audley End shortly after her last U.K. flight on 13 February 1995.

The next Spitfire to be sold by Historic Flying was TE476 – to Kermit Weeks very soon after its removal from the gate at R.A.F. Northolt, the aircraft moving directly to Personal Plane Services, Kermit's U.K. agent. A third aircraft was also sold, this time to Eddie Coventry of B.A.C. Windows who already owned and flew Yak-11 G-OYAK. Eddie retained Tim and the Historic Flying team to rebuild the LF XVIe Spitfire TD248, much of the work taking place alongside RW382, then nearing completion.

Eddie Coventry's Spitfire XVI had been recovered from the gate at

R.A.F. Sealand where she had guarded the station from a number of vantage points since her allocation to 1366 Sqn A.T.C. in April 1959.

Spitfire TD248 was built against contract B981687/39.C.23(c), specifically the seventeenth order, which specified 1884 Mk IX Spitfires, dated 19 March 1944. The aircraft were built at the Vickers-Supermarine's Castle Bromwich factory as a mix of 850 Mk IX and 632 Mk XVI aircraft between December 1944 and June 1945. Some of the production run was cancelled before work began on them.

TD248 was allocated construction number CBAF-IX-4262 and built as an L.F. XVIe with Packard Merlin 266, was accepted by the R.A.F. on 11 May 1945 and finally delivered to 6 M.U. at R.A.F. Brize Norton on 16 May. After preparations for service duty at the M.U. she was allocated to 695 Army Co-operation Sqn, based at R.A.F. Horsham St Faith in Norfolk, on 5 July 1945, wearing the codes 8Q-T. No.695 Sqn had been formed only eighteen months earlier with the amalgamation (at R.A.F. Bircham Newton) of Nos. 1611 and 1612 Flights – carrying out anti-aircraft co-operation duties. The unit had used Henleys, Martinets and Lysanders for target towing and had also begun to use Hurricanes for gun-laying practice. Spitfire Mk Vbs and then Spitfire Mk XVIs gradually replaced the Hurricanes. Towards the end of 1948, they were complemented by target-towing Beaufighters. The squadron was renumbered 34 on 11 February 1949.

Spitfire TD248 suffered some damage at the hands of 695 Sqn on the last day of 1947 although the exact details are not available. Repairs to the aircraft were extensive – TD248 was unable to rejoin the squadron until 13 May 1948. By the time she rejoined the squadron, their codes had been changed to '4M' (and she was allocated the individual squadron letter E). The aircraft continued to serve with 695 (then 34) for a further three years, eventually moving to No. 2 C.A.A.C.U. based at R.A.F. Little Snoring, on 31 August 1951.

A further three years passed before TD248 was put into storage with 9 M.U. at R.A.F. Cosford on 27 May 1954. It was declared non-effective on 14 December the same year. On 4 October 1955, 610 (County of Chester) Sqn R.Aux.A.F., based at R.A.F. Hooton Park, took the Spitfire on charge

and allocated it the codes DW-A and posted it to static display duties on the station.

The year 1957 saw the gradual disbandment of the Royal Auxiliary Air Force. No. 610 Squadron was disbanded as a unit on 10 March 1957. TD248 was stored at Hooton Park until 8 April 1959 when No. 1366 (Chester) Sqn Air Training Corps, based at R.A.F. Sealand, took the aircraft on charge. Allocated instructional serial 7246M – coincidentally the next in sequence to RW382 which wore 7245M at R.A.F. Leconfield, No. 30 M.U., based at Sealand, took charge of the aircraft from 31 January 1961, positioning TD248 outside the Officers' Mess. Exposed to the coastal elements, by June 1967, the cockpit canopy had deteriorated so badly it was painted silver.

Refurbished by 30 M.U. in 1975 and again in 1979, placed on top of a pole in an action pose at the station main gate, TD248 was repainted after the later work in 610 Sqn colours as DW-A.

It remained aloft until rescued by Tim Routsis in 1988. The aircraft was removed from its plinth at Sealand on 14 October 1988 and transported away to join the queue for restoration. At the time of her assessment, the cockpit was noted as having been gutted, with the blind-flying panel missing and with just temperature and oil pressure gauges, and brake pressure and flap indicator dials remaining. The throttle quadrant, trim wheels and undercarriage selector were still in place, in addition to the spade grip.

Shortly after her recovery from R.A.F. Sealand, TD248 was purchased by Eddie Coventry and was registered as G-OXVI to B.A.C. Aviation Ltd on 22 August 1989. Restoration began in October 1988 and, by 1 September 1990, when Historic Flying moved into its new hangar at Audley End, the fuselage and tail cone were jigged and under restoration. The fuselage was completed in April 1991 and painting, systems fit and the installation of the tail cone were completed soon after.

The paint scheme chosen by the owner was a welcome change from the

(BELOW): Now the systems are installed in the fuselage, paintwork is complete and the aircraft is ready for final assembly. This is Mk XVI TD248.

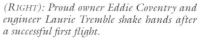

normal camouflage paint work. The scheme originated from a distinctive red and silver Spitfire F.21 of 41 Sqn as it appeared at the Blackpool airshow in 1946 and 1947. November 1991 saw the tail and fuselage mated, and systems fit in full swing. The wings were awaiting rebuild at this stage and the decision was taken to restore them with normal tips.

After successful ground running, the first flight of the newly rebuilt TD248 took place at Audley End at 14.00 hrs on 10 November 1992 with Sir John Allison at the helm. A Permit to Fly for the aircraft was issued in March 1993. Fittingly, the aircraft's display debut was at R.A.F. Sealand where she performed in front of an invited audience to mark the seventy-fifth anniversary of the Royal Air Force – on 1 April 1993. The U.K. weather was so bad that day that many of the other R.A.F. anniversary flights scheduled had to be cancelled – including the much publicised mass '75' formation of modern fighter aircraft. That pilot Charlie Brown felt able to fly the display at Sealand was as much due to his faith in the aircraft as the vagaries of the British weather.

Late 1989 saw discussions with another warbird enthusiast, Guy Black of Aero Vintage, raising the possibility of Historic Flying taking on the restoration of a Spitfire rescued many years earlier by Robert Lamplough.

(ABOVE AND OPPOSITE ABOVE):
Mk XVI TD248 out on the hard stand for inspection and engine runs.

The Spitfire in question had had a very active service career in the U.K., Czechoslovakia and finally in Israel, having eventually been rescued from an Israeli kibbutz and shipped to the U.K.

Agreement between the two parties saw the Mk IX, serial TE566, move from a small airfield at Ludham in Norfolk, where it had been undergoing restoration with Ralph Hull, to Historic Flying early in 1991. Much of the metal-work had been

(RIGHT): Proud owner Eddie Coventry and engineer Laurie Tremble shake hands after a successful first flight.

(BELOW): *Some adjustments can be carried out while the engine is running. In this instance, Martin Henocq has just adjusted the idle running on the engine of Mk XVI TD248.*

(BELOW): *Full power on. The moment of truth. Sir John Allison goes through the final power checks before deciding whether the aircraft is fit for flight. It was, and moments later was airborne. First flights are an evocative moment for all those concerned with the rebuild.*

completed at Ludham, and Historic Flying began the systems fit and took the aircraft through to its first flight in mid-1992.

TE566 had formed part of the seventeenth order for 1884 Mk IX Spitfires dated 19 April 1944 against contract B981687/39/C.23(c). Built as a mix of 850 Mk IXs and 632 Mk XIVs, some 402 machines were cancelled, which is why the numbers do not balance. TE566 was built at Castle Bromwich with the constructor's number CBAF-171363. Taken on charge by 33 M.U. R.A.F. Lyneham on 15 June 1945, final fitting and short-term storage pre-empted its allocation to No. 312 (Czech) Sqn on 3 August.

Assignment to 312 Sqn was significant in that the unit was to become part of the nascent Czechoslovakian Air Force and would retain the aircraft allocated to it at the time. TE566 was ferried to R.A.F. Manston where she was painted in Czech Air Force colours. The Spitfires assembled at Manston were to be flown across Europe to Czechoslovakia in waves. The first formation left the U.K. on 7 August 1945, although they were delayed in Germany, where they refuelled, due to bad weather, the wave eventually arrived in Prague on the 13th. The second group of twelve, including TE566, which wore its Czech Air Force codes DU-A alongside the Czech roundels, left Manston *en route* for Achmer and landed some 90 minutes later to refuel before pressing on to Prague, arriving some two hours later. The R.A.F. Aircraft Movement Record for TE566 dates its handover to the Czechoslovakian Air Force as 30 August 1945, the same date all three R.A.F. Squadrons were incorporated into the new Czech Air Force. No. 312 Sqn became the 2nd Air Division, 4th and 5th Fighter Regiments.

By 8 September, all the Spitfires had been flown to Prague's Ruzyne airport, though it was not until the 23rd that individual squadrons moved to their own bases. No. 312 Squadron was assigned to the Ceske Budejovice airbase in Southern Bohemia, and TE566 was flown there from Prague by a Squadron Leader Manak. TE566 later became part of the *Letecke Vojenske Akademie* – (LVA) the Czech Air Force Flying Academy, wearing a code in the A-700 range.

In early 1948, the newly formed state of Israel realised that they were in dire need of world-class armament if they were to survive. After discussions with the Czech authorities, it was decided the pool of Czechoslovakian Spitfires would supplement the Israeli defensive capability particularly well.

Aircraft selection – there were a total of seventy-six Spitfires in good condition spread around Czechoslovakia at the time – and crew training commenced in a climate of deteriorating Czech–Soviet relations.

The Russian overthrow of the Czech authorities served to increase Israeli resolve to complete the purchase – despite the increasing number of problems and bureaucracies which were being put in their path. All non-Soviet weaponry, including the aircraft of the Czech Air Force, was ordered to be replaced by Soviet machinery, making it almost impossible to complete the transaction.

The mix of Mk IXs and Mk XVIs selected grew to fifty-four during the summer of 1948, a list which included TE566. At this time, the Israelis began to turn their attention to the problem of getting the aircraft to Israel.

Enter Sam Pommerantz, one of many foreign volunteers, determined to meet the immediate needs of the Israeli Air Force by flying some of the aircraft to Israel under their own power. The Spitfires had an unrefuelled ferry range of about 960 miles, very small compared to the proposed route to Israel.

It was obvious that the aircraft would need to be heavily modified. The Spitfires were ferried to the factory at Kunovice in Southern Moravia during late-summer of 1948 and modification/rectification work began in September. The target was to cover the 1400-mile leg from Kunovice to Titograd in Southern Yugoslavia, in one go. Everything removable was removed from the airframes and replaced with auxiliary internal fuel tanks.

Weaponry and other surplus equipment was shipped or ferried in transport aircraft and by sea. Ninety-gallon external slipper tanks were fitted, providing the required range. On 22 September 1948, six of the modified Spitfires and a C-54 transport plane departed Czechoslovakia *en route* for Podgorica in Yugoslavia. All six made it – though one was damaged beyond repair during a forced-landing because the undercarriage would not come down.

The remaining five, still with their C-54 escort, left for Israel on 27 September. *En route,* two of the aircraft developed fuel problems and force-landed at Maritza airfield on Rhodes where they were interned. The remaining three, with the C-54, flew on to Israel. Through the winter, small groups of Spitfires made the flight to Israel in the hands of a band of volunteer pilots. During one period, they were unable to refuel in Titograd, which required a further auxiliary tanks fit. This extra internal storage put the all-up weight of the Spitfires beyond the design limits of the aircraft.

The contract for the dispatch of the Spitfires from Czechoslovakia to Israel was formally signed by both parties on 7 October – two weeks after deliveries had commenced. By early 1949, all the Spitfires had left Czechoslovakia, either by air or by sea, having been dismantled and dispatched by train to ports in Yugoslavia, Romania and Italy, and shipped to Haifa after the first armistice in early 1949, then to Israel. It would appear TE566 travelled sedately to Israel by sea, not being recorded as being present there until early 1949. Coded as 20-32 and operated by 101 Sqn of the I.D.F.A.F., the Spitfire was noted as having been registered 4X-FOB. Further details of her service in Israeli hands are scant.

Spitfire TE566 was offered to a kibbutz at Alonhim as a playground attraction for the children, and it was in this location that Robert Lamplough discovered the aircraft in 1976. Robert had discovered a number of Spitfires around Israel at this time, all of which he recovered. Following recovery, TE566 arrived at Duxford in December 1976, where she was stored. Still bearing evidence of her Israeli activities, with the Star of David, the code number 32, and the R.A.F. serial – sometimes very difficult to prove – carried clearly over her fuselage.

TE566 remained stored at Duxford until 1981 following sale to Guy Black of Aero Vintage. Guy transported the machine to Steve Atkins's Vintage Airworks workshops in St Leonards-on-Sea in Sussex where restoration work began in 1982 alongside another Spitfire project, MJ730, which had been coded 20-66 when in Israeli service. This aircraft had been recovered from Israel at the same time as TE566 but was in a much worse condition. Slowly over the next five years, progress was made on both aircraft. TE566, registered as G-BLCK on the U.K. register, was moved out of storage from Sussex to Ludham in Norfolk in May 1986, where Hull Aero was commissioned to complete the work to flying condition.

Owned by the Historic Aircraft Collection, work on the aircraft commenced with the jigs for fuselage and tail cone before those items could be rebuilt. The Spitfire's wings had been delivered to Ludham in sections and whilst sorting out the pieces it was discovered that the units were type C wings. The original E wings had been transferred to Trent Aero at East Midlands airport where MJ730 was being worked on. During work in Sussex, the wings of the two aircraft had been inadvertently swapped.

The first wing was completed after twelve months work, and work on the second began immediately. It was early 1989 before the wings were mated to the fuselage for the first time. During this period, an overhauled Merlin 68A had been procured from Aviation Jersey and made available for installation in the fuselage. In early 1990, a number of other Spitfires arrived at Ludham for Ralph Hull's attention and progress on TE566 slowed accordingly. Spitfire TE566 was moved to Audley End in early 1991 for completion to flying condition.

Progress was rapid. Mid-November 1991 saw the painted aircraft with the wings in place – having first had wheels and radiators fitted, and the engine – having been completed. Initial engine runs took place during April 1992 and the first flight, again in the hands of Sir John Allison, took place on 2 July 1992 from Audley End airfield. Just two days later, it was on display at Duxford's Classic Fighter display where its beautifully re-produced Czech paint scheme attracted much interest. The following year, it took part in the Czechoslovakian Memorial Airshow over Prague, an event which created a real stir in a country starved of real warbird activity. On both show days – 26 and 27 June – TE566, flown by Charlie Brown, opened the proceedings flanked by Czechoslovakian L-29 and L-39 jets.

The Spitfire also took part in the D-Day commemoration flights which took place over the beaches of Normandy on 6 June 1994. The Duxford-based Old Flying Machine Company operated the Spitfire over the 1995 show season. Whatever her immediate future, it is apparent that TE566 has had a rich and very varied past.

Whilst work was underway on RW382, TD248 and TE566, a fourth machine was contracted for completion and raised a new challenge for the team at Historic Flying, for it was very different to the others. A Griffon-engined Mk XVIII, owned by Rudy Frasca, owner of a flight simulator company, in Champaign, Illinois, it was one of two Spitfires which had recovered together from India.

Discussions between Rudy, who had started the rebuild in his own workshops in Illinois, and Historic Flying led to the arrival of TP280 at Audley End in May 1991. Work started immediately on the aircraft and the long-nosed Spitfire was to emerge from the workshops in pristine condition just over a year later.

(BELOW): Leading the line-up at Duxford's Classic Fighter airshow is high-back Mk IX TE566. Directly behind is the low-back Mk XVI RW382. A proud moment for the team. On this day they had three Spitfires at Duxford, the third being the Mk XVIII TP280.

Spitfire TP280 was manufactured in 1945, having been ordered in August 1944 as part of the twelfth order against contract Air/1877/C. 23(c). Out of an order for 300, she was one of only 26 machines built by Supermarine at Southampton and carries a 6S construction code: 6S/676372. Supermarine put her to work in March 1945 as a 'super production prototype', although the precise nature of the task is not clear. No. 39 M.U. at R.A.F. Colerne was the first Royal Air Force receiving unit, TP280 making its appearance in June 1945 and oddly going straight into store.

Allocated to the Far East Air Force in January 1946, TP280 was dispatched the following month to 76 M.U. at R.A.F. Sealand for crating and a move to Karachi. Dispatched from the docks at Birkenhead, TP280 arrived in Karachi in late March. Taken on charge in April, there was apparently no immediate need for the aircraft as she was stored again until July 1947. From here, the aircraft was to be shipped back to the U.K. and possibly scrapped but, in the event, TP280, in company with other late mark Spitfires, was assigned to R.A.F. Mauripor in November 1947. One month later, the Indian Air Force came into being as an armed military force in its own right and on 31 December 1947, TP280, having been assigned serial HS654, became a founder member of the new air arm.

Details of Indian Spitfire service histories are difficult to trace: TP280 is no exception. Discovery of the codes NG or N6 during her later rebuild indicate service with 14 Sqn, Indian Air Force, but this is not proven. In 1977, the Indian authorities put eight of their surplus Spitfires up for sale.

Abandoned at a number of military sites around the country since the 1950s, the aircraft were in generally poor condition. Eight aircraft were auctioned as a single lot by the Indian government, comprising two Mk XVIs, a single Mk VIII and five Mk XVIIIs. A number of sealed bids were received from collectors in both Britain and America. Brothers Ormond and Wesley Haydon-Baillie had their bid accepted and they

suddenly found that their Aircraft and Naval Collection now had the task of recovering the eight airframes from India.

TP280 had ended her Indian career posing as a decoy jet aircraft in revetments on the perimeter of Kailakunda Airbase. Her tail unit had been propped up to give the appearance of a tricycle undercarriage, prop blades had been sawn off, and many major items were missing – rudder, cockpit canopy and fairing, cowls and prop spinner not least amongst them. Three other Spitfires shared the same fate, TP298, SM845 and the aircraft which is known to this day only by its Indian Air Force serial HS649, all four being recovered by Wesley Haydon-Baillie. Sadly, brother Ormond was killed in a Mustang accident in Germany before the Indian recovery operation began.

Recovery commenced on 1 October 1977. All eight aircraft were dismantled, crated and transported by rail to Bombay for dispatch to the U.K.

American Rudy Frasca, renowned as a warbird collector, was contacted by Haydon-Baillie after he had shown interest in two of the Spitfires. Rudy purchased TP280, and TP276 which had been recovered from Barakpor coded HS653. He also purchased an extra set of wings – those that came with the two aircraft had seen better days. Both Spitfires were shipped to Rudy's airfield at Champaign, Illinois. Close inspection revealed TP280 was the best of the two airframes and so Spitfire TP276 was consigned to long-term storage while work commenced on TP280.

Initially, the restoration was carried out by volunteers with appropriate metalwork and airframe skills. The wings were contracted for rebuild to Steve Atkins's U.K. based Vintage Airworks in Sussex. The tail cone was rebuilt completely by Steve Vizard's Airframe Assemblies on the Isle of Wight and shipped to the U.S.A. in early 1989. The Griffon engine was zero-timed by Vintage V-12s in California. Two of the part-timers became full-time workers on the project in 1989, both having been United States Air Force airframe instructors. This advanced the restoration considerably.

Late in 1990, Rudy Frasca made the decision to ship TP280 to the U.K. for Historic Flying to finish the rebuild and get her back in the air. In May 1991 TP280 arrived at Audley End and the work of collating and assessing the accompanying components began. The fuselage appeared complete and the wings were awaiting installation. The fuselage and tail unit were undergoing systems fit in late 1991 after the aeroplane was placed on the U.K. civil register as G-BTXE.

The painted mainplanes were fitted to the fuselage shortly afterwards and the rebuilt engine, a modified Griffon 65, was installed early in 1992. Rudy had requested extra fuel tanks to be fitted in the gun bays of TP280 and an internal tank fitted in the fuselage. This raised the total fuel capacity of the aircraft to almost 170 gallons. The wing modification was standard but the fuselage installation was not and the Historic Flying team laboured long and hard over the problem of fitting a large tank through a small fuselage hole. Propeller blades were rebuilt by Skycraft and Hoffman, and the other parts of the propeller were overhauled by Dowty. Craig Charleston undertook the majority of the installation work.

After some deliberation, Rudy settled on a distinctive 60 Sqn paint scheme with black and yellow striping on the forward portion of the cowling, the personal markings of Group Captain Duncan Smith, and the simple code letter Z. Clive Denney undertook additional research and prepared drawings and templates so the paint scheme would be as close to the original as practicable, including the matt paint. The result was quite stunning.

After the aeroplane was issued with a permit to test by the U.K. C.A.A., Sir John Allison took her into the air on 5 June 1992, landing at Duxford again, coinciding with the Classic Fighter Display – this was becoming a habit! The test-flying programme was also undertaken from Duxford shortly afterwards.

(ABOVE): Proud owner Rudy Frasca with the Mk XVIII at Duxford shortly after the aircraft's first flight.

Rudy Frasca flew TP280 four times in the U.K. before dismantling and packing her for the journey by sea to the Great Lakes. After a short road journey to Champaign, where she arrived in September 1992, Historic's Chief Engineer, Paul Mercer, and Tim Routsis reassembled the aircraft. Oshkosh 1993 saw her American show debut and she attracted a great deal of attention in the warbird park. U.K. audiences would, however, have to make do with the very brief appearances she put in at Duxford during the month between her first flight and her return to the U.S.A.

Discussions with Historic Flying's near neighbours, the Duxford-based Fighter Collection, in the latter half of 1992 were to pay dividends as 1993 dawned. Three Spitfire projects in store with the Fighter Collection were to be restored to flying condition by Historic Flying over a projected period of two to three years. Two of the machines were former Indian Air Force Mk XIVs. The third, however, was a real gem and would provide Historic with more than just an insight in to the restoration of Tim Routsis's own Mk V, BM597. This was EP120, one-time gate guard at R.A.F. Wattisham, and arguably the highest-scoring Spitfire still extant. However, of the three airframes in the contract, one of the two Mk XIV aircraft, NH799, was the first to take to the air.

Built at Aldermaston in 1945 as part of the third order for 225 Mk VIII Spitfires contract Air/1877/C.23(c) which materialised as 23 Mk VIIIs, 191 Mk XIVs and 11 Mk XVIIIs – NH799 was delivered to 9 M.U. at R.A.F. Cosford in March the same year.

Following assignment to the Allied Command South East Asia's Operation *Tiger*, the

(RIGHT): No. 60 Squadron insignia hand-painted on the tailplane. Intensive research is undertaken by the team to reproduce accurately the original markings carried by the aircraft or the airframes that it is representing (Mk XVIII TP280).

(ABOVE): Final checks prior to first flight . . . moments later the aircraft was airborne (Mk XIV NH799).

anticipated invasion of Japan, NH799 was moved to No. 215 M.U. at Dumfries on 22 May. On 30 May, it was packed awaiting dispatch to Karachi, finally being shipped aboard the S.S. *Samsturdy* on 2 July. Twenty-six days later on 9 August, NH799 was taken on charge by Allied Command South East Asia (A.C.S.E.A).

Following the American atomic bombing of Hiroshima and Nagasaki, and Japan's subsequent capitulation (VJ day came on 15 August 1945), NH799 was noted as being present in India in the 30 August census and again in the Indian census of May 1946. Reports of a flying accident indicate service with 9 Sqn which reputedly wrote it off on 27 February 1947. It was, however, certainly fit enough to transfer to the newly created Indian Air Force ten months later on 31 December 1947.

Further operations with the Indian Air Force are not recorded and the next known chapter in its history was brought about by Doug Arnold who recovered it and shipped it to the Warbirds of Great Britain workshops at Blackbushe in 1981. The airframe was stored there until the group moved its base of operations to Bitteswell in 1985.

Work began on the fuselage in 1986 when the Fighter Collection acquired the airframe. The wings were complete and some of the fuselage metal-work had been restored. The components were stored, alongside the fuselage and wings of SM832, in the T2 hangar at Duxford until the summer of 1993 when Historic Flying was contracted to finish the rebuild.

Shortly after the start of work, Sir Tim Wallis's Alpine Fighter Collection, based in Wanaka, New Zealand, became the new owner and the aircraft was completed by Historic Flying for The Fighter Collection on behalf of the Alpine Fighter Collection! Completion of the restoration of this airframe was to take Historic Flying just six months. Spitfire NH799, registered G-BUZU, flew for the first time since her service with the Indian Air Force ended, on 21 January 1994 when she transferred to Cambridge Airport from Audley End in the hands of Sir John Allison. Two days later, she arrived at Duxford where the 10-hour test-flying programme was to be completed.

The aircraft had been finished in 130 Sqn colours, being camouflaged in grey/green and had invasion stripes, yellow-edged fuselage roundels, large wing roundels, and was coded AP-V.

It was critical that the aircraft arrived in New Zealand for an appearance at the 1994 Warbirds Over Wanaka Show and this kept the test-flying focused. The Spitfire was dismantled, crated and dispatched for New Zealand on 14 February. Unpacked and reassembled in New Zealand, it had been registered ZK-XIV in time for flight trials on 31 March and to keep its appointment with several thousand New Zealand Warbird enthusiasts at the Warbirds Over Wanaka Show on the 1–3 April.

Sadly, the aircraft was written off in a major accident on 2 January 1996 which saw its pilot and owner, Sir Tim Wallis, hospitalised with severe injuries.

Spitfire SM832, the second of the two Mk XIVs to be restored for The Fighter Collection was ordered originally for the Royal Air Force as a P.R.

(ABOVE): Final engine runs before first flight (Mk XIV SM832).

XI Spitfire, part of the eleventh order against contract Air/1877/C.23(c). The order was dated 12 April 1944 and specified 150 P.R. Mk XI Spitfires, later adjusted to 81 Mk XIVs and 51 F.R. Mk XVIIIs with several aircraft having been deleted from the order.

SM832 was built as an F.XIVe by Supermarine and allocated construction number 6S/663452. Flying for the first time from Chattis Hill in March 1945, shortly afterwards on the 13th, she was accepted by 29 M.U. at High Ercall. Eight days later, she was transferred to 222 M.U. at R.A.F. High Ercall and prepared for shipping to Bombay. The 26 March saw her at Hull docks for shipping aboard the *Highland Prince* bound for Bombay, arriving there on 14 May.

She was stored until struck off charge on 31 July 1947, although she was noted in both the census of 30 August 1945 and the Indian census of May 1946. The Indian Air Force purchased SM832 from the R.A.F. and nothing more is known about her until she appeared, *circa* 1972, guarding the gate at the Indian Military Academy at Dehra Dun. Rescued by Wesley Haydon-Baillie of the Aircraft and Naval Collection, SM832 was later purchased by Doug Arnold's Warbirds of Great Britain in 1978, taken to Blackbushe and registered G-WWII in July 1979.

Work began on the aircraft almost immediately, the plan being to restore the aircraft as a Mk VIII Spitfire. This involved removing the Griffon engine bearers and replacing them with Merlin equivalents, and a Mk IX

tail unit was rebuilt to fit the Spitfire at this point. Little work was carried out on the aircraft after Warbirds of Great Britain's move to Bitteswell, and the aircraft was transferred to The Fighter Collection in August 1986.

Spitfire SM832 was stored at Duxford until 1988 when it was purchased by Charles Church (Spitfires) Ltd and was extensively rebuilt by Dick Melton at his workshops in Micheldever. Dick began the job of returning the aircraft to its original Mk XIV configuration with a Griffon engine and an original Mk XIV tail unit. The rebuild utilised the recently rebuilt Mk XIV wings from RR232 which had been purchased from Australian Peter Sledge in 1986.

Following the unfortunate death of Charles Church in the crash of Spitfire Mk V EE606, SM832 was again acquired by The Fighter Collection in early November 1991. The airframe was complete and mostly rebuilt, the Griffon engine having been completely restored. Systems fit had not commenced, although the wings were complete. Spitfire SM832 passed into the care of Historic Flying at about the same time that NH799 moved to Audley End. The aircraft flew again on 22 May 1995, again with Sir John Allison at the controls. Still retaining her original registration G-WWII, she was finished as a 17 Squadron, R.A.F. Spitfire, specifically as Sqn Ldr 'Ginger' Lacey's aircraft (then the 17 Sqn C.O. in Malaya, 1945) appearing in public for the first time at the 1995 Flying Legends airshow.

The Griffon-engined Spitfires are much less common at airshows than their Merlin-engined counterparts. These two examples were both described by T.F.C. pilots as 'pure animal' to fly.

The next Spitfire for The Fighter Collection, EP120, was rebuilt at Audley End from mid-1993 to June 1996, although she flew briefly during September 1995 before engine and propeller problems kept her grounded over the winter and well into the Spring.

Spitfire EP120 was ordered by the Air Ministry on 23 August 1941, as part of a batch of 904 aircraft. Forming part of the fourth order against contract B981687/39/C.23(c), an order for a series of Mk Vb and Vc machines, delivery to the R.A.F. commenced on 26 April 1942 with Mk Vb serial EN763. Manufacture of this range took place at Castle Bromwich and delivery of EP120 to 45 M.U. at Kinloss, following flight testing at Castle Bromwich, was on 23 May 1942. EP120 was constructed with full span wings and a Merlin 46 engine, and was allocated construction number CBAF-2403.

On 4 June, EP120 was flown from Kinloss in Scotland to Ibsley, near Ringwood in Hampshire, to join No. 501 (County of Gloucester) Squadron. No. 501 Squadron was part of the Ibsley Wing which, in turn, formed part of No. 10 Group. At the time of EP120's arrival, the Wing was led by Wg Cdr I.R. 'Widge' Gleed. He was replaced on 15 July by Wg Cdr E.P.P. 'Pat' Gibbs who was to pilot EP120 on her first German kill a month after his arrival. EP120 was put on the strength of A Flight, 501 Sqn on 3 June, and assigned Squadron codes SD-L.

The Spitfire was damaged in an accident at Ibsley, at 13.10 hours on 16 July. Category AC damage was caused both to the airframe and to the engine when, in the hands of Pilot Officer R. C. Lynch, it struck Spitfire AB403 of 118 Sqn on a taxiway at Ibsley. The damage, the exact nature of which is unknown, was repaired on site over a period of about three weeks. The accident report noted *Spitfire AB403 was stationary some distance off the runway after bursting a tyre when EP120 taxied into it*. AB403 was declared to have suffered Cat. E damage (complete write-off) at the time, indicating how severe the impact must have been, although this was reassessed at a later date and the machine was salvaged and eventually returned to duty.

Repairs complete on 5 August, EP120 was returned to 501 Sqn, probably to B Flight, coded SD-Y. Her first flight following her return did not take place until 14 August when she was scrambled at 04.55 hours with Sgt H. R. Kelly on board, to intercept inbound raiders at 20,000 ft off St Alban's Head. From 14 August to 19 August, EP120 flew only five times, three of those operations being on the 19th, the day of the large-scale Dieppe raids, when the squadron was covering withdrawal of the Operation *Jubilee* forces.

The first two operations of the day were escort duties flown with Flt Sgt. R. J. Long at the controls. The third saw EP120 flown by the Wing Leader, Wg Cdr E. P. P. Gibbs. On this occasion the task involved protecting a shipping convoy off the beach at Dieppe, and the Wing was in action as soon as they arrived at their station at about 15.20 hours. After brief skirmishes with a number of FW 190s, the Wing Leader and other pilots sighted three Dornier Do 217s breaking cloud at the southern end of the convoy and commenced attack.

The Spitfires gave chase. Wg Cdr Gibbs was able to bring EP120 to point-blank range on one of the Dorniers and emptied his magazines into it. He did not see the outcome as he was attacked by a FW 190, picking up cannon shells in the tail and wing. Shaking off the Focke-Wulf, he dived to sea level heading north at speed, meeting 501 Squadron's Yellow Section at low level and leading them back to Shoreham. Despite Wg Cdr Gibbs not witnessing the Dornier crash, confirmation from Sqn Ldr Sing and Fg

Off Scott, 501 Sqn Yellow 1 and Yellow 2 respectively, supported Gibbs's claim of a Dornier destroyed.

The Cat. AC damage to the aircraft caused EP120 to be left behind when 501 Sqn moved on to R.A.F. Middle Wallop five days after the Dieppe operation. Following repair, EP120 was allocated to a new unit, 19 Sqn, on 9 September. No. 19 Sqn was based at Perranporth and operating under 10 Group control when EP120 joined it. The squadron's main duties were standing Atlantic patrols, although exercises away from Perranporth during EP120's attachment were not uncommon.

No. 19 Sqn had re-equipped with newer Mk V Spitfires in August, having had their early build Mk Vs since November 1941. EP120 saw her first operational sortie at 17.30 hours on 24 September, taking part in a patrol off the Lizard to intercept low-flying German intruders. No contact with the enemy was made on this sortie. Allocated to A Flight, under the command of Flt Lt D. J. Cox D.F.C., EP120 was coded QV-E for her posting with 19 Squadron, not QV-H as she was subsequently painted during her later gate guarding days at R.A.F. Wattisham.

During EP120's service with 19 Sqn, all Mk Vb Spitfires were upgraded to enhance their performance against the new German FW 190s. Supercharger impeller blades were cropped to further improve engine performance at low level, and the elliptical wings were clipped to enhance manoeuvrability. In comparison with the new Mk IX Spitfires then being made available to front-line squadrons, the tired Mk Vs were adjudged by the pilots to be clapped out. The unofficial designation for these aircraft thus became 'clipped, cropped and clapped'. Remarkably, EP120 flew sixty-one recorded operational sorties with 19 Squadron in seven months service, although contact with the enemy was infrequent, most sorties consisting of patrol work for shipping convoys sailing up and down the English Channel.

Eventually, 19 Sqn exchanged their full complement of aircraft with 402 Sqn, flying from Fairlop to Digby on 22 April 1943 to make the exchange.

No. 402 (City of Winnipeg) Sqn was popularly known as the Winnipeg Bear squadron due to the totem pole and bear in the squadron emblem, and was part of the Royal Canadian Air Force, based at Digby in Lincolnshire at the time of the exchange. Here, coded AE-A, EP120 was flown mostly by the Squadron Commanding Officer. This was initially Sqn Ldr Lloyd V. Chadburn who, on promotion to Wing Commander, handed over 402, and his aircraft, to Squadron Leader Geoffrey Wilson Northcott D.S.O., D.F.C., veteran of the Malta campaign. Wg Cdr Chadburn kept his ties with 402 Sqn when he took command of the Digby Wing which comprised 402 and 416 Sqns. Sqn Ldr Northcott arrived with 402 Sqn on 18 June 1943, having been promoted after completing an instructional tour with 53 O.T.U.

EP120's first flight with her new unit, at the hands of Flt Lt M. Johnston, was on operations providing rearguard support for bombers attacking the Dutch coast on 14 May. Sqn Ldr Northcott's first sorties were on 22 June when he flew twice. The first flight was aborted due to engine trouble.

From 23 June, his second flying day, Northcott adopted EP120 as his mount, an association that was to span seventy operations. Five days after joining the squadron Geoffrey Northcott claimed his first kill, a feat achieved flying EP120. The object of his attentions was a Bf 109 defending a German convoy from a Beaufighter attack off the Dutch coast. Northcott shredded the wing root and fuselage of the Bf 109, which began smoking heavily and plunged into the sea. The claim was for a 'probable' but Northcott was later awarded a confirmed kill.

EP120 made a brief visit, along with seventeen other squadron Spitfires, to 3501 Servicing Unit at Cranfield from 1 July to 6 July 1943 for modification work before returning to Digby and operations on 18 July.

19

On 2 August, the Wing was tasked to provide support to Beaufighters attacking convoys off Den Helder. The Wing flew to Coltishall to refuel before commencing escort duties and were on station abeam the convoy at 11.00 hours, having flown towards Den Helder under thick cloud at sea level. Later turning north to find the enemy shipping off Texel, the Wing spotted six Bf 109s to the north-east of the convoy. The 109s were attacked by 412 and 402 Sqns. Wg Cdr Chadburn accounted for one, another was downed by a 416 Sqn pilot, and Sqn Ldr Northcott in EP120 claimed two destroyed, using an estimated 30 cannon and 300 machine-gun rounds to destroy both machines. This action raised Northcott's tally with 402 Sqn to three and was to earn him a D.F.C.

On 22 August, 402 Sqn, acting as top cover to Marauders tasked with bombing Beaumont-le-Roget, saw the formation attacked over the target by fifteen plus FW 190s. Eight more FW 190s joined the fray from ahead a few minutes after the British formation left the target area. No. 402 Sqn met these aircraft face to face. Northcott selected the lead 190, shooting it down with a short burst of cannon and machine-gun fire.

Another FW 190 was added to Northcott's score on 4 September, again while supporting Marauders on a bombing mission, this time over Lille. Forty plus mixed Bf 109s and FW 190s attacked near the target, later driven off by 402 Sqn, though some of the German aircraft penetrated to the bombers. When the coast was reached at Le Touquet, twenty or so FW 190s climbed into the formation from the south-east and were engaged by the escort. No. 402 Sqn broke the enemy formation, which attacked in line astern having been mistaken for a formation of Spitfires despite the fact that their cowlings were painted white. Sqn Ldr Northcott attacked one of the FW 190s which continued to climb into the dogfight, the other 190s having flicked over and dived earthwards. Using cannon and machine-gun fire, he had the satisfaction of seeing his fire strike the FW 190 before its port wing tore off. The 190 crashed into the sea off Le Touquet. Four enemy aircraft were claimed destroyed by 402 Sqn in that action and a further FW 190 was claimed 'damaged'.

Northcott was to add one more Bf 109 to his score with EP120 and he damaged another Bf 109 on 3 October. He had to wait until 3 November to make his last kill however, when 416 and 402 Sqns were escorting seventy-two Marauders during an attack on Schiphol. The Wing sighted a number of Bf 109s *en route* to the target and defended an attack by the Germans. In the defensive action, Northcott claimed one of the nine enemy which fell to the Wing that day.

No. 402 continued to perform escort and shipping reconnaissance operations throughout the winter months and was posted to Ayr for air-firing armament practice camp over the Christmas 1943 and New Year periods.

On 12 February, 402 Sqn was ordered to leave Digby and move base to R.A.F. Wellingore. On departing Digby, EP120 suffered a major accident with Warrant Officer (II) Norman P. Murphy causing Cat. B damage to his C.O.'s aircraft. No details have so far come to light about the accident, but it ended the aircraft's association with the squadron.

EP120 flew seventy-nine operational sorties with 402 Squadron, accounting for the destruction of six enemy aircraft (four Bf 109s and two FW 190s), causing damage to a further enemy machine, a Bf 109, in the time she spent with the unit. All victories were at the hands of Sqn Ldr Northcott, who accounted for another FW 190 whilst flying another squadron aircraft.

Following the incident at Digby, EP120 spent time back at her birthplace undergoing repair. Arriving at Castle Bromwich on 21 February 1944, she did not depart until 24 June, moving into store with 33 M.U. at R.A.F. Lyneham.

After a four-month stay with 33 M.U. EP120 was assigned on 12 October 1944 to her last flying unit, 53 O.T.U. part of 9 Group based at Kirton-in-Lindsey. Serving here until the middle of May the following year, with a brief gap in service after a minor accident when a Vickers-Armstrong crew performed repairs on site on 19–20 April 1945. Normal service was then resumed until mid-May when the unit was disbanded.

On 2 June 1945 EP120 returned to 33 M.U. until 13 July following a transfer to No. 4 School of Technical Training (S.o.T.T.) at R.A.F. St Athan. She was allocated maintenance serial 5377M and used for training newly inducted mechanics.

Once EP120 had completed her service with the S.o.T.T. and had spent some time on the gate at the station, she was moved to gate guard duties at R.A.F. Wilmslow in Cheshire. She remained in an all-silver paint scheme until the station was closed in 1960. A maintenance serial change to 8070M, preceded a move to R.A.F. Bircham Newton in February 1960, again for instructional duties and further gate guarding until 1964.

R.A.F. Boulmer was the next receiving station and EP120 saw some tender loving care after the harsh treatment of the instructional workshops and the ravages of the English weather. Senior Technician John Ayling spent considerable time restoring EP120 using a Mk XVI Spitfire as a source of spares. The Mk XVI had been moved on to the dump at R.A.F. Dishforth, home of 60 M.U., only a matter of months before Ayling began removing pieces from it. This donor machine was TD135 which is still very much alive.

Once restored, EP120 guarded the gate at R.A.F. Boulmer until early 1967 when it was recruited by Spitfire Productions Ltd and moved to R.A.F. Henlow. Basic restoration work, a new paint scheme and a static role in the film *Battle of Britain* followed.

EP120 remained a static Spitfire – the term used was 'set dressing' – for the duration of the filming, bearing the codes AI-B and AI-N and the R.A.F. serial N3312 during its exposure to the cameras. It acquired wing-tips to make the general appearance fit that adopted for all the film Spitfires. Once filming was complete, the R.A.F. was left with a large number of maintained and some airworthy Spitfires. It had to find homes for these and EP120 was allocated, along with Mk V BL614, to R.A.F. Wattisham.

From arrival on 14 December 1970 to her departure on 30 January 1989, EP120 did not guard the gate at Wattisham all year round. During the summer months, bearing the codes QV-H – a tribute to her 19 Sqn days, despite her being QV-E during that time – she was inside the gate but during the winter she was moved into a hangar and looked after and maintained with the result that the airframe was in much better condition than many of its *Battle of Britain* contemporaries which saw subsequent gate guard service.

Following the M.o.D. decision to store historic aircraft, EP120 was moved from Wattisham to R.A.F. St Athan for storage alongside a number of other aircraft and well out of the weather to prevent further deterioration. Three years later, in an arrangement with The Fighter Collection, the M.o.D. released EP120 from its charge.

The last week in January 1993 saw EP120 arrive at Duxford for temporary storage prior to her complete restoration. She arrived painted overall grey, her engine still in place and fitted with a three-bladed metal propeller, her wings having been removed. Over the years, the cockpit had been robbed of most major components, although rudder pedals, control column (minus handgrip) and some instruments remained, and the canopy and bulletproof screen were crazed beyond repair.

A full rebuild awaited her. Audley End and Historic Flying were to undertake the restoration which was completed during late summer 1995. After considerable research, EP120 was painted in the colours of 402 Sqn, coded AE-A, bearing a Squadron Leader's pennant and the victory markings of Sqn Ldr Geoffrey Northcott.

After the rebuild and following the usual extensive ground runs, EP120 flew again, probably for the first time since 2 June 1945, on 12 September when Charlie Brown, complete with huge grin, flew her from Audley End.

Engine and propeller problems kept her grounded until the summer of 1996 when, after a series of engine runs at Duxford, she was test-flown ready to appear at the 1996 Flying Legends airshow where she was described by one of the most respected Spitfire pilots in the world as 'one of the best I have ever flown'. Testament indeed to the restoration skills of Historic Flying's engineers and Peter Rushen, The Fighter Collection's Chief Engineer, who also contributed significantly to the aircraft's restoration.

Following talks between Reynard Racing and Historic Flying, another Spitfire was to be put through the rebuild process at Audley. Adrian Reynard had owned other Spitfires in the U.K. before acquiring a Mk XVIII, serial SM845, from David Tallichet but had forsaken the other machines for the chance to own and operate the Griffon-engined Spitfire.

Originally forming part of the eleventh order for 150 Mk XI Spitfires, dated 12 February 1944, against contract Air/1877/c.23(c). Spitfire SM845 was included in the resultant mixture of Mk XIVs and Mk XVIIIs built between February 1945 and January 1946 with serials in the range SM843 to SM845, SM939 to SM956 and SM968 to SM997.

SM845 was constructed with the mighty Griffon 66 engine. Taken on charge by the R.A.F.'s 39 M.U. at R.A.F. Colerne on 28 May 1945, she remained there until her allocation to India and 76 M.U. at R.A.F. Sealand on 13 December the same year. Here she was packed for her sea voyage to India. The S.S. *Sampenn* departed the U.K. on 19 January 1946 and arrived in India on 11 February. SM845 was taken on strength by A.C.S.E.A. sixteen days later following reassembly and test flying. No

(ABOVE): Clive Denney puts the finishing touches to the fuselage artwork on The Fighter Collection's Spitfire Mk V EP120.

(ABOVE): Another example of the artistry of Clive Denney – Czech Air Force insignia on Spitfire Mk IX TE566.

record of her A.C.S.E.A activities in India exists. Apparently, she was returned to the U.K. for restoration work at Vickers before acceptance into Indian Air Force service.

Several Mk XVIII Spitfires went through this process before flying with the Indians, and it is possible that the Indian authorities contracted directly with Vickers to cover such work. Airworthy, SM845 returned to the Indian Air Force on 31 December 1947 with the serial HS687.

Her service with the Indian Air Force is not a matter of public record but it is thought the machine was one of the eight Spitfires recovered from India by Wesley Haydon-Baillie's Aircraft and Naval Collection in 1977. SM845 was located at the same base where TP280 was recovered, Kailakunda, and in a similar condition.

In company with the other three Spitfires recovered from Kailakunda, the wreck was dismantled, packed and transported to Bombay by train, then taken to the U.K. as sea freight, arriving in 1988. The Spitfire was originally purchased by Marshall Moss and Dick Boolootian of California. Following transportation to the U.S.A. the machine remained in its crate at Lancaster, California for some time. Eventually, in 1984, SM845 was acquired by David Tallichet who had Ken Sternberg of Tulsa, Oklahoma start restoration work on the airframe in his workshops. SM845 was to share these workshop facilities with TP298, another recovery from India. Both aircraft were moved to Casper, Wyoming towards the end of 1985.

One of the many Tallichet aircraft, a collection later sold, SM845 was acquired by U.K.-based Adrian Reynard and registered as G-BUOS on 19 October 1992. Restoration work with Historic Flying commenced at this time and the aircraft was resident in the Audley End hangar by spring 1994 when extensive reskinning work commenced on the wings. The fuselage and wings were completely rebuilt, almost from scratch. The wings were completed in mid-1994. After a break in activities, work on the fuselage was recommenced in early 1996. While a small number of Griffon-engined Spitfires fly in the U.K. – most notably the Mk XIVs operated by The Fighter Collection and the Mk XIXs of the Battle of Britain Memorial Flight – SM845 will be the first flying Mk XVIII resident here for some years.

While work on the wings of SM845 was underway, another Mk V arrived at Historic Flying. Spitfire AR614, a fairly complete Mk Vc, had been acquired by Sir Tim Wallis from the Old Flying Machine Company which had been working on the aeroplane away from the spotlight of Duxford. Installed at Audley End, work was started on the fuselage in late 1994. Built in 1942, AR614 had seen a great deal of wartime activity and had served very briefly in the same squadron as the Old Flying Machine Company's more famous Mk IX Spitfire, MH434.

Built by Westland Aircraft Ltd, and forming part of the first order against contract B124305/40 which specified 300 Mk I Spitfires, AR614 was included in the mix of 50 Mk Is, 140 Mk Vbs and 110 Mk Vcs built by Westlands between July 1941 and September 1942. The order was placed in August 1940 but AR614 was not completed by Westland until August 1942 – some two years later! Allocated the Westland build number WASP 20/288, AR614 was built as a Spitfire Vc with a Merlin 46 engine. On 22 August 1942, AR614 was delivered to 39 M.U. at R.A.F. Colerne for fitting for operational duty and assigned to No. 312 (Czech) Squadron based at R.A.F. Harrowbeer on 11 September.

No. 312 Sqn had formed on the 29 August 1940 with Czech personnel. Equipped initially with Hurricanes, the squadron was assigned to Speke to defend areas around the Mersey. They had been brought south in May 1941 to join the offensive and had made a name for themselves with their tenacity and fighting skills.

Spitfire AR614 suffered Category AC damage on 7 November in the hands of pilot Flt Sgt S. Tocauer when a tyre burst during the take-off run from Church Stanton. Tocauer switched off the engine immediately but one of the undercarriage legs collapsed. AR614 went down on one wing causing extensive damage to the radiator, undercarriage and propeller.

Though repairs began the same day, AR614 was not back on charge with 312 until February 1943. Mostly flown by the Squadron boss, Sqn Ldr Vybiral, it was during this time, while leading the Czech Wing on 14 May, that AR614 was hit and damaged. The Wing was attacking twelve German E-boats and a number of small vessels at St Peter Port, Guernsey when they encountered intense return fire. One shell hit AR614's fuselage, just aft of the cockpit, exploding and destroying the radio. She limped home after the attack which had left one other Czech pilot dead.

The initial Category AC damage was later reassessed Category B, and AR614 was sent to Air Service Training in June 1943 for repair. The work was completed at the end of August. Following test-flying, AR614 was transferred to 6 M.U. at R.A.F. Brize Norton on 9 September to await assignment. Held at the M.U. for just over a month, she was assigned on 20 November to 610 (County of Chester) Sqn Auxiliary Air Force based in Devon.

Two months later, on 30 January 1944, AR614 was allocated to 130 (Punjab) Squadron at Scorton where she wore the codes PJ-E. Three days later, she was air-tested by Flt Lt B. Madden, who was later rumoured to be the first R.A.F. pilot to tip over a V-1 flying bomb with his wing-tip. No. 130 Sqn was disbanded eleven days after this flight, on 13 February, and AR614 was transferred to 222 (Natal) Sqn at R.A.F. Acklington on the 16th. Interestingly, 130 Sqn lived on after their disbandment when, on 5 April 1944, 186 Sqn was renamed 130 Sqn and took on the Squadron codes of AP, replacing the original PJ codes.

Five days after the transfer, the machine was again damaged – Category AC again – after a flying accident, although there are no further details of this prang. A repair party was able to restore the machine to full health on site but it was to be 31 March before AR614 was back on charge with 222 Sqn. This state of affairs continued until 2 September 1944 when a move to 53 Operational Training Unit (O.T.U.) immediately followed attention from No. 3501 Servicing Unit.

It would appear that 3501 S.U. wasted their time with AR614 as she was pranged again fourteen days later, again suffering Category AC damage. She was repaired on site by the second week of October and returned to duties with 53 O.T.U., apparently incident free. In June the following year, she was retired to 33 M.U. at R.A.F. Lyneham and placed in storage. Her period of rest and recuperation was short-lived, however, as by 13 July she had been allocated the instructional serial 5378M and posted to the hell of the School of Technical Training at R.A.F. St Athan, South Wales.

The horrors and indignities of her time at St Athan have never been recorded and details are unlikely to be found now. However, R.A.F. Padgate near Warrington was to sport a new gate guard during 1949 which was displayed with the ambiguous maintenance serial 371M. The machine stayed for about two years before moving on to the gate of R.A.F. West Kirby where it displayed further confusing identities.

The maintenance serial 7555M was issued to the machine when it moved on to the gate at R.A.F. Hednesford in January 1958 and was retained when, later the same year, a further move took it to R.A.F. Bridgnorth in Shropshire. It was displayed here in an all-silver scheme until 1963 when it was removed to an ever-growing scrap heap at 60 M.U. R.A.F. Dishforth.

Later that same year, the R.A.F. offered for sale by tender two Spitfires, a Mk XVI and a Mk V from the 60 M.U. treasure trove. The Mk V was quoted as being 5728M despite the fact that this serial was allocated to BM597 at that time. A closer inspection of the aircraft brought to light a number of squadron codes, including the KU-V of 53 O.T.U., the combination of which pointed only to AR614. The 371M serial which had

(ABOVE): Spitfire Mk V AR614 displays its identity underneath the paintwork just aft of the starboard roundel.

begun the confusion in fact related to 6371M, which the aircraft had been allocated towards the end of its stay at St Athan. Photographs of the aircraft at this time show the code actually being worn as being 871M.

The sale of the two machines was completed and AR614 was bought in 1964 by the Air Museum of Calgary, Canada. Packed and crated, it was soon shipped to Canada but was stored on arrival, still in its crate, for a number of years. The museum was experiencing difficulties at this time and eventually it had to part with the crated Mk V. In 1970, it was purchased by Donald Campbell of Kapukasing, Ontario, who stored the aircraft for many years before commencing a long-term restoration programme. Despite its delayed start, work was definitely underway in 1986.

After some detailed negotiations, the Old Flying Machine Company at Duxford bought AR614 from Donald and in December 1992 returned the machine to England. Away from the workshops at Duxford, a restoration to full airworthy condition was begun. On 19 March 1993, it was registered to Ray Hanna of Classic Aviation Ltd as G-BUWA. Ownership passed to Sir Tim Wallis's Alpine Fighter Collection in 1994 and the aircraft has now been completed by Historic Flying at Audley End.

The newly installed engine was successfully run for the first time in late August 1996 and first post-restoration flight followed very shortly afterwards. AR614 is the second Mk V Spitfire to have been restored by Historic Flying.

Having mentioned BM597 several times so far, it would seem appropriate to deal with the history of the machine at this point. Spitfire BM597 is the oldest of all the Spitfires that have been through the workshops at Audley End, having been delivered into R.A.F. hands literally a month earlier than EP120, and only four months earlier than AR614. It was built as part of the batch of 1000 Mk III Spitfires that comprised the third order against contract B981687/39/C.23(c). The order was built as Mk Vbs from November 1941 to May 1942. She was built in early 1942 at the massive Castle Bromwich Aircraft Factory (hence the CBAF number which often prefixes the serials of such aircraft – in BM597's case the construction number CBAF-2461 was allocated).

No. 37 M.U., at R.A.F. Burtonwood, was the first R.A.F. unit to receive the aircraft, an event which took place on 26 April 1942. Operational preparation completed, the aircraft was assigned to 315 (Deblinski) Sqn, a Polish unit which was based at the time at R.A.F. Woodvale on the Lancashire coast.

No. 315 Sqn had been formed at R.A.F. Acklington on 21 January 1941 as a fighter squadron, and moved to Speke in mid-March that year to become operational with Hurricane Is with the general charge of protecting Merseyside. The unit graduated to Spitfire IIs in July 1941 when it was relocated to R.A.F. Northolt, and then to Spitfire Mk Vs in August. Flying from Northolt, the squadron was heavily involved in the air war over southern England and flew many fighter sweeps in the airspace of northern France.

After nine months of such intensive operations, 315 Squadron was withdrawn to R.A.F. Woodvale on the Lancashire coast for a breather and this is where BM597 caught up with it. Still operational, the unit flew sorties over the north-west of the U.K. and the Irish Sea for five months before being returned to the thick of the fighting. On 5 September 1942,

(LEFT):Inside the wings of Spitfire Mk V AR614 the stencilled identity of Spitfire EE768, also a Mk V, can be clearly seen. It is understood that AR614 had one wing replaced during one of its visits to Maintenance Units for repair after flying accidents. It became a ground instructional airframe in July 1945 when it was transported to R.A.F. St Athan. Note the extensive corrosion in the aluminium main web and steel blast-tube areas. However, other items, such as the catch, turret and door structures were refurbished and refitted.

317 (Wilenski) Sqn, another Polish unit, arrived at Woodvale thus allowing 315 Sqn to return to R.A.F. Northolt.

This they did the following day with, one imagines, considerable hangovers following the inevitable party in the mess that night. It is not clear whether all the aircraft of the two squadrons were swapped at this point but BM597 certainly made the transition from 315 to 317 without leaving Woodvale.

No. 317 (Wilenski) Sqn had been formed on 22 February 1941, again at R.A.F. Acklington, as a Polish Hurricane squadron, being equipped with Mk I Hurricanes. In June, it moved south to R.A.F. Colerne and began to take part in sweeps and bomber-escort missions over northern France. Further moves to Fairwood Common and Exeter, where the Squadron was re-equipped with Hurricane Mk IIs and then Mk Vb Spitfires, preceded its replacement of 315 Sqn at Northolt on 1 April 1942, and then its displacement of them again from R.A.F. Woodvale in September the same year.

Spitfire BM597 was to suffer some damage in a flying accident while with 317 Sqn, the damage being assessed at the time to be Category B and noted to have occurred on 13 February 1943. Repairs were to take place away from Woodvale and it was effectively taken off the strength of the Polish squadron at that time. It was not until the first week in June 1943 that the aircraft was again available to the R.A.F., 33 M.U. at R.A.F. Lyneham taking her on charge.

Her stay with the maintenance unit was short as BM597 was allocated to the Vickers South Marston works on 26 June to participate in a number of modifications and trials. The fuel systems were first modified and tested, followed by alterations to the elevators and rudder. The testing culminated in trials of wing stiffening modifications and the fitting of Mk III I.F.F. bomb-carrying shackles to the wings. The results of these trials were no doubt recorded at the time but have not yet come to light in either the Public Records Office or the R.A.F. Museum.

Vickers completed their testing by 23 November when the aircraft was returned to 39 M.U. at R.A.F. Colerne for a period of storage. Long-term storage must have been envisioned for the aeroplane as she was sent to 222 M.U.'s Packing Depot at High Ercall in early January 1944. Her return to 39 M.U. was not until 14 April and she was to remain at R.A.F. Colerne for nearly a year.

No. 58 O.T.U. was to be her last operational unit. She joined it on 2 April 1945 from Colerne and remained in service with it until 16 October the same year, effectively seeing the war come to a close while still being flown operationally. When it was finally decided to end her flying career, BM597 took on the maintenance serial 5713M and was transferred from 58 O.T.U. to the mercies of No. 4 School of Technical Training at R.A.F. St Athan in South Wales.

Ironically, despite the known hazards of the Schools of Technical Training for recently retired aircraft, it was probably this move that saved the aircraft from the attentions of the scrap men. The detailed movements of BM597, and more importantly the dates of her movements, start to get a little hazy at this point in her history. That she arrived on the gate at R.A.F. Hednesford, in Cannock Chase in Staffordshire, is undisputed, but whether she arrived in 1945 as one source would have it – thereby making her the first Spitfire to be used on the gate of an R.A.F. station – or whether the move was made after a period of use at No. 4 S.o.T.T. has not yet been established beyond doubt in the many sources used in this compilation.

Photographic evidence shows her to be at the station, which initially housed No. 6 S.o.T.T. and later concentrated solely on basic recruit training, around 1955. She is shown in an all silver finish without codes and apparently without a serial, and she remained on site up until the point at which Hednesford was closed. That R.A.F. Bridgnorth was the next

station to benefit from BM597's accumulated gate guarding skills is not challenged. However, the best that can be done to date her service at the station is a photograph of her at Bridgnorth 'sometime in the late 1950s'. Again, she is shown in an all silver finish without codes or serials.

The same source is adamant that BM597 was moved on to R.A.F. Church Fenton in 1964, following the closure of Bridgnorth as an R.A.F. station. It would appear that she may have been lucky to do so as other inmates of Bridgnorth, specifically the Meteor F. Mk III EE405, were scrapped on site as the station was shut down. Support for this date is offered in a photograph from a separate source, which shows BM597 on gate guard at Bridgnorth in 1960.

However, other sources are equally adamant that the move to R.A.F. Church Fenton was made some time in 1957. Checking the date for the closure of R.A.F. Bridgnorth would appear to offer the only absolute solution to this particular issue, as photograph captions cannot be wholly relied on in such important circumstances.

We are back on firmer ground by 1964 when the aircraft was definitely established at Church Fenton. She had had a little colour put back in her cheeks with a full camouflage paint scheme over the ageing silver scheme. No. 609 (West Riding) Sqn R.Aux.A.F. was honoured with the application of the codes PR-O (codes she still wore until the start of the fuselage restoration at Audley End) and her maintenance serial 5718M had been applied on both sides of the rear fuselage. Church Fenton was to relinquish its prized gate guard in March 1967, when it was removed from the gate to R.A.F. Henlow for use in the filming of the epic *Battle of Britain*.

Producers Harry Salzmann and Benjamin Fisz created the aptly named Spitfire Productions Ltd and set about building themselves a credible pair of air forces – British and German. They were ably assisted by Gp Capt Hamish Mahaddie who had been a founder member of the R.A.F.'s famous Pathfinders during the war. He had now been tasked with finding enough aircraft to make the set of the film look as though Spitfires, Hurricanes and Bf 109s had never gone out of production. He found over 100 Spitfires in the first ten days searching and his efforts, to a large degree, can be considered to have created the warbird industry we know today.

Despite his best efforts, however, there could never be enough aircraft to fill the airfields in the way demanded by the producers of the film, so a production unit was created at Pinewood Studios to build full-size Hurricanes, Spitfires and Bf 109s out of wood and plastic – the unit even ran to a full-size Heinkel 111 weighing 6 tons! These facsimile fighters were fitted with motorcycle engines that were sufficiently powerful to allow the aircraft to 'taxi' and, of course, it was to be the replicas that would take the explosive brunt of the many attack sequences planned for the film.

BM597 was moved from Henlow to the studios at Pinewood on 23 October 1967 to become the Spitfire model for the production unit to copy, the master for all the glassfibre moulds used to create the Spitfire Production's air force of Spitfires. Many of these dummy Spitfires still exist in museums around the country and all the survivors owe their good looks to BM597.

BM597 returned to R.A.F. Henlow in August 1968 and eventually made it back to Church Fenton in the early part of 1969, where she was restored to the gate. There she remained for the next six years until 1975 saw the relegation of R.A.F. Church Fenton to care and maintenance status. R.A.F. Linton-on-Ouse provided a new home for the aircraft at that time, a custody which was to last until 8 September 1979. R.A.F. Church Fenton had to be reopened early in 1979 and, when the cobwebs had been dusted off sufficiently, BM597 was rescued from her temporary home at Linton and transported back to the gate at Church Fenton.

It was here that Tim Routsis surveyed the aircraft in 1988 and from here that he removed it on 26 May 1989. The aircraft was remarkably complete and in extremely good condition at that time. It was stored immediately after its removal but despite having to wait to begin restoration Tim registered it as G-MKVB soon after he acquired it. R.A.F. Church Fenton was allocated a glassfibre replica Mk VIII to compensate for the loss of BM597, although the plastic Spit is painted as the Mk I L1096.

Work was able to begin on BM597 at Audley End in earnest in early 1993 with the removal and gradual rebuild of the tail unit. Work on the fuselage and wings started shortly afterwards, as time and resources allowed, and the engine was packed and posted away to be rebuilt. In early 1997 the work on the project moved into top gear and by May the airframe was substantially complete. By July an immaculate Merlin 35 (rebuilt by Andrew Wood of P. and A. Wood, Great Easton) was in place. The first engine runs were undertaken on the 16 July and by the 20 July the aircraft had flown and was well into its flight-test programme.

The other Spitfire which has not yet been dealt with, and which formed part of the original deal between Tim and the M.o.D., is TB252, the highbacked Mk XVI Spitfire which was rescued from the gate of R.A.F. Bentley Priory in November 1988. Spitfire TB252 was built at Castle Bromwich during late 1944 and early 1945 following the seventeenth order (for 1884 Spitfire Mk IX aircraft) against contract B981687/39/C.23(c). She took the constructor's number CBAF-IX-3801 and was built, despite the reference to IX in the number, as one of the 632 Mk XVIe aircraft eventually produced against that order, being completed with clipped wings, a high back and a Packard Merlin 266 engine.

From Castle Bromwich, the aeroplane was moved on 6 January 1945 to No. 9 M.U. at R.A.F. Cosford where it was prepared for service. She was held briefly before being allocated to No. 329 (Cigognes) Squadron of the Free French Air Force at the Dutch airfield of Schijndel, which was known to the Allies as airfield B.85, on 1 March 1945. No. 329 Sqn had only been in existence as an R.A.F. unit for a little over a year at this point, being formed at Ayr in early January 1944. The unit had arrived in Scotland from North Africa where it had fought under its Armée de l'Air title of Groupe de Chasse I/2.

After providing cover for the D-Day landings, flying from Kent, the unit moved into France during August 1944 and to Holland the following September. TB252 was soon in the thick of the fighting, its activities being brought to an end after literally one week when it was damaged and needed field repairs. These were carried out by No. 411 Repair and Servicing Unit (R.S.U.) from 8 March at Schijndel. On completion of the work, which lasted until 15 March, the aircraft was taken on to the strength of No. 341 (Alsace) Sqn of the Free French because 329 Sqn had moved back to R.A.F. Turnhouse the day after the accident.

No. 341 Sqn had also been formed from personnel of the Free French Flight, but this time at R.A.F. Turnhouse, in January 1943 and was moved to Schijndel to replace 329 Sqn on 9 March, thus inheriting TB252 in her damaged state. The squadron had previously seen action from Biggin Hill and over the Brittany coast while based in Cornwall, and through France and Belgium following the D-Day invasion in June 1944. In mid-April, TB252, now carrying the squadron codes NL, moved with the squadron to airfield B.105 at Drope and then on to B.152 at Fassberg on 6 July.

The squadron gave up its aircraft on 7 November when it left R.A.F. control and passed to the administration of the Belgian Armée de l'Air. The subsequent movements of TB252 would indicate that she did not leave Belgium at this time but remained there awaiting a decision on her next allocation.

She briefly served with No. 135 Wing after the war, joining them on 29 November 1945, then passing to No. 350 (Belgian) Sqn of 146 Wing at Fassberg in Belgium on 15 January 1946. At this point, the aircraft was

considered to be on loan to the Belgian Air Force. With the squadron codes MN-J, it was to fly with the Belgians from a number of Belgian bases, Fassberg and St-Denijs Westrem not least among them, before an accident in early October 1946 forced its return to the U.K. and the long-term attentions of No. 151 Repair Unit. No. 61 O.T.U. was to be the next home for TB252, but such was the damage done in the accident in Belgium that it was to be 29 May 1947 before she was taken on strength at the O.T.U.

No. 61 O.T.U. was based at R.A.F. Keevil where a lot of the Spitfire production test-flying had taken place throughout the years of the war. TB252 was still training R.A.F. pilots when the unit was redesignated 203 Advanced Flying School. It was not until 18 January 1949 that she was moved again. This time, she was seen to be surplus to requirements and the move was to storage at Old Sarum.

Many a Spitfire, and probably many other types, had suffered a slow death by burning at Old Sarum at about this time. The fire dump at the station had been used for fire-crew training for some years and the consumption of airframes in this training can only be viewed now after a good stiff drink. How TB252 came to avoid the fiery death is not known but she was on that station for some four years before being placed in longer-term storage at R.A.F. Lyneham's 33 M.U. a move which was dated 27 February 1953. It is likely that she was allocated the maintenance serial number 7257M at the time she was moved.

From Lyneham, TB252 moved to R.A.F. Odiham, near Basingstoke, on 12 September 1955, where she was to be used for ground instruction duties. Just before this move, she had another maintenance serial allocated, 7281M, but this was cancelled soon after and she arrived at Odiham as 7257M. Her stay at the station was just short of four years when, on 21 August 1959, she was placed on display at R.A.F. Acklington with an all silver paint scheme and the squadron codes RR-M.

Her tailwheel was removed and replaced with an extended support which served to raise the tail so that she was displayed in a vaguely level pose. She managed to avoid call-up for use in the *Battle of Britain* but moved to R.A.F. Boulmer on 1 August 1969 for further display duties. The maintenance serial 8073M was issued at about this time, although it was never worn.

Duty at Boulmer was to be short-lived. On 5 December 1969 the Spitfire was moved again, this time to R.A.F. Leuchars. Early in its stay in Scotland, TB252 acquired the colours of No. 340 (Ile de France) Sqn of the Free French, being displayed as GW-H and wearing the legend 'Lucky Nine' with five swastika kill markings. The legend apparently referred to the sum of her individual serial numerals, i.e. 2+5+2 equalling 9, although the origin of the aircraft's luck was not recorded. She was displayed inside the station for much of the time she was in Scotland, a residency which was to last for some sixteen years.

In 1985 moves were afoot in the Ministry of Defence to present a Spitfire to the San Diego Air and Space Museum where it would appear in honour of the American Eagle Squadrons. The presentation was, in fact, an exchange for a North American Mustang for display in the R.A.F. Museum at Hendon. The Spitfire selected for the exchange was Mk XVI SL574 which was on display guarding the gate at the historic headquarters of No. 11 Group, R.A.F. Bentley Priory.

In 1986, SL574 was transferred from Bentley Priory to R.A.F. Halton where it was to be refurbished before its presentation to the American authorities in October 1989. The resulting vacancy at Bentley Priory was filled by TB252 which was replaced at Leuchars by the F.21 Spitfire LA198 which had been moved from R.A.F. Locking in Avon. After the Spitfire shuffle was complete, R.A.F. Locking was allocated a former Red Arrows' Gnat to fill the gap on the station's gate. This move was to be the last for TB252 before being acquired by Tim Routsis in mid-1988 and her subsequent transport to the workshops of Vintage Fabrics on 9 November the same year.

The aircraft was in very good condition when it was removed, being almost totally complete – rather surprising after its ground instructional service at Odiham and very nearly thirty years on a number of R.A.F. gates.

Initially, Bentley Priory was to have F.21 Spitfire LA226, then in store at R.A.F. Shawbury, to replace TB252. This decision was rescinded in favour of one of the glassfibre Spitfires produced for the purpose by Feggans Brown on behalf of Tim Routsis. The Mk VIII Spitfire, painted as Mk I K9926, was assembled during 1990. TB252 moved in September 1990 to the newly built hangar at Audley End and was stored alongside BM597. Restoration work to airworthy status commenced on this airframe in late 1997.

(Below): Spitfire Mk XVIe TB252 at Audley End, June 1992. This aircraft was removed from the gate at R.A.F. Bentley Priory where it had served as gate guardian for a number of years. Best of the gate guards, it was untouched due to positioning outside the senior officers' area of works.

While Historic Flying are widely known for its restoration work on Spitfires, it also carries out maintenance work on already airworthy examples, and on machines other than Spitfires. However, we will continue to concentrate on the Spitfires which have passed through the doors of the Historic Flying hangar and turn our attentions to one of the longest-serving Spitfires anywhere in the world, serving the R.A.F. in a number of guises since early 1945. The story of the Mk XIX PM631 is inextricably entwined with the story of the Battle of Britain Memorial Flight.

Production of the P.R. Mk XIX Spitfire PM631 commenced with the sixth M.o.D. order against contract Air/1877/C.23(c), which was submitted on 2 June 1942. The initial requirement was for 592 Mk VIII Spitfires and, after several amendments, was finally settled at 227 P.R. Mk XIs and 124 P.R. Mk XIXs. These aircraft were eventually constructed between February 1944 and May 1946 – up to four years after the initial order. Spitfire PM631 was completed at either Aldermaston or Chattis Hill in the early part of 1945, having taken the constructor's number 6S/683528. The specification for the standard Mk XIX included provision for 20 gallons of fuel to be carried in the leading edge of each wing, and

the use of the basic Mk VIII fuselage with Mk XI wings. The price of each aircraft was not to exceed £7500, although this limit was raised to £8980 shortly after the order was accepted.

It is likely that PM631 was pressed into service with her manufacturer shortly after completion and well before being released to the R.A.F. The Aircraft Movement form (AM78) records involvement in preproduction trials of the Coffman starter modifications mooted by Supermarine. The system was finally removed from PM631 in 1990 when a 24-volt electrical system replaced it, enabling electric starting. She was also involved in trials of a number of alterations to the pilot's harness arrangements before delivery to 6 M.U. at R.A.F. Brize Norton on 6 November 1945, too late to see wartime service with the R.A.F.

Although there is some confusion about PM631's activities at this point, it seems likely that she was stored at Brize Norton until 6 May 1949 when she was assigned to 203 Advanced Flying School at Keevil flying in an all silver paint scheme. The school moved to Stradishall on 19 July 1949, two months later being renamed 226 Operational Conversion Unit (O.C.U.) PM631 remained there until 13 January 1950 when she was flown back to Brize Norton and placed in storage, until 30 June 1950 and a move to 9 M.U. at R.A.F. Cosford. She spent about three weeks with the station flight at R.A.F. Bückeberg in Germany from 15 January 1951 before returning to the U.K. and further storage at Cosford.

On 2 July 1951, PM631 was issued to a civilian organisation, a division of Short Brothers and Harland, contracted by the Air Ministry to operate a weather-assessment flight from R.A.F. Hooton Park. The flight was designated the THUM (Temperature and HUMidity) flight and issued with four R.A.F. Spitfire P.R. Mk XIXs, the type being selected for its range, stability and general suitability for the job.

Initial aircraft allocated to the flight included PM549, coded A, PM577, coded B, PM652 coded C and PM631 coded D. Both PM549 and PM652 were lost in fatal flying accidents within a short period and were replaced by PS853 and PM651. The latter aircraft lasted a month before suffering damage beyond repair. It was replaced by PS915, which itself still flies today with the Battle of Britain Memorial Flight despite a lengthy period of gate guarding.

Eleven days after arrival at Hooton Park, the flight was moved across the Mersey to R.A.F. Woodvale where the Spitfires continued to be used for high-level meteorological work. Shorts' task was to gather data each morning on conditions in the upper atmosphere (to about 30,000 ft) over a point north of Worcester. Each climb took about 45 minutes. The data collected was then taken by the Spitfire to Liverpool airport, Speke, and passed to the Met. Office.

By 1956, the Air Ministry was looking to replace the Spitfires at Woodvale, although an alternative aircraft type had yet to be designated. A Mk 24 Spitfire was tried and rejected. Eventually, the Mosquito TT.35 was chosen as much for the spares availability as for its inherent stability. The last Spitfire THUM flight was made from Woodvale by PS853 on 10 June 1957.

Following an airshow at Woodvale on the 12th, the Spitfires were readied for return to R.A.F. operations. From the THUM flight at Woodvale, PM631, PS853 and PS915 were due to be flown by their civilian pilots to Duxford on 14 June 1957. However, PS853 suffered an engine failure resulting in John Formby making a forced landing on the grass at Woodvale. A pit in the ground caught an undercarriage leg after a successful touchdown and the aircraft ended up on its nose.

Meanwhile, PS915 was causing pilot Frank Richards some difficulty and he too landed back at Woodvale. The cause of PS915's reluctance to leave was cured in very short order and PS915 and PM631, in the hands of THUM pilot Eric Richards, made it to Duxford later that same day with

PS853 joining the pair some days later.

There preparations were made to add the three Spitfires to the single Hurricane, LF363, of the Historic Aircraft Flight at Biggin Hill in Kent. On 11 July, the three Spitfires were flown from Duxford by Group Captain 'Johnnie' Johnson, Group Captain 'Jamie' Rankin and Wing Commander Peter Thompson who was at the helm of PM631. The Flight officially became the Battle of Britain Flight on that day, though a number of commentators were quick to point out that the three Mk XIXs had not even been in service at the time of the Battle.

Early in 1958, the Battle of Britain Flight was forced to move its base when the Ministry of Defence saw fit to close Biggin Hill as a Royal Air Force front-line station. By this time, PS915 had been relegated to gate guard duties at R.A.F. West Malling.

Fortunately however, two Mk XVIs joined the Flight and the two XVIs and the two XIXs, with the attendant Hurricane, took up brief residence at R.A.F. North Weald in Essex on 28 February 1958. By the end of May that year, the Flight moved to Martlesham Heath in Suffolk, after the closure of North Weald on 16 May. Spitfire PS853 was moved to the gate at the C.F.E. at West Raynham. The two Mk XVIs were transferred from the Flight a year later when, within a matter of a few days, they both suffered landing accidents, one the celebrated stumping-by-Spitfire at the Oxo cricket ground in Bromley while a match was in progress.

The remaining aircraft in the Flight spent four years at Martlesham Heath before it, too, closed and forced the Flight to move to R.A.F. Horsham St Faith on 3 November 1961. Horsham was closed on 1 April 1963 and the Flight was again relocated, just a few miles down the road to R.A.F. Coltishall. Here, PS853 was at last reunited with the Flight and, on 15 September 1965, Jeffrey Quill himself delivered a 'rescued' Mk V Spitfire to the Flight.

From flying solo, PM631 was now joined by PS853 and AB910, and it was not long before the 'baby Spitfire', Mk IIa P7350, was dramatically rescued from the scrap man and made available to the Flight.

Whilst with the Flight at Coltishall in January 1964, PM631 was pressed into service at R.A.F. Binbrook in Lincolnshire, taking part in combat trials against a Gloster Javelin of No. 64 Sqn. This unlikely combination was intended to allow the C.F.E., and the Javelin pilots of No. 60 Sqn located in the Far East at the time of the Indonesian confrontation, to develop suitable tactics for using the Firestreak missile in jet versus piston-engined fighter dogfighting scenarios. Three years later, another secondment from the Flight saw PM631 and her pilot, Flt Lt J. Armstrong, being used in the *Battle of Britain*. During the aerial filming, PM631 bore the serials N3316, N3317, N3319, N3320 and N3326 and codes AI-L, EI-K, EI-N and DO-G. However, being Griffon-engined and having five propeller blades, she was not allowed to get too close to the cameras in case the look required by the director was compromised.

In late summer 1968, Spitfire Productions moved an aerial filming unit to Montpellier in the south of France in an attempt to beat the worsening British weather which was delaying the final air-to-air sequences. The move paid off, and the sequences were soon on film using French sunshine instead of the absent British equivalent. The film unit consisted of nine Spitfires, PM631 amongst them, three Hispano Buchons (representing Bf 109s), and the B-25 camera ship.

On the day the armada was due to return to the U.K., PM631 suffered propeller damage when a stone was thrown into it by the prop wash of another aircraft. Damage was limited to a missing chunk of propeller blade but the damage was bad enough to warrant remedial treatment at Montpellier. The other eleven aircraft flew back to England and PM631 had two inches sawn off the tip of each of her propeller blades to remove the affected part and balance the propeller to within flying tolerances.

While sounding somewhat unorthodox, this mod was standard during the war years in cases of similar damage. The R.A.F. was rather less supportive of the action in this particular case. Their strident objections to the treatment received by PM631 were sufficient to warrant Spitfire Productions replacing the five blades from the Mk XIX with pristine examples before handing back the aircraft. When the company's spares holding was sold off after filming was complete, the shortened blades found their way to Spencer Flack who used them on the restoration of his bright red Spitfire Mk XIV, NH904, without problem.

Spitfire PM631 returned to the Battle of Britain Flight at Coltishall in 1969 to have the rest of her film make-up removed in favour of a gloss camouflage finish and the 113 Sqn codes AD-C.

The year 1976 saw the Battle of Britain Memorial Flight, as the Flight

(ABOVE): Mk XIX of the Battle of Britain Memorial Flight, post maintenance work and total repaint.

was now known, take up residence at R.A.F. Conningsby in Lincolnshire, a home it still occupies today. The opportunities for the Flight to perform before the public began to increase gradually with a consistent number of hours being flown by each of the aircraft over the following years.

On 5 March 1986 – the fiftieth anniversary of the first flight of the prototype Spitfire – PM631 was flown by Squadron Leader Paul Day in the first official R.A.F. flypast over central London since the 1959 ban imposed following SL574's unfortunate forced-landing on the Bromley cricket pitch. In 1984 she had been painted as a 91 Sqn aircraft, coded DL-E, with full invasion stripes around fuselage and wings to commemorate the fortieth anniversary of the D-Day landings. These markings were seen by the French during her flight over the Normandy beaches on 6 June 1944 and by Londoners who viewed her flight in 1986.

At the end of the 1989 season, during which exactly 14 hours were flown by PM631, a major overhaul of the aircraft was undertaken at the Cranfield Institute of Technology in Bedfordshire. The opportunity was taken to replace the ancient cartridge starter mechanism on the Griffon 66 with a 24-volt electrical starter system. This work meant that the whole electrical system had to be uprated. The alteration enabled the Spitfire to land away from Conningsby after displays whereas previously she had been tasked with fly-out and fly-back trips, dependent on cartridges for starting. She returned to the Flight from Cranfield following air-tests on 10 April 1990, having been resprayed in S.E.A.C. camouflage colours (11 Sqn). S.E.A.C.

roundels and the simple code letter N were applied to the aircraft and the name *Mary* was added to the port engine-cowling.

Spitfire PM631 arrived at the Audley End hangar on 21 November 1995 for a major strip-down and service. With the engine out, it soon became apparent that the fuel tanks would need to be replaced. This achieved, and a new paint scheme applied (No. 681 Sqn P.R. blue markings), the Battle of Britain Memorial Flight's longest-serving Spitfire was returned to the unit she had served since July 1957, ready for the rigours of her thirty-ninth display season.

Historic Flying Limited is still continuing the work to increase the world's population of airworthy Spitfires and will no doubt continue to do so while there are still airframes to build.

The Commercial Approach – Comments by Tim Routsis

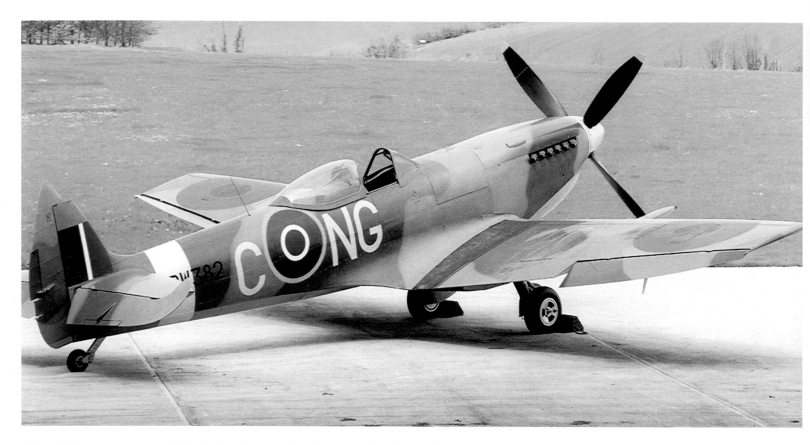

(ABOVE): Grace, symmetry – the Spitfire has it all. It seems almost incongruous that it proved to be one of the most efficient fighting machines of its time.

'Because it's a toy and it's a dream, it would be very sad to let either the toy or the dream founder on the rock of financial reality.'

The Spitfire is a remarkable example of man's ingenuity. Having once been built to fly, the ingenuity of man can rebuild the aircraft to airworthy condition and make it fly again. When they were first built, the financial resources of the nation underwrote the cost. That is no longer the case and the resources have to be found from elsewhere. Nowadays, a single businessman or a small consortium picks up the bill for putting a Spitfire back into the air.

Each airframe requires the attention of two teams of skilled artisans. They spend between 10,000 and 13,000 man-hours on the restoration. The propeller is the single most expensive part; it is even more expensive than the Rolls-Royce Merlin that drives it. The restoration process means that, in effect, each Spitfire that is rebuilt becomes a prototype, each with its own particular problems to solve. No two Spitfire restorations are the same. The overall success of the restoration is determined by how the project is managed from day one – not very glamorous but a harsh reality that has to be faced.

'If you were to look at the pile of bits that just arrived out there, and allowed yourself to dwell for too long on the difficulties that may lie ahead, you would become very depressed very quickly.'

The airframes described in this book broadly fall into two categories: untouched airframes and partly restored airframes.

Untouched Airframes

These are generally in a parlous condition, bereft of a huge number of components but their structural integrity is good. They are not exactly in factory condition but they are still unadulterated products of the factory. With this sort of airframe we have a good starting point from which to work on the restoration process. A survey of the airframe is conducted immediately to ascertain which mods and what repairs have been carried out during its life. In addition, the survey is intended to spot any corrosion or physical damage suffered by the airframe.

Partly Restored Airframes

These airframes always give the most trouble. There are basically three problem areas: part lineage, metallurgy, and dimensional integrity.

Part Lineage

Nowadays, the criteria for replacement parts is very clear: only components that have a known provenance can be used in the restoration of a Spitfire.

(*ABOVE*): *Work commences on carefully dismantling the port wing from Spitfire Mk V BM597 in the autumn of 1994. This shot shows the structure of the Spitfire wing. This is the first major work that has been undertaken on the wing since it was built at Castle Bromwich. All existing tubing and wiring is replaced with new stock which will ensure the aircraft's longevity. A large proportion of the original material was reused, e.g. rear spar, most of the ribs and open boom section.*

(*ABOVE*): *Two wing sections from Spitfire Mk V AR614 prior to work commencing on the rebuild, autumn 1994. Though some work had been done on the fuselage in Canada, the wings remained untouched and were undoubtedly the worst examples that Historic Flying had attempted to restore up to then. It turned out that these wings came from two different aircraft – note wooden fairing strip on one and metal on the other.*

(*BELOW*): *Original 'As Received' condition of EP120.*

(*ABOVE*): *Roughly daubed on the inside of the gun-bay panel is the serial BM597 which was almost certainly applied by R.A.F. armourers to facilitate swift refitting to the correct aircraft during rearming turnarounds.*

(ABOVE): The airframe on arrival had been partially restored using American-gauge rivets. The work was of a suitable standard and reused. The standard work process had to be changed to accommodate the earlier work. Mk V AR614.

Without knowing the provenance of a part there is no way to verify that it is a genuine part. If it is not genuine it should not be used. Engineers find themselves reusing parts that are fifty plus years old and unable to use one that is only six years old because there is no documentation to prove its authenticity.

Metallurgy

An airframe inspector can quickly see if a bolt is correctly torqued up and secured properly with a split pin but he cannot tell what it is made of. Until recently, there was a certain arrogance about modern materials and technology: they are superior in every respect to anything of wartime vintage. However, many ingenious materials were manufactured during the war regardless of their cost because they were essential at the time. Many of these materials are no longer made. While some of the modern substitutes have some of the required properties, none of them have exactly the same properties as the wartime originals. A modern material may have, for example, the required mechanical properties but lack the necessary formability to shape it. Thus, it is not always possible to make a substitute part that conforms to the original specification.

When original parts are available it is usually more economical to use

these rather than refurbished or remanufactured substitutes. However, as time passes, new unused original parts become fewer and fewer. There are situations where original components are beyond repair and a replacement part cannot be found. Then a replacement has to be made by a skilled artisan. This involves researching original drawings from which new drawings are made, making appropriate tools to manufacture the part, and finding someone capable of making it. Then, of course, it has to be fitted to the airframe. All this could take as long as six months. The advent of computer numerically controlled machining, when it can be used, enables the process to move along a little more quickly.

Dimensional Integrity

On arrival, the integrity of each airframe is checked in the appropriate jigs. When previous restoration work has been carried out on the airframe, all the relevant paperwork must accompany it to prove that the work done and the materials used meet the required standards.

'The more depressed you are in the early stages of the project, the more likely you are to see it through to a satisfactory conclusion.'

Financial Aspects

From very early on, it becomes obvious very quickly that the project is soaking up a lot of money. Some owners agree to fixed monthly payments for the duration of the project. Others agree to a fixed price at the outset and only pay on completion of the project. Progression of the work is, therefore, entirely dependent on the financial input from the customer.

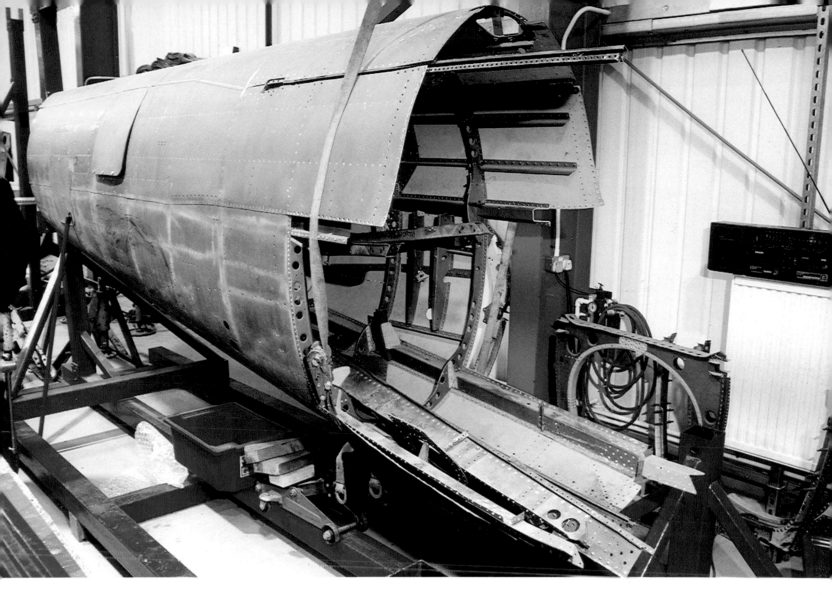

(ABOVE): *Mark XVIII SM845 during disassembly. The aircraft had been partially restored in America prior to being delivered to Historic Flying. Both wings and fuselage were completely rebuilt by Historic Flying.*

Organising the Project

The first stage is to break it down into manageable pieces so that each can be considered and understood in its entirety. The major difficulties can be analysed and solved. It does no good to avoid them because you will only find yourself bogged down in the treacle of delay later on if you do, without necessarily knowing what is at the root of the hold-up.

The two teams working on the airframe are the Structures Team and the Systems Team. The Structures Team is subdivided into smaller groups that work on the wings, fuselage and tail. Their work is carried out concurrently or sequentially depending on the financing arrangement.

By virtue of the number of different systems and the skills required to work on them, the Systems Team is more subdivided than the Structures Team. Systems are a complex and diverse field. Historically, airframes and engines, given the right amount of attention, give little trouble, so it is fair to say that, in the main, the owner's perception of his aircraft's reliability is based on how well the systems work.

'If you're looking for a painless restoration, you're going to have to be fastidious in the method and hierarchical in approach.'

As each component is finished it has to be properly tested before it is

(LEFT): *The wings from Spitfire Mk V EP120 in the double jig.*

(ABOVE): TD248 prior to being cowled up. Note that the difference in paint finish drastically alters the appearance from that of a camouflaged aeroplane. Paint schemes are chosen by respective owners.

ABOVE): Between the wheels can be seen the chin scoop on Spitfire Mk XVI prior to fitting. This is a complex piece to manufacture due to the curvature of the unit. It is made from five different pieces and is handcrafted. Note that the side cowlings have also been installed.

(ABOVE): Top cowling installation also requires a degree of patience due to inaccessibility. The cowlings require trimming to such a degree to ensure a good fit that painting is left until last.

(ABOVE): Cowlings fitted to an aircraft stay with it for life. They are hand-tailored and are not interchangeable with another airframe. Note also cannon outer barrels have been installed.

fitted. Once tested and passed, the components are combined to make modules. The modules are combined to make the systems. Each complete system is tested before it is installed. If this method is not followed, serious delays can result if a component fails. For example, something goes wrong in the hydraulic system and the consensus of opinion is that it has 'gotta be the ram shuttle valve'. It will take well over a day, more likely two, to uncover this little beast and once uncovered it will probably take no more than 10 minutes to fix it.

'When these aircraft were built, maintenance wasn't considered . . . it wasn't even given a thought.'

When you consider that it takes two men two days to remove all the cowls and fillets, then replace them, you can see the veracity of that statement. Lacing together the two teams is a foreman, a first-class warrior whose job it is to peer into the cracks and see what has been dropped in there. The work ethos of a team is an almost pathological desire to find all the problems at the beginning and start resolving them as a priority. Working in this methodical way, the only problems remaining at the end of the project should be the unforeseen difficulties that no amount of planning and analysis could have highlighted. The same ethos should apply throughout the entire project from start to finish.

Probably the only person who sees the totality of the work is the pilot and he will ask questions like 'Does the tacho waver? Are all the instruments on the blind-flying panel working? Is the pitot working? Is the lateral trim just right?' If the answers to these are 'no, yes, yes, yes, yes' there will be a lot of happy faces and a pilot who appreciates that everyone went that extra mile to produce the thoroughbred he now sits in.

(LEFT AND BELOW): TE566 showing top and chin cowlings installed with the radiator fairing now in place after engine runs. The first flight is now imminent. In this case, the Spitfire was airborne a week later.

(ABOVE LEFT AND RIGHT): Cowling completed on TD248. Work spent on this aspect of Spitfire finishing is an investment for the future – it facilitates easy and rapid removal and replacement of cowlings during flying operations.

(BELOW):This cowling section requires maximum use of the traditional metal-master's skills to achieve a perfect and accurate shape.

(BELOW):Job done! Painted chin cowls on TD248. The reflection in the finish says it all.

(ABOVE, BELOW AND NEXT PAGE):
Tim departs Audley End en-route to Duxford.

The roles of these aircraft have inevitably changed since the war, the airframes are worked less hard and maintenance standards are high. Modern operators of the aircraft are less willing to accept snags than were wartime pilots. What would have been deemed an acceptable leak rate in 1940 demands immediate remedial action today. This brings us to the question: is there anything in the aircraft that would benefit from modification or redesign?

'Mostly, we see ourselves as restorers; modify or redesign and you'll end up with something but you won't be able to call it a Spitfire.'

You have to bear in mind that when the aircraft was conceived, the design teams were 200 to 300 strong and these were the best people available. By and large, their decisions were based on the best information available at the time. It is not always the case that the best decision then is the best one for today, but those people understood more about the aircraft than we do now.

There are, however, exceptions. There are uncontentious areas such as the materials used for seals. A properly researched and documented modern material will far outlast the original. However, it is a fact of life that you will attract a lot of attention if you deviate from the specification; few people will question your adherence to it.

'Why did I get involved? Oh, I suppose it was one of those itches that you have to scratch. The good side is that I got to do a lot of things other people don't even get a look at.'

First Flight

It was six years in coming and it was not a let-down. It was a very sharp moment, a magic experience, far more memorable than any other event in my aviation career. I remember sitting at the end of the runway at Duxford strapped into RW382 and thinking I don't mind messing up and I don't mind dying, just let me do it honourably! It was the sort of occasion when Albert climbs on to your shoulder and says, 'You really want us to do this . . . this is absolutely your last chance.' It was great.

Messing with the Messer

'The last time anyone did this in a real Messerschmitt Bf 109 and a real Spitfire it was wartime.'

One year, Charlie and I took a Messerschmitt and a Spitfire to La Ferté-Alais in France. It was the first time the Bf 109 had been out of the U.K. and in the tower before departure David Henchie said, 'Make a mess of it and don't even think about coming back. Just keep flying east!'

We poked off. The fuel gauge on the Bf 109 packed up mid-Channel, quickly followed by the radio. Needless to say, Charlie had a very focused view about who was going to be the first to land in Calais.

Coming back the sky was 8/8 blue. We had left La Ferté at around 08.00 hours on the Bank Holiday Monday. Down at 400 ft, the wheat was golden yellow. As we poled along in echelon, people waved at us. The crackle on the radio broke into my thoughts; it was Charlie. 'What do you imagine the poor people are doing today, Tim?'

3
The Structure of the Spitfire

(Above): Mark V Spitfire EP120.

Across the world there are more than fifty Supermarine Spitfires which have been rebuilt by their owners to fly. This is in excess of twenty-five per cent of all the Spitfire airframes extant – an excellent average compared to other warbirds. The numbers of newly rebuilt fliers and recently discovered airframes in various states of completeness is increasing by the month. From the United States to New Zealand, India to Australia, and, of course, in Great Britain, the birthplace of this legendary fighting aeroplane, Spitfires are being restored and flown. This airworthy population has never been so healthy, despite humble and almost desperate beginnings in the 1950s and 1960s after the Royal Air Force moved into the jet era and foreign air forces gradually followed. Despite accidents in recent years which have resulted in the total loss of a few airframes, the numbers of airworthy Spitfires continues to increase. However, to put this into perspective, less than one per cent of Spitfires built are in existence today.

Displaying airworthy warbirds to the general public has increased dramatically over the last decade, the U.K. scene alone offering an airshow of some description on almost every spring, summer and autumn weekend of the year. Major shows span an entire weekend and attract up to 50,000 people in the two days, though generally the figures are closer to half this. The U.K. shows still tend to be conservative when compared to the magni-

tude and coverage of some of the events offered in the United States. Notable amongst these, the Experimental Aircraft Association's annual Oshkosh Convention is very well attended with every type of aviation interest catered for to some degree.

Warbirds are generally well represented in any show as they provide a first-class spectacle for the crowds without the noise, relative expense and more specialist support of their jet equivalent. Currently they cater for a large, discerning, but sadly reducing, proportion of the public – the veterans who flew and maintained them during the war years. To engage in conversation with these people is a joy: their reminiscences are as fascinating as they are understated, with memories pouring out the closer they get to the aeroplanes. The depth of understanding they still have about the operation or maintenance of the aircraft is always in focus and remarkably undimmed by the intervening half-century.

The enthusiasm veterans demonstrate for the aircraft on view is subtly different to that so evident from every other component of the airshow audience. For them, the nostalgia factor is still at work. Despite the colour, spectacle and obvious appeal of any warbird gathering, which embraces families as well as the more dedicated aviation enthusiasts, the veterans have an edge because they understand what it was like to fly or maintain the aircraft. They have a greater appreciation of the technical attributes, an understanding of the essential mechanics and a healthy respect for all the elements of the machines they once trusted with their lives.

Spitfires are not single entities, able to purr or growl around the sky by some divine decree. Every inch of aerial progress is a hard-won conflict of man-made systems against the most basic elements, conquering the imbalance of metal against air. That the Spitfire was designed and built to fly is beyond contention. That it performs this so beautifully is testament to the genius behind the total co-operation of the many separate and distinct assemblies, systems, controls and instruments that make up the airframe.

Describing the engineering involved in the Spitfire as an aircraft can be readily accomplished here – much more easily than giving interested parties a chance to fly in one. There will be little surprise, then, that we have elected to do the former and will regrettably leave the latter to those with more suitable bank balances and hard won qualifications.

So what mystery lies beneath the skin of the Spitfire and how do we begin to detail the mechanical organs and copper arteries, the howling V-12 heart, the metal limbs and their lethal fingers of machine-guns and cannon? On the basis that most small aircraft get simpler the further you get from the nose, we will make a start with the tail assembly and gradually work our way forward to the more complicated bits. What is described here applies mostly to the early Spitfires; later variants often introduced different solutions to the problem of additional weight and vastly increased power, and these will be noted where relevant.

Tail Section
The tail section of every Spitfire was designed to detach from the rear of the fuselage at a transport joint and is actually held in place on the last of the fuselage frames with fifty-two bolts. Therefore it is not easily detached and there are very few instances of Spitfire accidents caused by the loss of this section without enemy assistance. Removing the tail in more relaxed

circumstances on the ground gives access to the tailwheel assembly and to the internal structure of the tail section itself.

There are access hatches cut into the skin around the tailwheel which offer limited access to the tailwheel strut and the shock absorber itself. However, because they are so small, prolonged use of these hatches has been known to cut the engineers' wrists. The shock absorber, which is similar, but smaller, to those employed on the mainwheels, is attached to a trunnion block at the bottom of the nineteenth frame, on the tail side of the fuselage attachments. The top of the shock absorber is attached to the upper end of the swinging arm which, at its other end, carries the fully pivoting tailwheel. The arm itself pivots close to its centre on two brackets mounted on frame 20. The whole assembly allows the tailwheel to shunt upwards as it takes the static weight of the aircraft, and the impact of landing.

Later variants (mostly from Mk VII onwards) allowed the tailwheel to retract into the fuselage, closing two small tailwheel doors as it did so, using

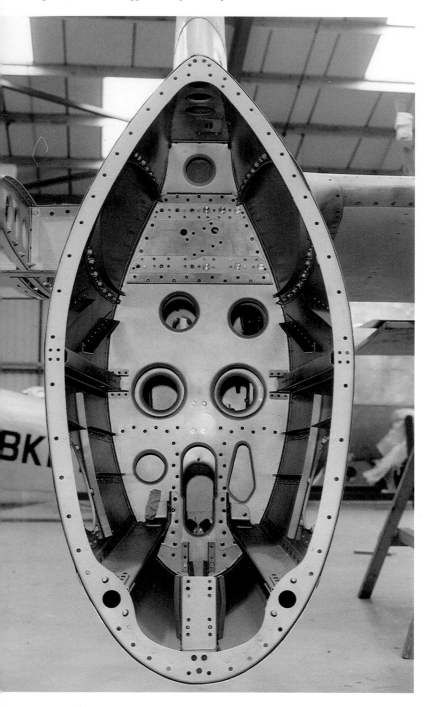

(BELOW): Tail cone photographed from the front. All-new A.G.S. (Aircraft General Spares) enhance the appearance of the newly rebuilt unit.

(BELOW): Shock absorber mounted within the inverted tailcone (Mk XVIe variant).

(ABOVE): Retractable tailwheel on Mk XIV airframe.

the main undercarriage gear selector. This further reduced the drag of an already clean airframe. Left 'hanging out' in the slipstream, the tailwheel revolves slowly – about fifteen times a minute!

Tail Fin

The fin of the Spitfire is effectively an extension of two of the frames from which this back end of the fuselage is constructed. There is a double frame hidden amongst the metalwork, which extends upwards, bent slightly backwards from the fuselage, to form the front fin spar. This provides the anchor point for the front horizontal spar of the tailplane. A similar arrangement exists immediately behind the front fin spar to provide a second vertical extension and the anchor point for the tailplane auxiliary spar. From these two vertical spars, a number of horizontal ribs provide one of the components of the classic Spitfire tail fin shape and more importantly the anchor for the sternpost to which the rudder is attached.

The metal skin of the tail fin is attached to the ribs in different ways,

(TOP RIGHT): The tail cone from Spitfire Mk V BM597 which clearly shows the corrosion incurred as a result of long periods exposed to the elements as a gate guardian. Despite this damage, frames 19 and 20 were repaired, the brackets were removed for renovation and cad plating, the rest of the material refurbished and all of these pieces were then reassembled to form the basic structure of the 'new' unit.

(RIGHT): Fresh from the jig is the refurbished tail cone of Spitfire Mk V BM597. The unit is dismantled and reassembled in a jig, replacing materials as required. It is interesting to note the construction which results in a very strong subassembly.

depending on which side of the tail the skins are located. Those on the port side are riveted, while those on the starboard side and on the leading edge are held by a number of wood screws, using sections of spruce which are bolted to the ribs as their base. The reason for this is simply that it would not be possible to rivet both sides of the fin to the ribs because there is no room for a hand-held bucking bar to rivet between the skins.

There is one small fillet plate which fits on the top of the fuselage at the point where it meets the tail fin. In the good old days at Supermarine it was known affectionately as 'The Little Bastard' for it was among the most difficult parts of the Spitfire metalwork to hand fabricate – there were no hydraulic sheet-metal presses in the early 1940s.

Take a look at the tail of a Spitfire next time you are close to one and you will see a piece of shaped metal about 10 inches in length; at one end it is curved to meet the shape of the fuselage and, at the other, it is bent almost to a V shape in order to accommodate the leading edge of the tail fin. A smooth curve of some 80° from a horizontal line to the near vertical has to be introduced to cover the transition from fuselage to tail. It is nearly as difficult to describe as it was to make and only a handful of Supermarine sheet-metal workers were able to turn their hands to the production of these parts.

From the late-production models of the Griffon-engined Mk XIV machines onwards, Spitfires had an enlarged tailplane to cope with additional torque introduced by larger engines and heavier propeller units. The rudder shape had changed once before – with the introduction of the pointed broad-chord rudder on Mk IXs, which was again necessary to counter the increased engine powers and torques. The broad-chord rudder was added to a standard tail unit but the Mk XIV tail was almost a complete redesign in shape, while the internal structure was broadly similar. From the introduction of Mk 21 Spitfires, the tail unit was a completely redesigned, higher and deeper unit providing greater lateral control.

Rudder

Rudders are essentially simple devices. A basic fabric-covered wood or metal frame is hinged at two or more points to the sternpost of the tail fin. There are two minor complications to this simple unit. One is the inclusion of a metal trim tab in the trailing edge of the rudder, and the second is the weighting in the 'horn' of the rudder which sits above the uppermost rib, forward of the two hinges.

The effect of this 'horn balancing' is to ease the load on the hinges, making the rudder smoother to operate. The trim tab is manipulated

(BELOW): Rudder attached to a Spitfire Mk V for fitting to check the bearing alignment prior to being removed and fabric-covered by Clive Denney. The metal skin on the horizontal stabiliser is temporarily held in place with gripper pins.

(BELOW): Spitfire Mk XVI RW382. Note broad chord rudder.

(ABOVE): The tailplane of the low-back Spitfire Mk XVI TD248 nearing final assembly. The circular plate at the bottom rear is known as the datum point. This indicates that the airframe is level for rigging purposes. The rod for operating the rudder is apparent in this view.

(ABOVE): Tail cone and horizontal stabiliser from BM597 showing the spruce attached to the ribs which is installed so that the underside skins can be screwed in place, thus making assembly easier. The jigged fuselage at the rear is BM597.

by a short rod which in turn is operated by the pilot turning a small wheel situated low on the port side of the cockpit. The effect is to provide rudder input to the direction of the aircraft without the pilot having to constantly move the rudder pedals. The rudder also houses the tail navigation light at the bottom of the trailing edge.

Tailplane

The tailplane is constructed in two halves bolted together where the spars butt together, inside the tail fin, to form a single cantilever unit. Two spars run the length of the tailplanes; the main spar is at the front and the auxiliary spar connects the trailing edges of the tailplanes together. It also provides attachment points for the elevator assembly. The ribs are attached to the spars and form the basic shape of the tailplanes. These are plates with flanged edges to permit the top and bottom skins to be attached.

The skins are each cut from a single piece of metal sheet and shaped to fit the rib structure before installation. The top skins are riveted to the ribs and the lower skins are attached with wood screws to sections of spruce which are attached to lower portions of the ribs, similar to the rudder construction although in later marks the lower skins are 'pop' rivetted in place. A leading edge strip is riveted to the upper skin and screwed into the lower skin to conceal the join. Small fillet plates are placed at the tailplanes and tail fin joint to maintain aerodynamic efficiency.

Elevators

Though the tailplanes are constructed in two halves and bolted together to form the complete unit, the elevators are constructed as single units and attached to the trailing edge of a complete tailplane construction. They are manufactured in a light alloy as symmetrical booms and rib

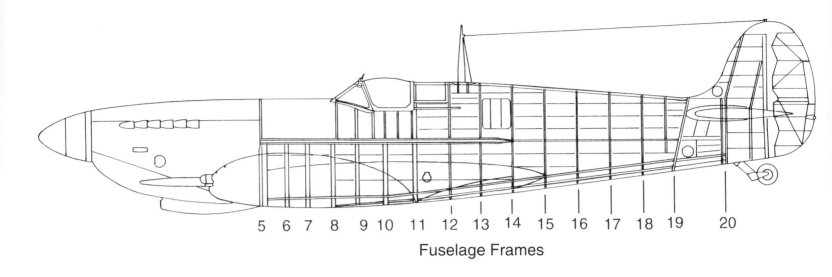

5 6 7 8 9 10 11 12 13 14 15 16 17 18 19 20

Fuselage Frames

frameworks, then covered in fabric. Later models had all-metal elevators following the discovery that control of the aircraft would be much more effective at high speed with all-metal elevators as the fabric was prone to 'denting' under high air pressure.

Like the rudder, elevators are fitted with horn portions at their tips. These are metal-covered on all marks of Spitfire, with fabric-covered metal trim tabs on each side. Operated by the pilot in the same way as

the rudder trims, but with a different wheel, the elevator trims allowed the 'hands off' attitude of the aircraft to be adjusted without constant use of control inputs.

Fuselage

The Spitfire fuselage is divided into three main units, one of which – the detachable tail unit – we have already dealt with, leaving the main portion of the fuselage, and the forward portion which contains the cockpit and fuel tanks. The fuselage itself is constructed entirely of metal, formed by a total of twenty longerons running along the length of the fuselage, four of

(BELOW): Spitfire Mk IX TE566 with wings installed prior to engine installation and final detail fitting. Elevator assembly prominent.

which are particularly important, and fifteen hooped or U-shaped frames to which the longerons are attached by rivets. The fuselage is therefore simply a squashed metal cylinder which uses sheet metal over a basic frame to supply all the necessary strength.

Main Fuselage

Starting at the tail and working forwards, the smallest frame comes first. Each frame has a unique number to identify it and the smallest frame (which is not actually part of the tail unit) is numbered 19. This frame is stronger than the others and carries around its perimeter the fifty-two bolt holes to secure the tail unit. It cants back to allow the tail unit sufficient room to carry the tailwheel strut and the shock absorber at its base.

Fourteen longerons are riveted at points around the outer edge of the frame. These extend all the way forward to the front of the fuselage, being reinforced by other longerons as the fuselage thickens and takes on the Spitfire shape. The frames forward of frame 19 are also riveted to longerons, so the fuselage takes on a cage-like appearance before the metal skins are riveted on.

This construction is manufactured inside an accurately constructed jig; all the frames are pinned and held precisely in place while the longerons are riveted around their circumferences.

Individual skins are shaped before being joined to the fuselage framework. This type of construction is known as stressed-skin as the skin sheets form an integral part of the fuselage, helping to fully absorb the forces imposed during flight. The skins are further strengthened by a number of Z-shaped stringers which are riveted in place to stiffen them before the skins are fitted to the fuselage. The fit of the skins has to be very precise,

(LEFT): *Fuselage frames are in position at this stage after overhaul and rectification work has been completed on mark XVIII SM845.*

(BELOW): *By installing the fuselage in a jig its structural integrity is guaranteed. Work continues on the aft fuselage section. Note the lower fuselage extrusions run all the way to the transport joint at the rear of the section.*

(ABOVE): *This rear side view depicts the completed framework prior to reskinning of the basic structure. All the skin panels are painted prior to assembly.*

(BELOW): *Here we see new skins being fixed to the basic framework. The skins forward of frame 11 have been etch-painted to prevent corrosion – this is the low back variant Mk XVIII SM845.*

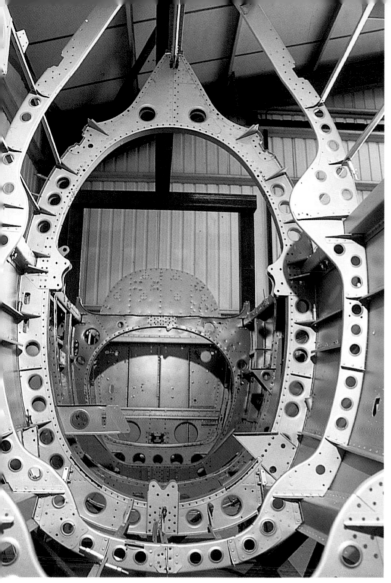

from the hand-cutting of the metal sheet, through all the skilled bending and wheeling processes, to the final riveting. An accurate fit is essential.

The main section of fuselage runs from frame 11 (immediately behind the cockpit door) back to frame 19 at the tail. On earlier Spitfire marks, frame 11 is full height, forming the back of the cockpit area, but on later versions of Mk IXs, Mk XVIs and later marks the fuselage was cut down to accommodate a bubble canopy for improved visibility. These marks had shorter fuselage frames from number 11 backwards than other marks, although number 19 remained unchanged as it formed the tail attachment.

In the high-back Spitfires, the area at the top of the fuselage between frames 11 and 12 was fitted with Plexiglas to afford the pilot some rearward vision. The area just behind this (between frames 12 and 13) was strengthened to take the radio aerial. Provision for the radio itself was made immediately below and slightly behind the aerial, between frames 13 and 14. A small shelf was built into the fuselage and an access hatch sited on the port side. Radios were not as reliable nor as small as they are today so easy access was imperative in the rough operational environment in which they were used.

The battery was also located in the fuselage. Careful positioning of this unit was vital so as not to adversely affect flying characteristics of the aircraft. It was placed on a shelf, similar in construction to that of the radio unit, between frames 17 and 18 in the early marks. It was subsequently repositioned as the weight distribution of later marks altered. A simple access hatch was built into the fuselage on the port side so the battery could

(LEFT): Looking down the fuselage centre section of BM597 (rear to front). Note the monocoque construction and the positions of radio and battery shelves.

(BELOW): Spitfire Mk V EP120 in the jig. Work is underway on the aft fuselage structure, in the area of frames 11 to 19. One frame at a time is taken out, refurbished and replaced before moving on to the next one. This is done to maintain the integrity of the structure. Note the original lower skins and a substantial number of ribs are still in place. Work continues to be carried out on the cockpit area. The access hatch for the battery is apparent in this view.

be unscrewed from its stowage point and removed reasonably easily from the aircraft.

Other major items of equipment located in the fuselage included oxygen bottles, flare chutes in the early variants and internal fuel tanks. Care had to be exercised when putting internal fuel behind the cockpit as the aircraft became very unstable in pitch if the centre of gravity was moved too far to the rear. The photo-reconnaissance Spitfires made most effective use of the metal cage of the fuselage when cameras were installed in the forward main fuselage in a number of configurations. Sighting was achieved through ports cut in the fuselage skin.

The P.R. aircraft were significantly different to all other marks. They were generally unarmed and often sported pressurised cabins which necessitated reinforced fuselage construction in the cockpit area and air compression devices driven by the engine.

The Forward Fuselage

This extends forward from frame 11 right up to the firewall at frame 5. The forward fuselage encompasses the cockpit and the fuel tanks and provides anchor points for the engine bearers and wings. This section of the aircraft bears the lion's share of the flying stresses and its construction reflects this. There is provision for extra bracing members and weight-bearing, with stiffening stringers to provide additional strength and rigidity.

The pilot might have considered himself fortunate to find himself in the middle of such formidable strength but, if he ever considered the construction, he could not help but notice that he was positioned immediately behind two large fuel tanks containing a total of 85 gallons of 100-octane fuel. A sobering thought.

The firewall was made of two sheets of metal between which was sandwiched an asbestos filling, stiffened with appropriately shaped metal members in horizontal and vertical positions. A shaped bulletproof panel was added to this arrangement to cover the top fuel tank. The bulk of the engine was intended to offer protection to the majority of the lower tank. The firewall was attached to frame 5 which in turn was attached to the front ends of the fuselage longerons many of which extend all the way back to frame 19.

At the base of frame 5 there are four channel-sectioned members extending across and beyond the sides of the bottom of the fuselage. These are joined by plate webs and form booms which carry attachment points for the main wing spars. Seven bolts hold the main wing spars in place in the upper and lower booms on each side of the aircraft. The upper boom takes three bolts and the lower boom the remaining four. Provision for jacking the aircraft up is also made on these booms by including two small hemispherical jacking pads on the underside of the lower boom.

The top longerons on each side of the fuel tanks are strengthened and run backwards to frame 14 in the main fuselage. The mounting points for the top engine bearers slot on to the ends of these longerons at frame 5. Additional bracing is provided at these same points on frame 5 with two diagonal struts running back to the centre of the especially strengthened frame 8. The struts dictate that the Spitfire has two fuel tanks as they slice the space between frames 5 and 8 in half, at a point halfway up the fuselage height.

The lower fuel tank has to be fitted on to the cork-lined mount points between frames 6 and 7 before the struts can be put into position and the upper tank is then slotted into position above this arrangement. The connections are made between the two tanks so that the top tank will gravity feed its fuel into the lower.

A large, thick cowling is positioned above the upper tank protecting it and completing the smooth lines of the Spitfire's upper external fuselage skins. The mount points for the lower engine bearers are located on the lowest main wing spar booms and bolted through the boom itself. Frame 5 is therefore the busiest in the entire aircraft.

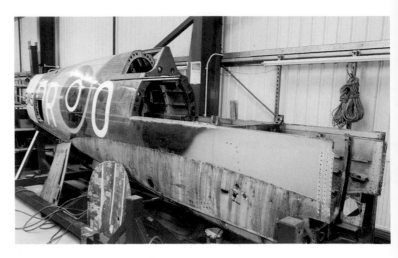

(ABOVE): *Spitfire Mk V BM597 during installation in the jig. The firewall and some of the centre fuselage ribs have been removed and work is about to commence on rebuilding that area. Note the surface corrosion on the unpainted skins due to exposure to the elements. Old skins are not usually suitable for reuse but the new skin is patterned from the old. All fuselage tanks were suitable for reuse.*

(ABOVE): *Further progress on the fuselage break-down is illustrated in this view. Note the difference between the cockpit area (painted cockpit green) and the silver paint in other areas of the fuselage section. This conforms to the original specification; green was used to counter excessive glare in the cockpit area.*

(ABOVE): *The rebuilt centre section showing extrusions installed and the degree of faithfulness to the original paint specification. Frames 5 to 11 are rebuilt first so that the rigidity of the airframe is maintained.*

(ABOVE): *Further on in the process the skins are now pinned in position.*

(BELOW): *Forward fuselage on Mk XVIII SM845.*

(ABOVE): *Close-up of the plate from Spitfire Mk V BM597 which is attached to the spar boom. This plate would have been riveted to the aircraft by an M.U. facility after modification or repair. The plate denotes that the top boom bolts are already 16 thou oversize; tolerance is 31.25 thou.*

(ABOVE): *Front fuselage and cockpit section basic structure complete, the Mk V awaits skinning of the rear sections before it is removed from the jig. The belly skin is not fitted until much later in the process. To fit it now would impede access to the fuselage.*

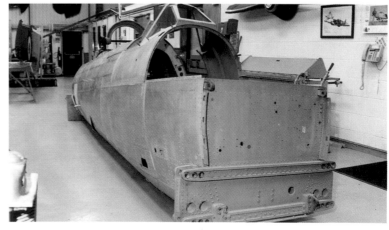

(ABOVE): *Main spar prominent on Mk XIV NH799.*

49

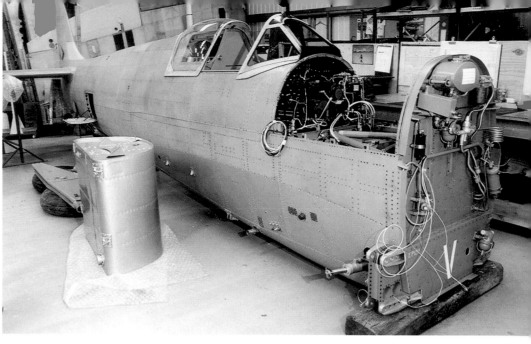

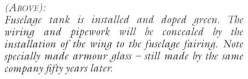

(ABOVE):
Fuselage tank is installed and doped green. The wiring and pipework will be concealed by the installation of the wing to the fuselage fairing. Note specially made armour glass – still made by the same company fifty years later.

(ABOVE): Spitfire Mk V EP120 with fuselage top fuel tank to the left. This unit has a capacity of 47 gallons. Windscreen and canopy are now installed but will soon be masked to prevent scratching and other damage. Lower tank in position with the diagonal bracing struts in place.

(BELOW): Instrument and systems installation continues apace and the wiring loom starts to take form on Spitfire BM597. A brand new stub spar is in place.

The Cockpit Area

The Spitfire cockpit construction begins at frame 8 and runs back to frame 11 which is the first of the full frames to form the high-back fuselage shape. It is heavily braced to maintain structural integrity. Just in front of the cockpit itself is an arch, curved to match the curvature of the fuel tank fairing, which forms the basis for the cockpit coaming immediately aft of frame 8. This arch is attached to the same two longerons that carry the engine bearers at their most forward point, and provides anchors for the instrument panel.

Further substructure provides support and shaping to the area of the cockpit coaming. On the port side this is interrupted at frame 9 by the inclusion of the cockpit access door. Hinged on the top of the port side longeron, the door can be secured in three positions – fully open, fully closed and a third position best described as ajar. This slightly opened position was used at take-off and landing when the cockpit canopy was moved to the rear, thus preventing the canopy from slamming shut and jamming in the event of a take-off or landing incident. Once airborne, the pilot would completely close the door and pull the canopy forward to the locked position for flight.

Brass canopy runners are positioned along the top edge of the door and into the fuselage aft of the door on the port side and along the starboard

(LEFT): Interesting shot of TE566 following installation of the fuselage fuel tank. Note the fuel tank cover is heavy-gauge aluminium.

(BELOW): Completely reskinned, the fuselage is now out of the jig and wiring and systems installation can commence. The unit is now much more accessible, and several craftsmen can work on the fuselage at the same time. Note the previously assembled tail cone has also been installed. No less than fifty-two 2BA bolts hold this component in place. The wings for this aircraft, Spitfire EP120, are in the background.

(ABOVE): View from just aft of the canopy rail into the cockpit area at an early stage of systems installation. At this point, the cockpit looks particularly spartan but closer examination will reveal some intricate pipework and wiring which is hidden after final assembly.

(ABOVE): The bulletproof screen.

(LEFT): Detail shot showing the interior of the cockpit access door. Prominent is the red-painted aid to escape – a crow-bar!

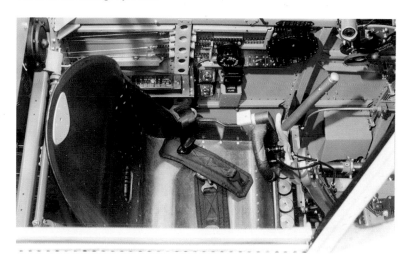

(ABOVE): Seat installed. Note Very cartridges to the front of the seat, readily accessible for the pilot. The silver radiator flap lever is new and manually operates the flap – distinctly different from the method employed in later models. Note fuse box located adjacent to pilot's seat.

side of the fuselage at the corresponding height. At the rear of the cockpit, a catch at the top of frame 11 locked the canopy open (although the effect of air pressure would keep the canopy open in flight), and a second catch would keep it in place when the pilot pulled it to the fully forward position.

All Spitfires canopies were jettisonable in flight, although the position of the jettison lever differed slightly in different marks. Cables were run from the jettison lever to four pins attaching the canopy to the runners. By pulling the lever, the pins would come out of the runners and the air pressure under the leading edge of the canopy was intended to do the rest. Comprehensive testing had to be carried out before a satisfactory arrangement was finalised, and the application of the pilot's fist was generally accepted as being very helpful in an emergency.

The windscreen of very early Spitfires was constructed from Plexiglass of normal thickness. Modifications were soon made to add up to 1.5 inches of bulletproofing to the windscreen. This was initially fitted externally but later designs allowed armoured glass to be fitted internally so that detrimental aerodynamic effects were eliminated. The windscreen assembly was bolted to the cockpit coaming with rubber strips between the two metal sections providing an effective waterproof seal.

(OPPOSITE):
A view of the aircraft from immediately aft of the firewall to the rear of the instrument panel. The ordered layout of the pipework and electrical wiring is apparent. Brake lever at rear of control column apparent in this aspect as is the rudder bar mechanism.

The pilot's seat was manufactured from papier maché and resin and was designed with a well to accommodate a seat-type parachute. Consequently, the pilot sat on this for the duration of his sortie, a far from comfortable arrangement. The seat mounting was attached to the bottom of the fuselage and could easily be removed from the aircraft should the need arise. The seat was height adjustable, allowing the pilot to raise and lower it as required. Compensators in the seat allowed it to be raised against the pilot's weight. Provision was made for further bulletproofing on the back of the seat with brackets allowing a small panel to be attached at the height of the pilot's head.

Forward of the seat are two small assemblies attached to the floor of the cockpit. One is built at the base of frame 9 which provides bracing to the cockpit floor and the mountings for the sliding rudder bar mechanisms and rudder bar. The second is slightly aft of this arrangement, forming the base of the control column, allowing fore and aft pivoting of the column. Other, much smaller assemblies, were attached to both sides of the cockpit and contained the cockpit controls and switches.

Wings

The Spitfire wing has always been the most striking recognition feature of the aeroplane. Technically – being both thin *and* strong – it was very advanced, although it is the shape which is the most obvious characteristic. The wing shape is everything to the silhouette and aesthetically sets the Spitfire apart from all its contemporaries, Allied and Axis. The elliptical wing shape was designed and developed on the Supermarine drawing-boards to address the practical issues of strength, control and stability however, and not to provide a simple artistic touch to the aircraft. For the reduction of drag, the ellipse was theoretically ideal.

The origin of the Spitfire's elliptical wing has been the subject of much speculation. Some commentators even suggest that the Heinkel He 70, a German transport aircraft which slightly predated the Spitfire, was used as a model. This was not the case. The Spitfire wing was much thinner than that of the Heinkel and taking a cross-section through a wing of each aircraft reveals entirely different structures. The Spitfire wing was also designed to carry armament, a feat the transport machine would never be required to perform.

Use of the elliptical shape was a practical solution to a number of problems. These included the requirement to stow the undercarriage in a part of the wing thick enough to accommodate it and to enable the fighter to carry four guns – which formed part of the initial specification. This was very quickly revised to a total of eight. Overriding all other factors was the requirement to keep the drag as low as possible by keeping the wing thickness to a minimum.

Earlier designs had adopted tapered wings; leading and trailing edges both leave the fuselage at an angle and are then joined in a sweep at the tips. The anticipated use of the Rolls-Royce PV-12 engine – later to become known as the Merlin – increased the projected weight of the aircraft (from the calculations made when the Goshawk engine was the favoured unit) and thus the loading on the wings. A leading edge which left the fuselage at right-angles better equipped the wing to maintain a wide chord at its root and so support higher loading. This helped reduce both chord and the supported load only gradually at first, and then rather more rapidly towards the tip. So, from the point of view of load, volume and drag, the elliptical wing was the preferred choice.

Designing the overall shape was just the first step. The wing needed to be strong enough to withstand the projected flying forces in combat and yet be light enough not to restrict the performance of the complete aircraft. It also needed to be rigid to help eliminate the problem of flutter as the speed of the aircraft neared its upper limit. The wheels and weapons also had to be fitted in somewhere.

The foundation for the mainplane construction is the main spar which is constructed of two sets of square box-section booms held together one above the other by a single thick plate web on the rear face of the assembly. The booms were manufactured from five metal square box-sections of different lengths. The root ends of the booms are virtually solid, while the tips are tapered and cut away to support the thin section and lighter loading at the tips. The extreme outer end of the boom has lugs attached to allow the wing-tips to be secured to the spars.

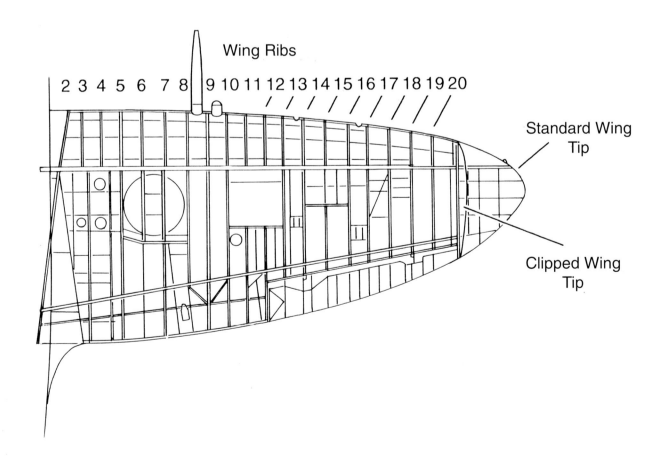

(ABOVE): Starboard wing structure on TD248. The main spar is shown in detail on the right-hand wing. The skeleton structure is seen prior to permanent riveting and reskinning. Note the red tags which denote unserviceable items. Green tags denote items that are serviceable.

(ABOVE): Completed wing section with protruding wing spar attachment points. Three wing upper attachment bolts and four lower attachment bolts are sandwiched between the spar booms. The bolts are driven through the entire structure to secure the wings. The jig alignment bushes have yet to be removed from the top spar.

(ABOVE): Wing tip structure under construction.

(ABOVE): The wing from former Indian Air Force Spitfire Mk XVIII SM845, which was worked on in the United States. On close inspection, it was decided to completely strip and rebuild the wings at Historic Flying. Again we can clearly see the spar.

Later designs of the Spitfire wing called for solid spars to support the increased weight of the aircraft and these were formed from lengths of solid metal, being drilled, milled and machined to give the same attachment points and fittings as their square box-section predecessors.

Dihedral is built in to the booms, and thus to the spar, giving the Spitfire its familiar tip-high appearance when viewed from the front. In fact, only 6° of dihedral was established as optimum for the fighter, although there were those who, at the time of the initial designs, wanted more in order to counter what were seen to be the apparent negative effects of having the centre of gravity of the aircraft above the wing attachment points.

Some twenty-one D-shaped stiffening ribs are attached to the front face of the spar. Attached to and supported by the thick upper and lower skins of the wing leading edge (and the web stiffeners between the booms on the spar), these form an extremely strong D-shaped box which runs the entire length of the wing. Known as the torsion box, this construction absorbs most of the wing loads and provided the key to creating an extremely rigid and very light wing. The shaped leading edge skins cover the upper and lower surfaces of the wing, and are riveted directly on to D-ribs and the top and bottom of the two main spars themselves.

Access points for internal work are incorporated in the leading edge skins, though the most obvious holes in the D-box were intended to accommodate the gun tunnels, which extend back through the spar web itself. The D-box had originally been designed to take the steam condensing load for the evaporative cooling system associated with the projected Rolls-Royce Goshawk installation but this proved unnecessary with the selection of the Merlin. Alternative cooling methods were required for the Merlin.

Very unusual at the time of design of the Spitfire, and not really appreciated except by those who flew it in anger, was the twist built into the

(ABOVE): The leading edge spar, D-section ribs and some skins from a Spitfire Mk XVIII which has a much stronger structure than other marks. The spar is solid rather than the laminated box-section utilised on all the other variants up to that time.

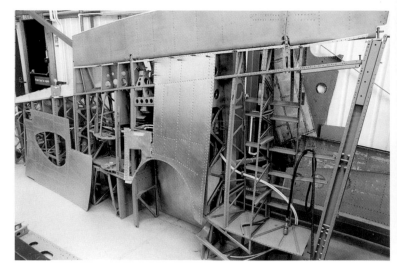

(ABOVE): Spitfire Mk XVIe wing structure aft of the D-section. This section was removed from the jig for installation of new main spars.

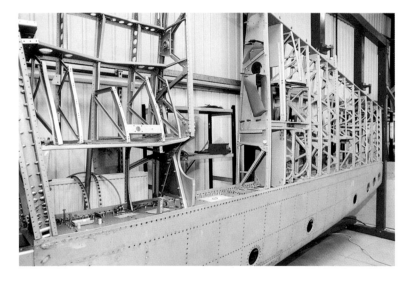

(ABOVE): D-section reskinned and aft wing structure about to be skinned on Spitfire Mk V BM597. At this stage, the wheelwell structure has yet to be built in.

(RIGHT): Aileron hinges minus shrouds. This is a highly stressed unit containing self-aligning bearings enclosed in a forged end, extremely complicated, on which the elevator pivots.

length of the main planes. Termed washout, it was to remain as an established design feature of the wing throughout the development life of the type. Acknowledged as one of the strongest contributors to the success of the machine as a fighter, it was responsible for making the Spitfire one of the most sober aircraft of its type on the approach to and during a stall. The wing root was inclined at a precise +2° to the oncoming air when the aircraft was flying normally. This angle was reduced to −½° at the tip of the wing, making the twist in the wing an invisible but very definite 2½°. In situations of high wing loading during combat, tight turns, etc., where the aircraft was close to its limits, the tip would be the last part of the wing to stall.

As the root stalled, the wing would judder warnings to the pilot of what would happen if the flight continued unchanged. As the ailerons are positioned on the outer portions of the wings, the pilot would be able to retain some control of the aircraft right up to the point of a full stall. Similarly,

the tips would be the first portion of the wing to recover from a stall, restoring aileron control to the pilot early in the recovery process.

The rest of the wing is constructed of twenty-one ribs which span the gap between the main spar and the auxiliary spar which is of much lighter construction. All the ribs are of similar construction, made up of channel-section booms and diagonal bracing bars. They differ only in their height and span: as the wing thins towards its tip, the rib height reduces. Two of the ribs are particularly important as they extend beyond the auxiliary spar which ends to accommodate them and is effectively split into three sections over the entire span of the wing, carrying the bearings for the two aileron hinges. These ribs are numbered 14 and 19 and are thicker and stronger than their immediate neighbours, absorbing the forces transmitted from the aileron itself.

Except for ribs 14 and 19, ribs 13 to 21 (which is nearest to the wingtip), do not extend back beyond the auxiliary spar as this space accommodates the aileron. Ribs inboard of number 13 break at the spar but are continued beyond it to form the trailing edge portion above the flap. These ribs are plate ribs with stiffening and have a trailing edge member which connects the rear-facing tips and provides anchorage for the rivets holding the trailing edge of the wing skin in place. Between ribs 5 and 8, provision is made for the circular wheelwell and ribs 2 to 5 are shaped to accommodate the undercarriage leg itself.

The leg is attached to the rear of the main spar web at the position of rib 2, being mounted on a pintle which is bolted to the spar. This permits the

(ABOVE): The almost complete wings (port side) of Spitfire Mk XVI TD248. Note the flexible fuel tanks on the work bench ready for installation in the already existing gun-bays.

leg to retract outwards and slightly backwards into the wheelwell. A fairing is attached to the inside of each undercarriage leg to keep the underside of the wing as smooth as possible when the leg is retracted, although there is still an area of wheel left exposed. The addition of an outer undercarriage door was not addressed until the redesign of the entire wing led to the introduction of the Mk 21 Spitfire very much later in the evolution of the machine.

The Spitfire's undercarriage arrangement has constantly been noted for its ability to surprise the unwary and the distracted pilot. It was kept deliberately close-coupled and arranged to retract outwards to reduce the bending forces on the main spar during landing. This it achieved, although it was widely acknowledged to be rather more delicate than the comparatively robust arrangements designed for the Hurricane. It was, however, significantly better than the Messerschmitt Bf 109, the undercarriage of which was actually attached to the fuselage and which demonstrated a definite tendency to 'dig in'. Most modern day warbird pilots can relate some

(ABOVE): Prior to reskinning, all tubing and wiring is installed as far as possible. Following this, trial fitting of undercarriage and radiator is undertaken. Actual installation takes place after the wing has been painted.

(ABOVE): Undercarriage pintle close up. The undercarriage leg pivots on the undersection. This photograph shows the original unit which was reused after inspection.

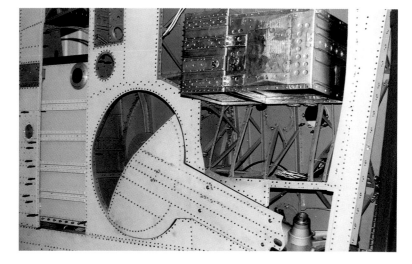

(ABOVE): Undercarriage leg in the retracted position clearly showing area where wheel is exposed. Radiator built by Anglia Radiators in Cambridge. Also of note is the fuel tank which is in the process of being installed.

(ABOVE): Spitfire wing with some of the coolant piping in the foreground. This is indicative of the number of components and amount of skill required to complete a Spitfire.

(ABOVE): Wing tip structure under construction.

experience of each type of undercarriage arrangement, the 109s having the most victims.

The upper skins and most of the lower skin is riveted both to the ribs and to the spars themselves. The outer portion of the skin is attached with wood screws to sections of spruce which are themselves attached to the ribs and spars. Access panels for the maintenance of machine-guns and cannon are positioned at various points in the upper and lower surfaces. Easy access to machine-gun and cannon ammunition boxes was ensured. Another panel was provided in the lower surface of the wing to house the landing

lamp, although the exact position of this hinged panel depended on the ammunition fit of a particular wing.

The tip of the wing was designed to be detached from the mainplane, the two lugs on the spar ends taking bolts which locate the corresponding lugs on the tips. The rib and spar portion of the tip are metal but the other

(BELOW): Spitfire Mk XIV following undercarriage installation prior to final painting. Note the orange fire-sleeving around the fuel line leading through to the wing bay tanks.

formers, ribs and internal stiffeners are fabricated in spruce. The upper and lower skins of the tip are screwed into the wood to secure them. Clipped-wing Spitfires had a reduced fairing strip secured to the main and auxiliary spars in the same way. Clipping the wings in this fashion improved the manoeuvrability of the Spitfire, particularly the roll, and, combined with engines configured for low-altitude work, was demonstrably effective at low altitude.

Climb rates at high altitudes were adversely affected by clipping. The service ceiling of the clipped-wing Spitfire was noticeably reduced when compared to that of a conventional unclipped wing. During dog-fights and prolonged combat situations, altitudes tended to reduce rather than increase, and the intention was to improve the odds in favour of the clipped-winged machine.

Extending the wing-tip to augment the ceiling was also tried with some success, though the Spitfire was less responsive at lower levels. The Mk VII Spitfire and some photo-reconnaissance variants used the extended tips to great effect for high-altitude work. However, development of the Merlin, and later the Griffon powerplant, meant that increased levels of power were usually on hand to improve climb rate and absolute ceiling without the need to resort to altering the wing shape.

The wing-tips also house the navigation lamps and other minor electrical components.

Ailerons

The ailerons are attached at two hinge points on the outer trailing edges of the wings and do not extend beyond the main wing into the wing-tips. Clipping the wings therefore had no effect on the size of the ailerons, a factor which aided the manoeuvrability of Spitfires with reduced wing-tips. The shaping of the ailerons was a vital design consideration, as the effective area of the aileron had to be considered in conjunction with the need to build in the elliptical shape of the trailing edge and the reducing chord of the wing over its outer portion. The area is surprisingly small when compared to the entire wing area.

The aileron is thicker and deeper on its inboard side, and is carefully sculptured to meet all wing contours. The units are constructed around a spar of channel-section metal bonded to the ribs of flanged metal plates. The whole assembly is covered in light alloy sheet which is riveted into position on the ribs. Lead weights were also riveted on to the leading edge of

the aileron to balance the full weight of the trailing aileron. Additional balancing is applied if required on a forward-pointing rod which fits neatly into the leading edge of the inboard end of the aileron.

The trademark of the Spitfire has always been the fine balance of the controls and the light pressures needed from the pilot to bring about major changes in attitude in normal flying conditions. The operation of the ailerons is a major factor in this respect.

Flaps

The flaps are constructed in two pieces because of the slight upward curvature of the underside of the wing as it meets the fuselage. The main portion of the flap is attached to the much smaller inboard portion to allow the two to move apart slightly as they move down from the normal (in flight) position and then to come together again as the flaps are raised. The wing is split laterally along the trailing edge of the inboard half so only the lower half will hinge down as the flaps are lowered. The flaps extend out to rib 12 on the wing, the point at which provision for the ailerons begins. The wing trailing edge is therefore split completely between flaps over the inner portion and ailerons over the outer.

The flaps are built around a tubular spar and a number of small Z-section plate ribs to which the metal skin is riveted on the underside to form the complete unit. Another Z-section strip runs along the trailing edge of the metal sheet of the flap and attaches to the ends of the ribs, completing the construction. The skins are contoured to complete the underside of the wing when the flap is in the closed position. The major portion of the flap is hinged at wing rib 8 and rib 12 at the outer end, and the smaller portion is hinged between ribs 2 and 3.

Flaps are lowered using a compressed-air system. This is controlled via a small two-position lever in the upper left quadrant of the main instrument panel in the cockpit. When in the 'up' position the flaps are locked to prevent them moving in flight. The first action of the main flap control-rod moves the locking pin to allow the flap to move downwards. Continued movement of the control-rod forces the flap to its fully lowered position.

However, raising the flaps from the 'down' position is not achieved pneumatically, as movement of the flap lever to the 'up' position simply permits stored air pressure to vent to the atmosphere. This unlocks the flaps and allows a combination of the slipstream of the moving machine and a

(BELOW): Spitfire Mk V wings from AR614, complete and ready for final finishing and fitment of systems.

(BELOW): Control column detail showing the gun button and highly polished Kigass primer pump (bottom right), all indicative of attention to detail. Flap lever in the 'up' position can be seen at top left, red and green undercarriage indicators are beneath.

small compression spring, which stores the necessary energy during the lowering cycle, to raise the flaps. The spring is fixed between the auxiliary wing spar and the flap and is strong enough to achieve the task unaided when the aircraft is stationary.

Undercarriage

Three main aspects to the undercarriage need to be explained here. First is the retraction and lowering mechanisms (there is also an emergency lowering capability). Second is the operation of the shock absorber and third are the braking operations.

Both undercarriage and brakes are operated through a combination of pneumatic and hydraulic systems, the latter to raise and lower the wheels under normal circumstances. The undercarriage selector lever is positioned on the right-hand side of the cockpit slightly above the pilot's knee and there are electrical and mechanical devices to give the pilot positive indication that the wheels are locked up or down at any point in the cycle. The mechanicals consist of small rods protruding through the wing upper surface when the wheels are down while a red or green light on the instrument panel tells him of the position of the wheels. The undercarriage lever is pulled back and moved slightly to the left to release it from the retaining gate before it can be pushed fully forward to raise the undercarriage.

At this point, the hydraulic system takes over, shortening the hydraulic jacks controlling the legs, raising them into the wheelwells. The mechanical indicator is connected directly to the legs and moves flush to the wings at this point. The hydraulics continue their operation to lock the undercarriage legs. The same pin is used to lock the wheels in both the up and the down positions, locking into the extension lever in the down position, and on to the strut itself in the up position. Once the undercarriage has been fully raised and locked, the selector lever moves itself slightly to the right and then back to locate itself on the upper gate in the selector quadrant. Electrical circuits are then completed to show a light behind the red coloured glass on the instrument panel.

The lowering operation is literally a direct reversal of this. The lever is pushed forwards and to the left to clear the gate, then pulled slowly backwards. The hydraulic system unlocks the undercarriage legs and powers the jacks to extend and move the legs down. Red-painted mechanical indicators protrude above the upper surface of the wing, providing a simple visual check. The wheels lock into the down position and the instrument panel shows a green light to confirm completion of the cycle.

(BELOW): Spitfire Mk XVI TD248 with undercarriage, wheels and brakes installed but minus radiator and systems which will be fitted after the paintwork has been completed. The close coupling of the undercarriage legs is illustrated here.

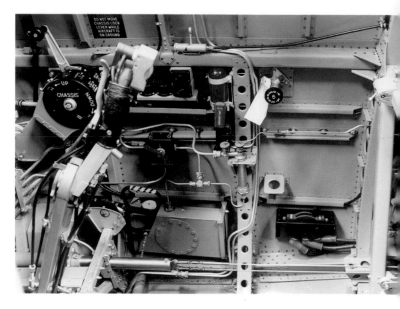

(ABOVE): The cockpit of Spitfire Mk V EP120 reflects the originality of the rebuild. The oxygen system has yet to go in. The undercarriage selector lever and CO_2 bottle for emergency lowering of the undercarriage are apparent.

There is a warning horn mounted on the throttle quadrant on the port side of the cockpit, which warns the pilot if he has retarded the throttle beyond twenty-five per cent of maximum without lowering the undercarriage. This small device has saved many a pilot – trainee and fully operational – from having the embarrassment of a wheels-up landing and the consequent expense of standing the squadron a barrel of beer to further underline his misdemeanour.

Emergency lowering of the undercarriage is undertaken with the aid of a bottle of high-pressure carbon dioxide, which is positioned near the pilot's right elbow on the cockpit wall. The bottle was connected to the undercarriage jacks and, in the event of a hydraulic system failure, it could be activated by the pilot breaking the seal with a small lever beside the cylinder. The pilot needed to remember to move the undercarriage lever to the 'down' position before pushing the small lever (marked EMERGENCY ONLY) forwards and down. The effect was to literally blow the wheels down with such force that they locked into place, allowing the pilot to land without further delay. This equipment was designed as a one-time measure, so forgetting to move the undercarriage selector lever to the down position could prove very costly.

Main Legs

The undercarriage struts are attached directly to the wing main spar at their upper end and provide shock absorption and damping through a combination of oil and air. Consisting of an outer cylinder and an internal ram and piston, the legs are attached to the spar to allow them to move outwards and slightly backwards on retraction. The outer cylinder also carries the extension lever at its top end which attaches to the hydraulic jack and provides sufficient leverage to force the leg and wheel assembly into the wing wheelwells with enough force to permit the locking pin to locate accurately.

The cylinder carries positioning attachments for the leg fairing. An oil-tight seal is maintained around the base of the cylinder, at the point the leg ram projects from it. The wheel assembly is mounted on a pintle at the base of the leg ram and the pintle is inclined slightly downwards to allow the wheel to touch the ground almost square, despite the angle of the leg.

The static weight of the Spitfire is supported by the volume of compressed air between the piston at the top of the leg ram and the outer cylinder. During touchdown, the air is compressed further by the upward movement of the piston and forced through small holes in the piston into the space between the piston and the outer cylinder. This space increases slightly as the compression takes place; the inner wall of the cylinder is tapered, being wider at the top than at the lower end. The oil adds to the shock-absorbing effect of the compressed air as it is forced around and through an internal valve plate, resisting further movement of the ram.

Once the impact energy has been absorbed, the compressed air at the top of the leg forces the ram back out. The oil in the strut is forced to flow back through the holes in the piston and a clever internal arrangement blanks off the original holes and brings a much smaller set into play. Thus, it is much more difficult for the oil to return to its static position and this increases resistance to the oil flow on the return stroke providing the damping effect, preventing the whole leg from oscillating and the aircraft from bouncing to a standstill.

Both oil level and the air pressure in the legs can be measured and adjusted reasonably easily by groundcrew in the field. A small screw device in the leg prevents the removal of the ram and piston from the cylinder of the leg without first bleeding off the compressed air.

Under normal static load the leg extension should be exactly 8.65 inches. The fully compressed and extended measurements are 5.15 inches and 10.05 inches respectively.

Brakes

Spitfire brakes are pneumatically controlled and operated by a small control lever mounted on the top rear-side of the control column spade grip. This lever controls the braking force, and a small retaining mechanism permits the brakes to be held in the fully-on position for aircraft parking. The lever operates a valve mechanism via a cable, and compressed air is delivered to the brakes through a series of flexible hoses attached to the exterior of the undercarriage legs.

There is a small valve connected to the rudder bar allowing differential braking by reduction of pressure to one or other of the brakes, depending on the position of the pilot's feet. The Spitfire is well renowned for tipping itself on its nose at the slightest provocation, and aggressive braking is high on the list of causes.

Radiators and Oil Coolers

For aircraft up to and including the Mk V Spitfire, only one radiator was fitted under the wing, located on the starboard wing between wing ribs 2 and 5. The port wing provided a home for the two oil coolers fitted to the early marks, similarly located. The radiator was housed in an open fairing allowing free passage of air through the radiator. An adjustable flap is fitted on the rear of the fairing so the pilot can control the degree of cooling applied. At extremely high altitude, it is possible for the pilot to almost completely close the radiator flaps to force warm air through a series of ducts to the guns in each wing, preventing freezing at a crucial moment.

In later marks of the Spitfire, two radiators were fitted, one to the underside of each wing, and the oil coolers were moved, to accommodate the greater cooling requirements of the more powerful Merlin and later Griffon powerplants. Radiator flaps after the Mk V were automatically controlled using thermostatic devices, eliminating the need for the pilot to constantly consider engine cooling. The radiator flap position on Spitfires up to and including the Mk V was set directly by the pilot with a large floor-mounted lever on the port side of the cockpit.

The internal and external shape of the radiator duct was critical to the low aerodynamic drag performance of the Spitfire, the large rectangular devices protruding from the underside of the wings should have had a pronounced negative effect on the drag, efficiency and performance of the aeroplane. To counteract this, the radiator ducts were shaped in such a way as to produce thrust from the compression of the hot air escaping from the rear of the radiators, to some degree compensating for the drag caused by their exposure to the airflow.

Work on this ducted radiator arrangement was undertaken at the Royal Aircraft Establishment as early as 1934, and Supermarine was quick to employ the significant advances offered. Supermarine had calculated that the Merlin engines under development at the time would produce about 420 kW of heat per minute which would have to be dissipated somewhere. It was calculated that the oil coolers would deal with approximately ten per cent of this. The remainder would have to be passed through the radiator.

The original idea of a purely water-based coolant system was superseded by the adoption of an ethylene glycol-based system. Ethylene glycol has a boiling point much higher than that of water and so the radiator could be run at higher temperatures without the risk of boiling the coolant. This meant the radiator could be smaller, much lighter (slightly less than half the weight of the water-based system) and more efficient. The Spitfire

(BELOW): Detailed drawings are essential for accurate construction, in this case, provided by Snap-on Tools! This photograph also shows to advantage the radiator, fairing, the newly installed brake unit and the bottom armament access panels.

(ABOVE): The lengthy and time-consuming process of installing the coolant pipes culminates with the successful alignment and fitment to the radiator. These pipes are bent on site to ensure a perfect fit. In this case, these are original. Cooling problems are one of the main headaches with the Spitfire. The large radiator is one of two main coolant units while the other smaller units are oil coolers.

gained the obvious benefit of adequate engine cooling without a performance penalty (weight or drag).

The radiators are connected directly to the coolant pump underneath the engine via pipes running back through the main spar. A further pipe containing a thermostatically controlled valve allows coolant to bypass the radiator until it is sufficiently warm to warrant cooling. This assists rapid warm-up of the engine which was vital in scramble situations.

A similar arrangement, and for the same reason, was applied to the two oil coolers mounted under the port wing. Oil from the engine passes into the rearmost cooler first, moving forward into the front honeycomb. Oil can be drained, if required, from either or both of the coolers without removing the fairing, and the two devices can be offered up to the wing as a single unit, held in place on a cradle arrangement.

The fairing is fitted around them for protection and governs the airflow passing through. To permit a second radiator to be fitted, on Spitfires beyond the Mk V, the oil coolers were removed from the underwing position and it is relatively easy to identify an early mark Spitfire by looking for the unbalanced collection of cooling devices on its underside.

Armament

As early as 1934, it had become evident to the Air Ministry that weaponry required by the new breed of fighter needed upgrading if the all-metal bombers being pressed into service by potential enemy air arms were to be shot down or critically damaged in a single pass. The original general specifications issued by the Operational Requirements section of the Air Ministry demanded just four guns and a target-in-sight time of about two seconds to deliver a lethal blow. Taking into account the projected increased combat speeds for the aircraft coming into service over the following five or ten years, it seemed unlikely that two seconds would be achieved by the average squadron pilot. In consequence, the Spitfire was born with eight Browning machine-guns, each firing 0.303-inch calibre rounds similar to rifle rounds.

Located in the wings, and with provision for 300 rounds of ammunition per gun, the design of the wing, which had been completed with a projected four-gun installation, proved to be remarkably adaptable. Space

was found between the existing wing ribs for both the extra guns and rounds, although a small blister was to be introduced to cover the outermost gun in each wing where the wing was at its thinnest.

The different armament layouts in the very versatile Spitfire wing gave rise to a small number of suffix letters to marks to indicate the fit. The original A wing contained four Browning 0.303-inch machine-guns, mounted behind the main spar, firing along blast tunnels routed through the spar and the leading edge D-box of the wings. The ammunition boxes sat in pairs between the guns, so there had to be a 6-inch difference in gun position to enable the outermost gun of the pair to sit slightly behind the innermost Browning. This permitted easy access to the two units from beneath the wing, ensuring there was enough wing space to allow the installation of all four guns.

Each gun was mounted on a pair of forks; the front fork was attached directly to the main wing spar and adjustable laterally, enabling the armourers to make small horizontal changes to the direction of fire. The rear mounting fork allowed vertical adjustment. Synchronising eight guns to focus fire on a single spot was a major task. As the requirement for the firing distance changed as air-fighting tactics developed, it was a task which had to be performed many times.

The guns were operated pneumatically from a small but important button on the spade grip at the top of the control column. A ring around the button could be rotated to either allow or prevent the button from being pressed, effectively giving 'fire' and 'safe' positions. With the ring in the fire position, pressing the button allowed the air pressure to operate the bolt action on the guns. Some air ducting was required in the wing to divert warm air from the rear of the radiator on to the guns to prevent them freezing in extreme conditions. At best, the eight-gun arrangement could pump about 2 lb of projectiles into an enemy aircraft, dependent on the pilot getting close enough and holding the firing position long enough to empty the magazines. The A wing armament was effectively a spray gun, offering an impressive rate of fire, but the impact fell short of a devastating punch.

The B wing went one stage further than its predecessor. Two of the Browning machine-guns were traded for a weapon of a higher calibre and destructive power. The B wing offered four Brownings, mounted in the two outermost wing positions, and two of the new Hispano 20mm cannon.

(BELOW): De-activated armament as fitted to Mk Vb BM597 illustrates the fastidious attention to detail pursued by the owners of these aircraft.

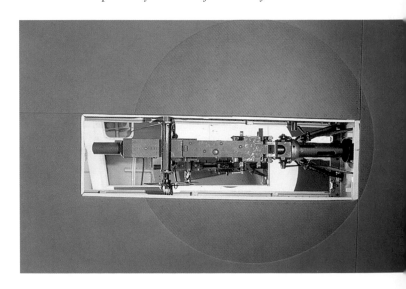

(ABOVE): Close-up of the cannon empennages. After installation on this particular aircraft, the surfaces of the wings were finished in preparation for a very high gloss metallic silver paint requested by the customer.

(ABOVE): Screw-thread for the cannon barrels and the high-gloss finish shown in this close-up of wing section on TD248.

The cannon was supposedly introduced to counteract the armour-plating which was beginning to appear on the backs of engines in Luftwaffe aircraft. Rifle-calibre ammunition was effective against unprotected engines but the more powerful cannon were needed to penetrate armour-plate.

Cannon-armed Spitfires were first evaluated by 19 Squadron based at Duxford. Stoppages and misfires continually hampered the guns' effectiveness, so the squadron C.O. demanded the reinstatement of Spitfire Ia's with their eight Brownings until the cannon stoppages problem was rectified. His demand was met. Following further modification, cannon-armed Spitfire Ibs were issued to 92 Squadron in November 1940, just too late to see any real action in the Battle of Britain.

The general B arrangement of two cannon and four Brownings was adopted on a large number of Spitfires from that time on. The Hispanos were mounted on their side, adjacent to the undercarriage wheelwell and

supported at both leading edge and frame 8, although the latter absorbed none of the recoil of the gun. Adjustments to the line of fire were made at the leading edge attachment through an eccentric bearing at a connection point. Cannons therefore could be harmonised independently of the machine-guns if the pilot desired, increasing his chances of inflicting damage on an enemy aircraft.

The circular magazine could hold up to sixty rounds of 20mm ammunition. It was of slightly larger diameter than the wing was able to accommodate at the mount point so cannon-armed Spitfires have characteristic blisters on the upper and lower wing surfaces, just outboard of the cannon themselves, to house the magazines. The Hispanos were cocked and fired by two separate mechanisms, both being pneumatically operated. Like the Brownings they replaced, the Hispanos also responded well to the warm air supply fed to them from the radiator ducts. The B arrangement wings proved to be popular and successful once problems with the cannon had been rectified.

The third variation in Spitfire firepower was the C wing. Rather than dictate the position of the cannon and machine-gun combinations during wing manufacture, the C wing permitted alteration of the arrangements in the field to suit pilot preference and, more practically, according to the availability of the weapons themselves. The result was a wing which could support the A or B arrangement or an entirely new configuration where two Hispano cannon were mounted in the inboard wing positions adjacent to the wheelwell. Cannon in this position dictated that an alternative ammunition feed be devised to enable both cannon to function alongside each other.

This was achieved by setting back the outer cannon by approximately 6 inches, and mounting ammunition boxes outboard of wing rib 10. The cannon were mounted between ribs 8 and 10. Ammunition feed was through a belt mechanism running over rollers. The positioning of the boxes allowed a total of 120 rounds per unit to be carried, double the capacity of the standard magazine in the B wing. To allow combinations of weaponry, the pneumatic system in the C wing Spitfire was upgraded to support the Browning fire-and-safe and bolt-action unit and the separate cocking and bolt-action unit of the Hispano.

Each gun type could be fired independently of the other, as with the B arrangement wing, if the pilot wished. Alternatively, he could elect to do as much damage as possible with fire from Brownings and cannon together. The clipped-wing version of the C arrangement, albeit identical to the standard C in every other respect, was designated D. Very few aircraft have this letter in their designation.

Later, an updated Browning machine-gun was introduced with a 0.50-inch calibre. The weapons were initially available during the production runs of the Mk IX and Mk XVI Spitfires, and reworked wing arrangements, with capacity for a single 20mm Hispano (inboard) and two of the new

(RIGHT): The cannon blister clearly shown in this view. High gloss on TD248 was achieved by the application of specialist paints and clear coats. Number of coats applied: one etch, two epoxy primer, three coats grey polyurethane, one coat green matt, two silver base coats, three coats clear lacquer.

weapons (outboard), was designated as the E wing. As a result, the L.F. Mk IX and Mk XVI aircraft became Mk IXe and Mk XVIe respectively.

The original wing design with the modifications detailed above served the Spitfire to the Griffon engine development, the Mk XIV, before a radical redesign was required. Spitfire Mks XVIII and XIX were already in manufacture during the redesign process and, after stringent testing, to reassure Air Ministry uncertainty, the Mk 21 Spitfire (roman numerals in designations were dropped at this point in favour of their arabic equivalent) was unleashed.

The leading edge torsion box was retained but additional torque boxes were introduced internally with load-bearing joints at the more exposed points – at the wheelwell openings for example. Bigger ailerons were required and this necessitated an increase in the overall wing area and incorporation of a laminar-flow wing, a design which introduced much lower levels of disturbance in the airflow over the wing.

Though the blunter ellipse wing was larger, it was stronger than before. The ailerons were extended out as far as the tip itself and formed part of the wing-tip, an arrangement which had been avoided in earlier marks. The spar was also redesigned for the Mk 21 wing. In an attempt to reduce the weight of the wing unit as a whole, and to simplify the process of spar production, the contractors manufacturing spar booms were asked to build a spar consisting of a single tube with walls that were thicker at the inboard

(RIGHT): Access panel over the R.A.F. roundel illustrates the difficulties faced by Clive Denney in ensuring that everything lines up on the completely assembled aeroplane!

end than at the outboard end and still permit the tip attachment points to take the weight and flying stresses of the tip itself. As a result, the spar became a single unit for the first time.

The radiators were redesigned and an attempt was made to replace the copper previously used with a lighter alloy. Insufficient numbers of these new units were available to get beyond the testing stage.

The Mk 21 wing armament was specified as two Hispano 20mm cannon in each wing. Guns were positioned immediately outboard of the wheelwells which carried a second undercarriage door to completely cover the wheel in the retracted position. There was no provision for Browning machine-gun fits. Wing to fuselage attachment procedures remained the

(BELOW): Superb finish on TD248's wing prior to fitting of the gun-bay fuel tanks. The white tape covers the rivet heads to prevent damage to the unit. Once final painting has taken place, it is a major effort to avoid scratching or damaging the finish. This is the 'E' wing.

same with the seven retaining bolts fixing the front spar to the lower portion of the fuselage frame 5 and the rear spar attaching further along the fuselage as before.

With its larger area tail, redesigned wings, cannon armament, Griffon engine and extended cowlings, a revised undercarriage leg arrangement and the huge five-bladed propeller, the Mk 21, Mk 22 and Mk 24 Spitfires were completely new aeroplanes compared to the Mk I which had entered service only a few years previously.

Spitfire Systems

The Spitfire has three major systems: hydraulic, pneumatic and electrical. The other systems, lubrication and cooling, are directly related to the engine, and will be dealt with accordingly.

Hydraulic System

The undercarriage is the only service which uses the hydraulic system which is consequently fairly simple in its design. A pump, driven by the engine, draws up fluid from the hydraulic reservoir and supplies a pair of hydraulic jacks with pressurised fluid. The operation of the undercarriage is dictated by which side of the jacks the fluid bears against which is, in turn, dictated by control inputs from the pilot.

The fluid reservoir is mounted on the fuselage frame 5 firewall and the pump is positioned on the lower starboard side of the engine with delivery via the undercarriage lever to the jacks. The pressurised fluid is delivered through a relief valve, mounted on the firewall, to ensure over-pressure in the system does not cause damage to the undercarriage quadrant in the cockpit, the pump itself or the jacks.

The valve on the early marks of aircraft was set to function, returning fluid to the reservoir, when pressure reached 1150 psi. The level of pressure required to correctly operate the undercarriage legs is considerable. A small filter is located in the hydraulic pipework as the fluid feeds back into the reservoir, reducing the number of foreign bodies collected by the fluid in its passage around the system.

The undercarriage selector is a complex piece of equipment with three small sliding cylinders and a number of connecting rods managing automation of the lever and transmitting incoming fluid from the pump to the correct service. The exhausted fluid is guided back to the reservoir again.

(BELOW): Compressed-air bottles and voltage regulator are installed in the same place on the newly rebuilt Mk V as they were on the Second World War version.

Some of the movement of the lever is made under positive pressure from the undercarriage system itself, with the unlocking and raising or lowering action carried out by the control inputs from the pilot.

The quadrant is mounted on the right-hand side of the cockpit, so the pilot has to take his right hand off the control column to retract the undercarriage after take-off. Trainee pilots could usually be identified by a small dip in the flight path of the aircraft as it climbed away after take-off, and in extreme cases this dip was a definite wobble. The movement of left hand to stick from the throttle and then right hand to undercarriage from the stick had to be practised to achieve a smooth action and consequent smooth flight path.

Pneumatic System

A larger number of services are supplied with compressed air than are operated by the hydraulics. The brakes, the Browning and Hispano weaponry, the gun camera, the retractable landing lamps (on the earlier models) and the flaps all require compressed air to function. Air supply is managed in much the same way as hydraulic fluid, with an engine-mounted pump driven by a gear on the rear of the camshaft on the back of the starboard bank of cylinders. Through non-return valves and cleaning devices (to remove oil, water or hydraulic fluid which may have become mixed with the air), air is eventually stored in twin containers mounted on the starboard fuselage wall, aft of the cockpit area.

Stored at 300 psi, the air is then delivered at a reduced pressure – the exact requirement from the systems depends on the mark of machine. The Mk Vc, for instance, requires a reduction to 200 psi, achieved through use of a reducing valve which allowed the pressure to be pre-set on the ground. Charging the cylinders from the ground is managed through a valve, the mounting position of which again depends on the mark of aircraft, which allows the engineers access to increase or reduce air pressure in the cylinders without the need to remove them from the aircraft.

Control valves for both the flaps and landing lamps are fed from the reduction valve. For the guns and the wing-mounted gun cine-camera, the supply is effectively one way. The camera was rigged to operate when the Brownings or the Hispanos were fired and took its supply from the air lines feeding these weapons. The air pipe to each of the Brownings ended in a Y-piece, the arms of the Y being fitted with wing-nut connections, flexible hoses delivering air to the fire-and-safe unit and the bolt-action unit on the gun. Hispanos had to be cocked and fired through separate units and this required two separate compressed-air feeds. Feeds for all gun types – and the cine-camera – came through the three-way fire button at the top of the control column, mounted on the spade grip.

Brakes mounted in the hubs of the main wheels are fed via a small hand lever mounted on the rear of the spade grip. Braking is generally fairly progressive, described as sharp on some machines, but as with all braking mechanisms of the day, prone to fade during prolonged use. Pilots usually allow the machine to coast on landing for as long as possible before making use of the brakes to control their return to the dispersal point.

Because of the long Spitfire nose, taxying has to be performed as a series of S-bend manoeuvres, the machine weaving from left to right down the taxiway or across the grass to ensure the pilot has forward vision from at least one side of the cockpit at any one time. Direction on the ground is controlled through a restrictor valve connected to the rudder bar on the aircraft, where left or right bootfuls of direction from the pilot reduces the passage of compressed air to the brake on the appropriate side. Turning right can be achieved with right rudder, restricting air supply to the left brake and allowing the right brake to work harder. This is known as differential braking and allows the Spitfire to manoeuvre accurately and in tighter confines on the ground than its contemporaries.

Electrical System

Like many other British and German fighters of the time, the Spitfire had a basic, but rugged, electrical system. A 12-volt system was fitted to the early marks, later marks sporting a more powerful 24-volt system. The benefits of the latter have resulted in the restored Spitfires being configured to run 24-volt systems, regardless of their original rating, avoiding the comparative delicacy of the lower voltage.

In the same way as the pneumatic system charged a reservoir of compressed air, the engine-mounted electrical generator supplies charge to the battery, mounted in a special compartment aft of the pilot on the inside of the starboard fuselage. The battery supplies the aircraft systems through terminal blocks and three fuse-boxes. Battery charging when the engine is running is controlled by a carbon-pile regulator, mounted behind the pilot's head on the rear of his headrest, smoothing the voltage signal from the generator and maintaining a constant charging voltage across the battery regardless of engine speed or system load. A suppressor prevents interference with the radio, and the pilot can monitor the health of his electrical system with a glance at the voltmeter mounted in the top right-hand corner of the instrument panel.

For running and checking the electrically powered services and for providing power for engine start, provision is made for external power via a three-pin socket usually mounted in the port wing fillet. Alternative locations are low on the engine (starboard cowling) or set further aft in the fuselage. The socket accepts a plug and power from a ground accumulator unit (trolley accumulator) or external engine-driven generator (Houchin).

It was perfectly normal for the aircraft to be started from internal power during the Second World War and in later R.A.F. service, but the Spitfires of today are usually equipped for external power to ease strain on batteries and internal wiring.

Of the three fuse-boxes, two are eight-way devices and the third is a four-way device, mounted on the port side of the cockpit, two just below the entry hatch and the third above the lower longeron. The boxes are supplied from the same terminal block which is powered from both the service side of the battery and the external power socket. This is designed to deliver a constant voltage and does not require further internal regulation.

The first box contains fuses 1 to 8, and serves navigation, flood and identification lamps, the gunsight, the fuel gauge, and undercarriage indicators and warning horn. There are positions for two spare fuses in this box in the Mk V aircraft.

The second box is the four-way device, containing fuses 9 to 12. Services supplied include the gun camera (while being triggered by the compressed-air supply to the guns, it is electrically powered), pressure head heater, radio connector and (at a surprisingly low 10 A rating) the fuse which manages engine start-up.

The third box provides power for the oil-dilution valve (used for assisting engine starts when a low oil temperature makes oil viscous and difficult to move around the engine), the ARI5000 radio and its detonation device (utilised by pilots brought down in enemy territory to destroy the radio to prevent frequency information and R.A.F. radio technology from falling into enemy hands). Last through this fuse-box on the early Spitfires was the power source for heating the pilot's gloves and boots! This was an interim measure before the days of cabin heating.

Electrics involved in engine start-up are simple regardless of the system voltage, centring around supply of power to the starter motor and boost

coil from either the internal battery or an external power supply. A single terminal block makes the power source irrelevant as battery and external supply are connected directly to it, the external power being mounted across the battery terminals. A feed is taken to the positive side of the starter relay and the starter and boost coil switches in such a way that allows the starter to operate without the boost coil being operative but not the other way round. Switching on the starter motor switch completes the connection across the starter relay providing voltage between the external supply terminal, which is fed from the negative battery terminal when internal power is being used, and the positive feed from the relay.

Currents in the range 300–400 A are not unusual at the instant that the starter motor begins to turn, though this current quickly dies away to less than 50 A. The engine-starting fuse resides on the low current side of the relay, and the 10 A value is more than sufficient to get the engine running. Simultaneously, the boost coil is activated, again via the starter relay supplied from the external terminal.

Pilots Notes for the Mk V dictate engine turning periods must not exceed 20 seconds, and that 30 seconds be allowed between starting attempts to allow the motor and associated circuitry to cool. Manuals also recommend that the prospective pilot of the Mk V 'work the priming pump as rapidly and as vigorously as possible' to get as much fuel into the engine in as short a time as possible.

The boost coil is held until the engine is running smoothly, when it is released and normal magneto ignition takes over. The pilot is advised to hold off opening the throttle for as long as possible, and certainly at least for half a minute, while the oil is pumped upwards to lubricate the upper part of the engine. Warm-up would then be carried out at fast tick-over. One can only wonder at how rigidly, if at all, these instructions were adhered to in the heat of a scramble.

The 'Office'

So what is it like to sit in the Spitfire cockpit? What can you see, what buttons are there to play with? The cockpit of any aircraft is the control centre and the Spitfire is no exception. There is so much to see, hear and feel through a myriad nerve endings. Then there is the smell. No two aircraft types smell the same. True, there is oil, hydraulic fluid, sweat, fuel and exhaust but each aircraft blends these common elements in a different way and then adds something of itself; the unique ingredient that makes the difference.

As the systems on these fighters are simple, so the display of information necessary for the pilot to operate it is kept equally simple. The switches and buttons required for the pilot to make his inputs and quickly evaluate the consequence are arranged around the dials. Immediately in front of the pilot is the blind-flying panel which includes the six most frequently used instruments, vital when contact with the ground or horizon is lost. Speed, height, direction and attitude are displayed with indications of rate of climb or descent, and information on turn and bank.

To the left of the blind-flying panel and running top to bottom on the main panel are the flap switch, navigation light switch, oxygen regulator and undercarriage position indicators with red and green 'designer' lighting. Below this are the elevator tab position indicator, triple-brake and air-pressure gauge, and two small switches to control the ignition magnetos.

To the right of the central panel are engine gauges – oil temperature and pressure, radiator temperature and boost pressure. The fuel gauge is nestled at the base of the panel, while the top houses the voltmeter. The engine booster and starter buttons are alongside two cockpit lighting switches beneath the blind-flying panel.

Above the panel, unfortunately positioned to do the most damage to the pilot's head and face in the event of a forced landing, is the reflector gunsight. Just below the panel is the horizontally placed compass. Its face is more than partly obscured by the control column spade grip and the pilot's hand on the grip. In the early versions, the compass needle exhibited a frustrating tendency to stick in the same position, especially after particularly harsh manoeuvres during combat. The engine priming pump – in Spitfires manufactured before electrical pumps were fitted – is to the right of the compass in a position that allows the pilot to pump fuel to the engine with his right hand at the same time as pressing the boost coil and starter buttons with his left.

The port side of the cockpit is dominated by the throttle quadrant, combined with the propeller controls and friction adjusters which allow the pilot to set the throttle to the required position. Behind and below the throttle are the trim tab wheels. The larger of the two controls the elevator. The smaller one, which has to be dialled fully to the right for take-off in a Merlin-engined aircraft, controls the rudder trim tab. Push-buttons and switches for the oil dilution pump, pressure head heater and camera gun were also located to the pilot's left side. Early marks of Spitfire had a radiator flap control lever mounted on the floor to the left of the pilot's seat, like an oversized handbrake. This was removed from later marks which had the thermostatically controlled radiator doors.

If the left side was centred around the throttle, the right side of the cockpit was organised around the undercarriage lever quadrant. Behind the undercarriage lever was the compressed carbon dioxide cylinder and plunger lever providing the motive force for undercarriage emergency lowering. Pilot oxygen controls were positioned nearby along with the pumps and cocks required for windscreen de-icing systems. External fuel capacity was managed from the starboard side of the cockpit, with fuel cock and jettison lever placed down at seat level. The main tank fuel cock was situated just below and to the right of the compass, below the flying control

(BELOW): Another close-in view of the cockpit area. Note the control column, webbing on the rudder pedals, as distinct from on the later models, and the radiator lever at lower left. This is the Mk V variant.

(BELOW): The completed cockpit of Mk XVIII TP280 makes an interesting comparison to that of the Mk V.

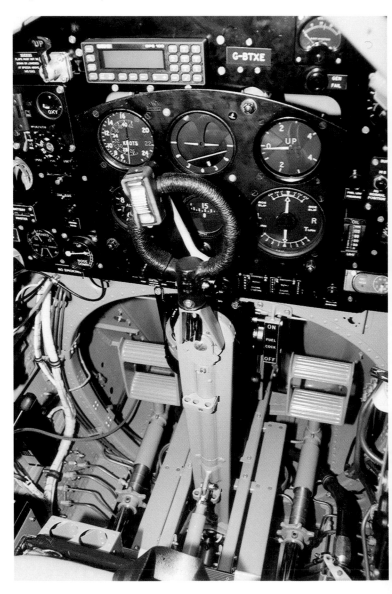

(ABOVE LEFT AND RIGHT): Bubble canopy on low-backed Spitfire Mk XVI RW382.

panel although, in later marks it was floor mounted on the port side of the cockpit.

The Spitfire cockpit is a busy, but not uncomfortable, place to be in normal circumstances. It is not as big as the cockpits in some of the American fighters, but it was not generally reckoned to be as claustrophobic as the Messerschmitt Bf 109's.

Described as 'like pulling on a large aluminium glove' and 'making the aircraft an extension of the pilot', the Spitfire cockpit layout was regarded as both sensible and usable in the heat of battle. The later low-backed variants allowed excellent all-round vision without making pilots feel exposed to the elements or enemy fire. Access to the cockpit on the ground was easy through the side hatch, and rapid exit in the air could be managed by sliding the canopy back or shedding it altogether, turning the aircraft on its back, unfastening the seat straps, then falling out of the aeroplane. If the Spitfire was falling out of control without showing an inclination to turn over, leaping over the side would usually be successful, although the tailplane of the aircraft could cause problems – a collision with it was not impossible.

The pilot was expected to sit on his parachute under normal circum-

stances. The base of the seat was shaped to take the parachute which also doubled as a very firm seat cushion, so was already strapped to the pilot which in the event of a bale-out could save valuable time.

Powerplants

The Spitfire without the Merlin would have been like Laurel without Hardy. Alternative powerplants could have been used but the effectiveness of the fighter would no doubt have been significantly reduced.

The original design put the evaporation-cooled Rolls-Royce Goshawk engine into the projected Spitfire airframe, immediately underpowering the aircraft and making the cooling system more prone to problems. It was a momentous amalgamation which saw the Rolls-Royce PV-12 engine developed alongside the early Spitfire. The PV-12 was a larger progression of the Kestrel engine, manufactured by Rolls-Royce during the 1920s. That the engine and the airframe were made for each other became obvious at a very early stage and all further development of the two were made on

(NEXT PAGE): RW382 with engine installed showing the close-fitting powerplant and kidney-shaped coolant tank.

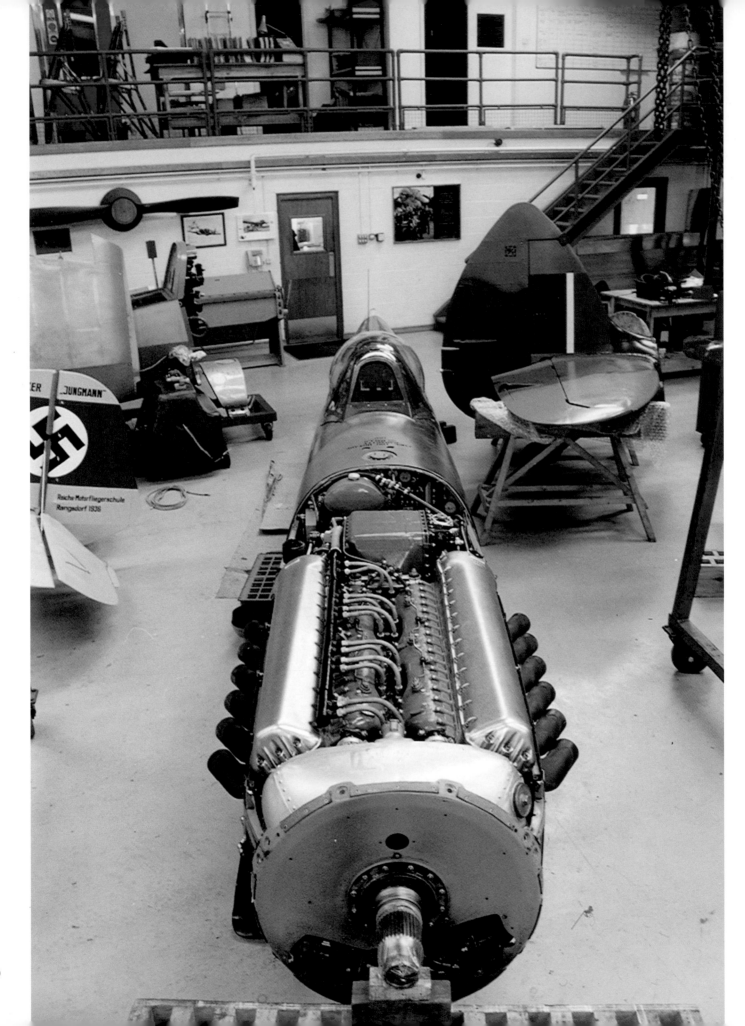

a collaborative basis. The Merlins produced by Rolls-Royce evolved to power aircraft as diverse as the Lancaster bomber, the York transport aircraft and the North American Mustang, but the only other engine to go near a Spitfire on a production basis was the Merlin's big sister, the Griffon engine.

In fact the Germans were the only other people to experiment with the motive power for the Spitfire. Captured Spitfires were air-tested against Luftwaffe fighters at various stages of the war as the aircraft became available, and some were even fitted with Daimler-Benz DB601 and DB605A engines which powered the Messerschmitt Bf 109s to take these flight trials even further. The effect of this fit was odd, as the German powerplant was an inverted-V configuration, putting the exhaust stacks low on the engine cowlings. The resulting nose bulge on the usually flat Spitfire top cowl made it look very clumsy. Ironically, the first design for the Merlin – extending even to a wooden mock up – had the inverted-V configuration, though it was demonstrated that many complications could be avoided with the final design if the engine was built 'the right way up'.

The Merlin Engine

The Merlin is a V-12 liquid-cooled powerplant with cylinders arranged in two banks of six, each being 60° apart to produce a classic V shape. Displacement is 27 litres and the power produced by these engines ranges from 1045 hp in the earliest version to 1580 hp in the later Packard Merlin 266s which powered Mk XVI Spitfires. Development of the Merlin began in 1932 using the Kestrel engine as a foundation, and working models of the engine were available for testing in October 1933. The first two were funded privately by Rolls-Royce themselves.

Flight trials in a Hawker Hart took place later the following year. The engine was advanced enough to power the Spitfire prototype, K5054, in March 1936. It was able to offer a reliable 1045 hp for its 1370 lb weight.

(ABOVE AND BELOW): These photographs of RW382 show the compactness of the engine, installation pipework, wiring and cowling framework (port and starboard views) This is the Packard built Merlin.

Improvements to the cooling system, supercharging arrangements and propeller reduction gearing were always in process but it was internal redesign which led to the largest power improvement with a jump from 1240 hp to 1470 hp after the Merlin 45 superseded the Merlin XX.

Maximum power from a Merlin peaked with the Merlin 63a, employed in

(LEFT): *Spitfire Mk V EP120 being prepared for engine installation. In the foreground, all the necessary ancillary equipment and items like Siamese exhaust stubs, flame dampers, etc. are assembled so the installation runs with everything to immediate hand.*

the Mk VIII, Mk IX and P.R. XI Spitfires, when 1710 hp was available for take-off and emergency power. Higher power and prolonged use of the emergency boost settings reduced engine life but during combat the extra power was invaluable.

The Merlin developed a reputation with the pilots during early operations for reliability. The decision to use a glycol and water mixture (30% to 70%) certainly assisted engine heat management but ailing engines could run for a considerable period even when the cooling system had suffered major damage. Such characteristics quickly endeared the engines to the pilots, especially when they were faced with ditching in unfriendly seas as an alternative.

(BELOW): *Engine bay detail on Spitfire Mk V EP120. This illustrates how the earlier marks were configured. The oil tank is new due to the lack of availability of original units. Note the larger gauge pipe required, there being only one radiator.*

The Griffon Engine

The Griffon was not, as is widely, believed, based on the Merlin or its predecessors. It is a development of the R engine originally employed by Supermarine in its Schneider Trophy Racing aeroplanes. Initial design of the Griffon began at the same time as the work on Merlin engine development. Concentration on the Merlin development dictated that bench tests of the prototype Griffon engines did not take place until mid-1940.

Rated at 1735 hp for the V-12, with 36.7 litres capacity at 1980 lb weight, prospects for the engine looked favourable. Equipped with a two-speed single-stage supercharger (Merlins offered a single-speed device), the Griffon went on to use three supercharging stages to produce a maximum power output of 2450 hp in the Seafire F.46 and Spitfire F.21 projects when Rolls-Royce replaced the conventional carburettor fuel/air induction with fuel injection systems. That the modified, developed Spitfire was able to absorb additional power without a major redesign is a tribute to its designers.

Engine Installation

Merlin or Griffon installation on the Spitfire airframe is a simple arrangement, belying the complicated-looking pipework and ancillary equipment visible when the cowlings are off. In the case of the Merlin, it is mounted in a cradle constructed of tubular steel in a U-shaped member to give added strength and rigidity under the rear of the engine. The cradle is bolted to the aircraft at the two datum longerons, the strengthened longerons which run rearward from the firewall, and at the base of the wing attachment booms.

Tapered bolts hold the cradle in place with the cradle itself providing four mounting blocks to locate and secure the 'feet' of the engine, each block offering two bolts to secure the engine. Additionally, the cradle supports ancillary equipment and has brackets and cut-outs to house these along the lengths of its tubing. Engine connections either pass forward through the firewall at frame 5 or through the webs on the mainplane spars at the base of frame 5.

(ABOVE): Final assembly in progress on TE566. Engine cradle is being prepared ready to accept the Merlin. Initial testing of the undercarriage began at this point.

On the port side, the spar web is pierced by oil pipes which carry hot engine oil to the underwing-mounted oil coolers. On the starboard side, the same method is used to convey hot coolant back to the radiator. On post-Mk V Spitfires, both sides carry coolant to respective radiators and alternative arrangements were made for oil cooling.

The firewall is cut in a number of places to permit fuel, compressed air, engine control rods and control cables to run forwards to the engine, and for engine instrumentation lines (for example, the rev counter attachment cables) to connect to the cockpit area. The engine is normally hoisted and lowered into place on the cradle which would have already been installed in the Spitfire. The firewall-mounted reservoirs, pumps and filters would already be installed, and cable, pipe and electrical connections would be ready to be made to the engine.

All 650 kg of Merlin is then located and secured. The task is complicated by the aircraft sitting nose high on the ground; the angle of the slung engine has to be adjusted to allow the cast feet on the engine to meet the cradle mounting points. Once the engine is secured, the oil tank (mounted under the chin of the engine) and coolant header tank (mounted over the nose of the engine) are fitted and the pipework for each connected.

Engine-mounted oil and coolant pumps push fluids around the engine

(ABOVE): Nixon-overhauled Griffon 65 shortly after installation and prior to further systems work (Mk XVIII TP280).

73

(ABOVE): *Installation of a Vintage V-12's Merlin into Spitfire Mk XVI TD248. The red engine casing was provided at the request of the original owner.*

(BELOW): *TD248 with wiring well advanced and close to mating with the wings. Note the oil tank on the underside of the Merlin by the sump which actually came from a Seafire. Cooling system pipework prominent in this view.*

and the cooling and cleaning systems, and these are connected into their respective header tanks. Most of the pipes that are visible when the cowlings are off are related to the cooling system.

Two magnetos are engine-mounted at the rear of the powerplant, above the carburettor and supercharger casing, and these are connected to electrical systems so the engine starting and boost coils can be operated alongside normal ignition procedures.

Fuel feed to the carburettor has to be established, in tandem with controls for the throttle and fuel mixture settings. The pipework for conveying fuel to the cylinders for engine priming is then connected, and cables and control lines installed. Propeller connections are made to permit prop speed control from the throttle quadrant in the cockpit.

An experienced team can fit a Merlin to a Spitfire easily within a day in the controlled conditions of an aircraft hangar. Wartime maintenance crews in wartime situations seldom had that luxury, often working out in the open

(PREVIOUS PAGE): Detailed systems shot, again emphasising the compactness of the engine installation and ancillaries. Note the number of detail brackets required to hold the pipework in place.

(RIGHT): Close-up of diaphragm, crankshaft spline and reduction gear on the Merlin.

(BELOW): Comparison shots which show differences between the Mk XVI and Mk XVIII. In the background are the wings from the Mk XVI and note that the wooden structure for the wing ellipses have now been attached.

and suffering from either the piercing cold of the Russian steppe or the searing heat of the North African desert.

Main Engine Components

Forward portions of both the Merlin and the Griffon engine casings housed the propeller reduction gears. This comprises a small number of large and finely machined gears serving to reduce the engine revolutions to speeds which could be transmitted safely to the propeller. Typically, the propeller would turn at slightly less than half the speed of the engine. On some of the later marks, the reduction gear was arranged to support contra-rotating propellers. This arrangement eliminated the torque which made the aircraft swing on take-off and, to a much lesser extent, on landing. The complications of building constant-speed devices and incorporating full-range blade movement into epicyclic drives had delayed this innovative solution so contra-props were only available during the latter stages of the Second World War.

The main crankcase and cylinder banks sit immediately behind the reduction gear. Each bank houses six cylinders with overhead valve gears including the rockers and gear-driven camshafts. The entire camshaft and rocker arm assembly can be removed from the head of the cylinder bank in a single unit, allowing access to the top end of the valves. Connecting rods are in six pairs, plain and forked, working on a fully balanced one-piece crankshaft geared at the forward end to drive the propeller reduction gear. At the rear end it provides the driving force to auxiliary systems including the supercharger assembly. The supercharger is a centrally-fed centrifugal device which sucks the fuel–air mixture through the upright, twin-choke carburettor located at the rear of the engine assembly. The carburettor is fed through the air inlet under the chin of the Spitfire, very often through a number of filters depending on the aircraft's theatre of operations.

In extreme cases, a Vokes filter was fitted to a large number of Spitfires destined for North Africa where the dry and sandy environment was not conducive to normal clean engine operation. The Vokes filter dictated a new characteristic chin cowl shape and gave so equipped Spitfires a pugnacious look. Under normal conditions, Spitfires operated with only stone guards and low-grade filters fitted to the carburettor intakes.

Two magnetos were sited on the outside of both cylinder banks feeding all twelve cylinders simultaneously. The loss of one of the magnetos, a not uncommon occurrence, while not crucial to the operation of the engine, often resulted in loss of power or a drop in engine revs. Magnetos were mechanically driven from the geared camshaft ends via a drive coupling so both devices were receiving the same input from the top of the engine. Initial magneto set-up and cam clearance adjustment on the valve heads, were both labour-intensive tasks.

Other pump-driven gear and ancillary equipment included an oil scavenge pump, and fuel and coolant pumps, all driven from the mass of gears at the rear of the engine. A layshaft allowed the coolant pump to be situated on the port side of the crankcase away from the ancillaries at the back of the engine. The electrical system generator is the one standard piece of equipment driven from the front end of the crankshaft, situated low on the right-hand side of the crankcase when viewed from the cockpit.

(ABOVE): Picture front to rear showing detail from the prop hub right back to the installed wing bolts, engine ancillaries and coolant pipework. The pitch change unit has now been installed and the oil tank's convoluted shape where it meets the sump can be clearly seen.

(ABOVE): Detail shot of cowling fittings showing G-clamps holding the cowls in place for an accurate fit. The oblong recess at lower right of the silver oil tank is a feature of the Seafire variant but, as is illustrated here, it can be also used on the Spitfire. The drain plug is located inside this oblong area. Below can be seen the air inlet.

(ABOVE): TE566 with the propeller installed. Close-up of the propeller boss, during a trial installation, and sump. Note the polythene was left in place to protect the blades during installation.

Camshafts are used to take ancillary gear drives, at a quarter of engine speed, including the drive for the engine rpm indicator which is taken from the rear of the port cam assembly, and there are further drives for additional pumps on the starboard side.

The starter motor is attached to the rear of the engine base, again on the starboard side, connected to the crankshaft through a number of gears and shafts. Gear ratios between starter motor and crankshaft vary depending on the mark of engine but are usually within 85:1 and 105:1, meaning the engine turns over once for every 85 to 105 revolutions of the starter motor.

As outlined earlier, the oil system is a simple arrangement with the nose tank feeding the oil pump, the oil flowing to the oil coolers in the wings via the numerous sheaths, jackets and oilways in the engine itself. Mechanisms are provided at the oil coolers to prevent cold oil from a newly started engine passing through and delaying the warm-up of the engine.

Oil diluters, which can be operated from cockpit switches, can be used in the event of the aircraft standing for a lengthy period of time in cold conditions. In many airworthy Spitfires today, the use of preheated oil pumped into the heads of each cylinder bank goes some way to reducing the wear on the top end of the engine on start-up if the engine has not been run for some time, thus increasing the time between overhauls.

The cooling system is slightly more complicated than the oil system. The coolant tank above the reduction gear casing pushes the 70:30 water–glycol mixture around the engine and out through the wing spar web to the radiator(s), under pressure from a coolant pump. Heated coolant is put to good use in the carburettor where it is used to preheat air being sucked into the engine as it is pumped around a small jacket to the main choke. The coolant header tank is maintained at 2.25 psi above atmospheric pressure with a small relief valve, allowing the tank to vent to the atmosphere if the pressure is exceeded.

A blow-by-blow account of all that happens in a Merlin or Griffon engine is impractical here. Suffice to say that the two engines were complex, sophisticated devices for their time.

(BELOW): Note the rocker covers have been removed. This angle emphasises the nose to tail aggression of the Spitfire.

Propeller

Engine development was critical to the initial performance of the Spitfire. The development of propeller units for the Spitfire is often ignored but it is a key element in the success of the type. At the time of the first flights of the prototype Spitfire, propellers came in one flavour. They were wooden, fixed in pitch and usually, though not exclusively, two-bladed units which had to offer a balance of performance to suit the wide variety of situations the aircraft was likely to encounter. Demands on engine and propeller are vastly different on take-off to those when cruising at altitude. These early propeller units were not fitted with constant-speed devices and the pilot had other variables to consider in efficiently operating the engine and propeller together.

The angle of the propeller blades on fixed-pitch airscrews was calculated to give about 3000 rpm with full throttle at 18,000 ft. This combination produced the highest speed in level flight. This also meant that the propeller could only achieve approximately 1900 rpm on the take-off run because the blades were set too coarsely for an optimum run. This coarse setting stirred the air up much more than was ideal, which prolonged the take-off run. This was because less of the engine power was effective, causing a pronounced torque reaction that forced one wing to sit low on take-off resulting in the air over the tail surfaces spinning more than was desirable. It is this effect which caused the Spitfire to swing on take-off. A torque reaction itself would not prevent the pilot from taking off in a straight line. This effect had to be rectified by harsh use of the rudder.

Even Jeffrey Quill, the Supermarine Test Pilot on the Spitfire, reported that, while it was possible to take off in a straight line by judicious use of the throttle, the Spitfires which sported the wooden props were better suited to flying from a grass airfield than they were from concrete runways.

A number of propeller configurations were tested on the prototype Spitfire. A unit with blades geared for the best take-off run had the engine overworking at height. A propeller designed for maximum level speed at altitude would cause the Spitfire to swing heavily on take-off. A prop with

(Below): TE566 ready for cowling. Rocker covers are removed so that work can be carried out on the camshaft (in compliance with a C.A.A. directive).

THE STRUCTURE OF THE SPITFIRE

a wider blade was trialled. It was designed to keep the speed as high as possible in flight and reduce airflow spinning over the tail unit on the ground. Another propeller was designed and built for demonstrations, when heights were kept very low and the take-off run could be seen by large numbers of people. Even a four-bladed unit was tried at this stage.

It was found that the take-off run could be reduced by about thirty-three per cent when a three-bladed, variable-pitch propeller was installed on the aircraft. However, this increased the all-up weight of the prototype by 325 lb and produced no improvement in handling qualities compared to the wooden propeller it replaced. This unit was made by Hamilton. Others were tried from Fairey Reed and de Havilland.

It was decided to fit the first fifty production aircraft with a new two-bladed fixed-pitch wooden propeller made by the Airscrew Company. The first seventy-seven Spitfires rolled off the production line so equipped. Development and production work on the de Havilland two-pitch propellers, which allowed the pilot to select take-off (fine pitch) or normal flight (coarse pitch) settings, had put the performance of the three-bladed metal propellers ahead of that of their wooden counterparts and these were subsequently fitted to Spitfire Is equipped with the Merlin II and III engines. At squadron level, they were well received, offering a speed of 350 mph at 18,000 ft, depending on the state of the engine and airframe.

Late in 1939, three-bladed props were available to Spitfire production lines, and twenty-two Spitfire Is were fitted with these units at Woolston. The aircraft were delivered to No. 19 Squadron. The biggest improvement in performance came about as a result of the fitting of de Havilland constant-speed units to the Spitfires which were already allocated to squadrons. De Havilland was able to achieve this task within two months of the request being made.

A four-bladed propeller was made available to a special Spitfire project as a one-off. The Airscrew Company designed and built a unit which would equip the 'Speed Spitfire' which was to attempt the world air speed record with a custom-modified production aircraft. A speed of 450 mph was anticipated for the aircraft using a Merlin III engine and 100-octane fuel, producing 2150 hp at sea level. Before it could make an attempt on the record, a German team raised the record to just below 470 mph, well outside the projected abilities of the Spitfire.

The first Griffon-engined Spitfire was the Mk IV and such was the increase in power output, even at the early stages of Griffon development, that the propeller had to be revised to a four-bladed device, a feature not to be seen on Merlin-engined Spitfires until the Mk VI. All marks until that point used the three-bladed constant-speed Rotol units which were preferred over the de Havilland equivalents. The four-bladed units were retained in all marks from VI through to the Mk XII. Only eighteen Mk XIIIs were built and they all sported the de Havilland three-bladed propeller which was driven by the low-altitude Merlin 32 engine.

The Mk XIV Spitfire was the first Griffon-engined Spitfire to enter R.A.F. service. The airframes for the Mk XIV were taken directly from the Mk VIII production line and the Merlin engine was replaced with the Griffon as an interim step towards what was seen to be a 'super' Spitfire. The early Mk XIVs had the normal Merlin-sized tail, although later examples countered the reduction in lateral stability caused by the extra three feet of engine with an increase in the area of both tail fin and rudder.

The propeller fitted to all the Mk XIV machines was a five-bladed constant-speed Rotol, and this fit was to be continued through the remaining Spitfire marks, with two exceptions. First of these was the Mk XVI Spitfire which was powered by a Packard-built Merlin 266 engine and which therefore adopted the same propeller arrangements as the Mk IX Spitfire – a four-bladed Rotol device.

The other exception was much more interesting, especially as none of the world's surviving Spitfires has yet been restored to exhibit the arrangement. Several F.21 Spitfires were fitted with the Griffon 85 engine which had epicyclic propeller reduction gears and would therefore drive twin three-bladed contra-rotating propellers.

Never really adopted to any great degree on the Spitfires that followed, the use of the Griffon 85 and the contra-props was popular with the Fleet Air Arm which used the arrangement on the Seafire 45, 46 and 47 following a decision in April 1947 to standardise on this arrangement to avoid the massive torque experienced with the five-bladed Rotol airscrews then in use. After this same month, Griffon 87 engines were available for use, offering 2145 hp at +25 lb boost, and, for the F.47 Seafires, the Griffon 88 with its fuel injection systems which took the rated power up to a massive 2350 hp. One can only imagine the effects of this level of torque on take-off from the deck of a heaving aircraft-carrier under steam in a choppy sea.

(Opposite): Massive five-bladed Rotol propeller and enlarged spinner. A far cry from the early Spitfire variants (Mk XVIII TP280).

4
The Griffon-engined Spitfires. (A pictorial record)

Similarities in the build process of both Merlin- and Griffon-engined aircraft are apparent in the preceding chapter. The main differences are the engine and its systeming, and of course that massive torque-countering rudder. Illustrated here are both Mk XIV and Mk XVIII machines.

(ABOVE): With fuselage rectification work now complete, the systems installation can now proceed. Shown here is Mk XVIII TP280.

(ABOVE): The painting of the fuselage is now complete and the electrician now starts to wire the aircraft. This is Mk XIV NH799.

(ABOVE): Contrasting the Griffon and Merlin variants, Mk XVIII TP280 is on the left and on the right is Mk IX TE566. The Mk XVIII, apart from being Griffon-powered, will have a low-back profile with a bubble canopy and retractable tailwheel.

(ABOVE): TP280 undergoing a hydraulic systems check prior to installation of the wings.

(ABOVE AND NEXT PAGE TOP LEFT): The wings are now in place on the Mk XVIII. Seen to advantage are the deeper radiators of the Griffon-engined variant. The larger engine requires more cooling. Initial reaction would be that the larger units would slow the aircraft but this is not the case. Due to the shape of the radiator fairing a ram effect is produced which not only counters the drag but also adds about 4 mph to the top speed of the aircraft. This is TP280.

(BELOW): At this stage, the tail of the aircraft has been mated to the fuselage and the windscreen is trial assembled. Shown here is Mk XVIII TP280.

(LEFT AND OPPOSITE TOP LEFT):
A detailed look at the firewall of the Griffon variant. This is radically different to that of the Merlin-engined aircraft. Top left is the gearbox which drives such ancillaries as the generator vacuum pump, compressor and hydraulic pump.

(BELOW AND OPPOSITE BELOW):
Mk XVIII TP280 during undercarriage retraction and testing.

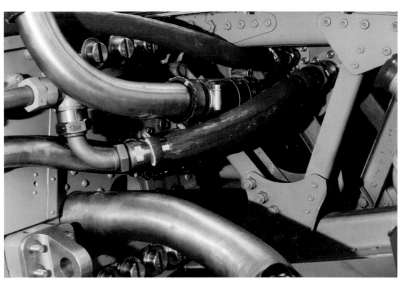

(LEFT):
Shown here is the pipework in the port leading edge. Those pipes covered in red fire-retardant material carry fuel from the newly fitted wing tanks. The seven wing retaining bolts can be seen top and bottom left of the frame. This is TP280.

(ABOVE): *Main fuel tank bays of the later aircraft have redesigned pipework in order to accommodate a larger welded fuel tank. This is a Mk XIV.*

(BELOW): *Constructional detail on Spitfire Mk V EP120. Note the oil tank on the mark V is exposed. It is an integral part of the cowling. This photograph has been included to clearly show the difference between the early Merlin variants and the later Griffon-engined machines.*

(FAR LEFT):
The engine complete with slab-sided bearers is now installed in the aircraft.

(LEFT):
Coolant pipes and cowling rails being trial fitted – necessary so that positions for clips and other system parts can be determined (Mk XVIII TP280).

(BELOW):
The colour scheme changes nothing – this is still a Griffon! This unit was overhauled by Dave Zeuschel and fitted in a Mk XIV (NH799).

(ABOVE): Main fuel tank bays of the later aircraft have redesigned pipework in order to accommodate a larger welded fuel tank. This is Mk XIV SM832.

(ABOVE): 2000 horses of serious power – built by the best – Rolls-Royce.

(BELOW): Nearly there! Oil tank in, wing fillets on, cowling rails fitted, prop on.

(ABOVE): The oil tank for the Griffon model is located behind the firewall, a markedly different location to that on the Merlin aircraft.

(ABOVE LEFT AND RIGHT): Complementing the powerful engine are the five blades of the Rotol propeller unit. These blades are manufactured by Hoffmann in Germany and returned to the U.K. where they are certified by Dowty Rotol (the successor to the original company).

(FAR LEFT AND LEFT):
The spinner of the Griffon variant is conceptually different as well as being larger, utilising a different process of manufacture.

(BELOW):
TP280 now largely complete, with cowlings removed for a final inspection prior to engine runs and first flight.

(ABOVE): One stage closer! The cowlings go back in place.

(BELOW):With everything in place TP280 is now ready for the next stage; first engine runs.

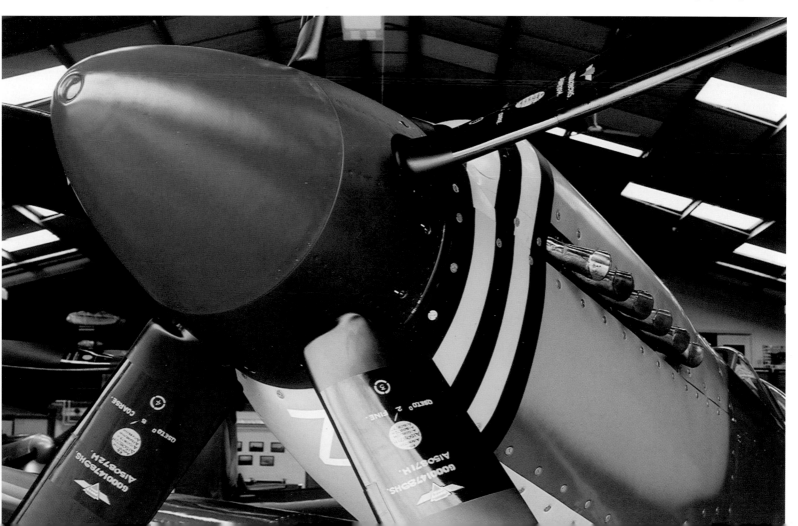

(ABOVE): A Mk XVIII tied down undergoing initial engine runs. Each aircraft is carefully tested on the ground to eliminate possible mishaps when the aircraft takes to the air.

(BELOW): With all flight testing completed Mk XVIII TP280 approaches the airfield at high speed and low level. "Hang on Saint Christopher!'

5
Design and Engineering Differences

(ABOVE): Spitfires both, but the Mk XVIII in the background clearly illustrates the growth potential. Transforming the aircraft from a little beauty to an absolute beast!

It has to be an extraordinarily hopeful, or naive, team of designers who imagine they can get it right first time when it comes to producing a front-line fighting aircraft. The success of an aircraft design, it has been said, is the ability of that design to undergo large numbers of modifications during its life span and not just how well it fits its initial purpose. To be really successful, it must offer something new and improved after each successive alteration, and keep ahead of the competition. So it was with the Spitfire.

Supermarine knew it had devised something special when the prototype aircraft took to the skies in the early morning of 5 March 1936 but the extent of the obvious success could only be considered when production of the last Spitfires ceased not too far short of ten years later. Over 20,300 Spitfires had been built in that time, the numbers of aircraft having been spread very unevenly over twenty-one different marks of the machine, depending on how successful they were. There were over 200 variations in

airframe, engine, propeller and general aircraft configuration conceived in the design offices and brought into being by the production managers and their teams in a surprisingly large number of locations around the south of England and, of course, in the huge production facility at Castle Bromwich in the Midlands.

The basic Spitfire airframe design was nothing if not flexible. The normal all-up weight jumped from a mere 6200 lb in the very early Mk I aircraft to 9900 lb in the Mk 24. This could be extended still further to 11,290 lb when the aircraft was fitted with an external 170-gallon fuel tank. The Mk 24 could manage 450 mph in level flight at 19,000 ft and could easily achieve over 510 mph when put into a dive. The Mk I was nearly 100 mph slower, reaching a little over 360 mph in level flight and about 430 mph in a steep dive. It is tempting to record that the basic aircraft design which could bend itself between these two points on the perform-ance scale was essentially the same with only strengthening modifications and increases in control area necessary to govern the successive increases in engine power. To do so, however, would be to distort the reality of the Spitfire's development well beyond acceptability.

There were times, in fact, when the changes were so profound that a change of name was seriously considered. The Supermarine Victor instead of the Spitfire Mk 21 was a real possibility and compromise had to be reached by introducing the use of arabic rather than roman numerals for the aircraft's designation. Many would still argue today that the Griffon-engined Spitfires were so unlike the Merlin-engined Spitfires as to warrant a different name for the aircraft.

We will not consider all of the variations of the Spitfire's pedigree here as the list is huge, but what follows is a view of each of the most important marks of Spitfire from an engineering perspective so that the differences between successive design changes can be charted, and the characteristics of the Spitfire prototype can be linked with all of its descendants.

The Prototype Spitfire, K5054

Work began on the Spitfire prototype in March 1935, just twelve short months before the famous maiden flight from Eastleigh airport. Throughout its development, the Supermarine team responsible for K5054 worked very closely with the Rolls-Royce team who were developing the PV-12 engine which was to become the equally famous Merlin. Less apparent, but just as vital, was the close working relationship with the Air Ministry and the Royal Aircraft Establishment (R.A.E.) at Farnborough. The result of this collaborative effort was the low-wing monoplane with all-metal stressed-skin fuselage and single-spar wing, moulded radiator and oil cooling ducts, two-bladed fixed-pitch propeller, tail skid and bare stalky undercarriage legs that was to form the cutting edge to Britain's defensive, and later offensive, strategy for much of the forthcoming war.

Other points worthy of note on the prototype machine were the engine exhaust ports which were vented straight to the atmosphere through flush-cut holes in the cowlings and the flat cockpit canopy which would very soon give way to the much more familiar rounded design which offered the pilot a little more room to move his head. The fundamental structure of the prototype is so similar to the detailed view given elsewhere in this book that the reader is referred to those pages to avoid replicating much of that information.

A number of modifications were made to the prototype machine, however, although test pilot Captain Joseph 'Mutt' Summers' famous request 'not to touch a thing' had been heeded for much of the very early flight-test work. By 19 March 1936, it had been decided to replace the engine cowlings with a new set which would offer a more complete seal around the engine. The originals were not airtight and, despite taping the joints to provide a seal, performance was adjudged to be suffering slightly. In a similar vein, the eighteen doors and hatches on the underside of the wing were causing airflow problems as they had been fitted before the installation of the seals and were projecting into the airstream and causing drag. Again, tape was used as an interim measure. Wheel fairings were also fitted to the undercarriage legs at about this point to further reduce the drag at the wing undersurfaces and work was undertaken on the ailerons and wing-tips which had both twisted.

The air intake on the underside of the fuselage was redesigned and rebuilt to be slightly shorter than the original. Finally, the slight indentations in the fuselage skin caused by the skin riveting process were filled to provide a completely smooth exterior on the aircraft, and the famous light-blue coat of high-gloss paint was applied to further improve the aerodynamics. With an all-up weight of 5439 lb the aircraft, in the hands of Jeffrey Quill who had tested the machine with a variety of different propellers, managed a maximum level speed of 349 mph before passing to Martlesham Heath for evaluation by the British authorities. Level-flight tests from the Suffolk airfield supported the Supermarine claim for a top

speed of 349 mph and further work was carried out into the effects of altitude on the Spitfire's speed. This was helped by the installation of a Merlin F engine, which was capable of developing 1045 hp, in place of the original Merlin C.

Other changes included the introduction of exhaust dampers over the open ports of the engine, a tailwheel to replace the skid, an engine-driven pump to raise and lower the undercarriage in place of the hand-operated system initially employed, and a reshaping of the horn balance on the rudder. It had been found that by pointing the exhaust gases towards the rear of the aircraft some small thrust gains could be achieved which helped nudge the speed of the aircraft upwards.

Following the application of large numbers of split peas to the airframe to simulate the domed heads of rivets, tests were carried out to determine the extent to which flush riveting was actually required for optimal aerodynamic performance. Only seven flights were actually made to test the effect of the gradual but systematic removal of the peas on the aerodynamics of the aircraft, but the testing must have been effective as not one Spitfire ever went into operations with a split pea stuck to it!

Prototype Spitfire K5054 was brought up to full Mk I production standard in September 1937 following an extensive modification programme. The machine continued to serve both Supermarine and the R.A.F., being formally taken on charge with the R.A.F. with effect from 23 October 1937, as a vehicle for a further series of tests into gun heating and the operation of the gun cine-camera. Two accidents befell the prototype, the second of which, on 4 September 1939, proved to be fatal to both the unfortunate pilot and the aircraft which had only flown for a total of 151.5 hours. K5054 had flipped over on to its back and was never flown again. She was declared obsolete the following month and found her way into storage at Farnborough where she made her last contribution to the Spitfire development programme by providing a ready fuselage for testing the location of early photo-reconnaissance cameras. It was not long after this work that she was destroyed.

On to the Mk I

The first order for Spitfires was for 310 machines, an order which was much larger than any that Supermarine or any other aircraft manufacturer for that matter, had ever had to deal with before. The order was placed on 3 June 1936 but it was not until two years later that the first production machine, K9787, was delivered to Rolls-Royce on 17 July 1938 where she was immediately employed in trials of the Merlin variants then under evaluation. The second machine was sent to Martlesham Heath for further gun trials, although this was only after she had assisted in the Rolls-Royce Merlin trials. It was the third production machine that was the first to find its way to an R.A.F. squadron.

No.19 Squadron, which was based at Duxford, became the evaluation Squadron for the new machines. Much valuable feedback from this pre-war evaluation was made available to the Supermarine design team, and a number of important changes were made to the machines during this period. The first seventy-four Spitfire Mk Is had Merlin II engines installed from the factory but Merlin IIIs, which had a 'universal' propeller fitment but no more horses, were fitted as standard in all further Mk Is. More important were the changes in the propellers fitted to the aircraft. The first seventy-seven were to wear the mahogany fixed-pitch two-bladed propellers which had been tested so thoroughly on the prototype. The remainder were fitted with the three-bladed, two-speed de Havilland propellers.

Before the end of June 1940, however, all surviving Spitfire Mk Is had been retro-fitted with the constant-speed three-bladed development of the de Havilland propeller and these alterations were of some significance to the performance of the aeroplane. The same modifications were made to Hurricanes at around the same time in a huge undertaking by de Havilland which saw its engineers touring all the fighter stations in England between late June and early August 1940, the start of the Battle of Britain.

Spitfire squadrons were instructed to armour-plate their aircraft when war finally came in September 1939. A deflector shield was to be fitted in the field to cover the fuel tanks and armour-plating was applied to the rear of the engine bulkhead. The bulletproof windscreen was introduced at this point, too. Further changes were made to the machines with the use of an engine-driven pump to replace the hand-operated unit used to raise and lower the wheels of the aircraft. It seems that the pump-driven hydraulic configuration on the prototype had actually been removed in favour of the hand pumps, which were carried forward to the first of the Mk I machines. Radiator changes were also made from September 1940 when Morris developed its QA radiator which owed as much to the cooling of car engines as it did to aeronautical development.

Of the 1566 Spitfire Mk Is which were produced, 50 of them being manufactured at the Westland factory and the remainder at Supermarine, only 30 were produced as Mk Ibs with a single 20mm Hispano cannon in each wing. The B wing is described in detail elsewhere in this book, but it is interesting to note that the cannon had already been appreciated as a more powerful weapon even at this early stage of the war. All other Mk I Spitfires were therefore Mk Ias by virtue of their being fitted with the standard four-machine-gun wing.

One aspect of the Spitfire's performance which is very easily overlooked is the fuel which was used. All the flying carried out by the prototype had been completed with the then standard 87-octane fuel and this was also used by the Mk I machines. The 100-octane fuel had been identified as a real possibility as early as 1935 following work in America into the reduction of the tendency of the existing fuel to pre-ignite in the cylinders (knocking) but it was not until 1939 that production of sufficient quantities for use by an air force could be guaranteed. Even then, supply of the fuel to the U.K. was to some extent dictated by the U-boat captains prowling the North Atlantic for tankers.

Three R.A.F. squadrons were able to make use of the fuel from November 1937 but it was not until September 1939 that the second production Spitfire, K9788, trialled the 100-octane fuel using a specially modified Merlin for the tests. A second Mk I machine was also used in the trials – but the Mk Is were the only Spitfire mark to go to war on 87-octane fuel.

As an aside, it was decided that an attempt on the world air speed record was to be made by a specially modified Spitfire. Two airframes were taken from the production line at Woolston but only one of them was actually modified to attempt the record. Spitfire K9834 was modified from Mk I standard with a redesigned cockpit, shorter span wings with a much rounder tip and a tail skid rather than a wheel to reduce the drag. Power was to be supplied by a much modified Merlin III using 100-octane fuel to give 2160 hp at sea level. It would drive a specially developed four-bladed fixed-pitch, propeller. The radiator under the starboard wing had to be enlarged to cope with the extra cooling requirements, and the exterior of the aircraft was prepared by filling in all unwanted holes including the cartridge ejector holes in the underside of the wings and by painting and polishing the whole fuselage. The top fuel tank was given over as a water reservoir for the total-loss cooling system which was to be employed in the record. However, after test-flights, and well before the record was seriously attempted by the team, there were doubts about the ability of the machine to meet its intended 450 mph target. The record had, by this time, been pushed to 469 mph by a German team flying an extensively modified Messerschmitt BF 109 and the British team had no alternative but to abandon its attempt. The aircraft was modified to take photo-reconnaissance cameras and, still in its specially applied blue and silver paint scheme, was to be flown over the Normandy beachhead on D-Day by Air Commodore J. Boothman, a member of the original Schneider Trophy winning team.

The Next Step – the Mk II

Externally, the Mk II Spitfire was identical to the Mk I but for a small tell-tale bulge low on the starboard engine cowling, just behind the three-bladed Rotol propeller. The Mk IIs were fitted with the Merlin XII engine producing 1175 hp on take-off, which was designed to run exclusively on the new 100 fuel. The Merlin XII was started by a Coffman type L.4 starter and it was this starter assembly, which was sited low on the starboard side of the engine, which caused Supermarine to include the small fairing lump in the starboard engine cowling. All the Mk I modifications were incorporated as standard into the Mk II's airframe from the Castle Bromwich production line, although there were a number of other small changes which were also made as the aircraft were being produced.

Not least amongst these modifications was the inclusion of nearly 75 lb of armour-plating in a small number of locations around the aircraft. Such plating had been identified as necessary by the operational squadrons and fitted to the Mk Is while they were in service. The Mk IIs were to carry protection straight from the production line. The Mk II was also to carry the externally fitted bulletproof windscreen as they were manufactured, these units being retrofitted to Mk Is during service.

The fuel tanks on the Mk II were self-sealing, using different types of rubber in a layered construction within the metal wall of the tank. Some of the inner, sandwiched rubber layer reacted with the fuel when the tank was punctured, swelling rapidly and effectively blocking the hole made by the passage of a bullet or shell through the wall of the tank. The method of sealing was not foolproof but it did offer the pilot a second chance at getting down on the ground with some fuel in his tanks, provided of course that he was not too badly shot up by the attack to achieve a landing.

In a drive to increase the range of the Spitfire in both defensive and offensive sorties, the fuel capacity of the machine was increased by adding external tanks. The fuselage-mounted 'slipper' tanks of varying capacities up to 170 gallons were finally adopted but not before a small number of Mk II aircraft had been produced with an integral wing-mounted tank of 40 gallons capacity. Faired into the leading edge of the port wing, these tanks could not be jettisoned in flight and were to prove very cumbersome in combat. However, Nos 66, 118 and 152 Squadrons were to use small numbers of these aircraft in operational sorties but their objections were not ignored by the commanders and the aircraft were very quickly replaced.

In all, some 920 Mk II Spitfires were built exclusively by the Castle Bromwich Aircraft Factory in the Midlands. Of these, 750 were built as Mk IIa aircraft with the four machine-guns in each wing, the remaining 170 being produced as IIbs with a single 20mm Hispano cannon mounted in each wing. The cannon were unpopular initially as they were very prone to jamming. However, a fault in the feed mechanism on the guns was unearthed and rectified, and larger numbers of the weapons found their way into popular squadron use. A minor modification was incorporated into all Mk II aircraft whereby the links, which connected the bullets together to form the ammunition belt, were collected as the bullets were fired, rather than allowing them to be thrown overboard and lost. This obviated the need to continually remake new links. A further seven Mk I airframes were modified to Mk II standards, adopting the B wing in the process.

Among these machines was K9788 – the second Spitfire ever produced and the machine which had acted as an engine test bed for Rolls-Royce. The Mk II Spitfire continued in squadron use up until August 1942 when

No. 111 Sqn was the last unit to retire its machines. The mark had lasted for exactly two years in operational service. No. 61 Sqn had been the first to take delivery of a Mk II machine with the arrival of P7282, in August of 1940, the height of the Battle of Britain.

About forty-nine Mk II Spitfires and a single Mk I were converted to perform another important task before being struck off charge. They were known variously as the Mk IIc, the Sea Rescue Type E (Spitfire) or, more commonly after 1942, the Spitfire A.S.R. Mk II. The A.S.R. stood for Air-Sea Rescue, and this was the role they were to perform. A small rack, designed to take two rescue marker smoke bombs, was fitted under the port wing and the two flare chutes mounted in the rear fuselage were modified to take and deliver canisters each containing a small dinghy and some food. The canisters would be dropped to pilots afloat in the Channel and the contents would greatly increase their chances of survival in an environment which could sap the life out of even the fittest pilots within two hours in summer and about 30 minutes in the winter.

Six Air-Sea Rescue squadrons operated the A.S.R. Mk II over the Channel and the northern Atlantic during the Battle of Britain and the early part of the war. While they were not able to directly assist any wet and salty pilot by picking him out of the sea, the smoke markers they dropped would increase the chances of Coastal Command or Royal Navy craft finding the man, and the dinghy and food would sustain him when he most needed it. The A.S.R. Spitfires also remained armed, despite being a non-combatant mark, being able to defend itself if called upon to do so.

The Spitfire Mk III

The Mk III Spitfire was very much an experimental beast, being devised at a time when a new and much more powerful engine was available from Rolls-Royce, and when the Ministry and Air Force officials were beginning to consider what should be done to maintain the position that the existing forces had been able to place them in. The concept of a superiority fighter was progressed by mating the new Rolls-Royce XX engine, which was capable of 1390 hp, 300 hp more than had been available on a Spitfire airframe before this time, to a much modified Mk I airframe. The use of the Mk I was deliberate in that the development and construction time of a new aircraft could be avoided and the project therefore could be delivered in a much more timely fashion.

The fuselage and engine mountings were strengthened and a retractable tailwheel was fitted to a Spitfire for the first time to improve the aerodynamics of the aircraft. The bulletproofing of the windscreen was fitted internally, again for the first time on a Spitfire, in an attempt to reduce the drag introduced by the external fit. More armour-plating in the fuselage was introduced. The undercarriage was strengthened, provided with full doors to reduce the drag of the under surface of the wing and, in a vain attempt to reduce the machine's tendency to tip over on its nose, the angle of each leg was further increased so as to move the wheel axles another two inches further forward.

The most evident change to the aeroplane came about when the Supermarine design team removed the wing-tips in an attempt to improve the roll rate of the aircraft at low level. This was achieved – but the clipped wings introduced problems of wing loading. Six square feet of wing had been removed in the redesign and the remaining wing had to support a heavier aeroplane. The length of the take off run was now noticeably longer. Dowding himself was to pronounce his dissatisfaction with the clipped wings. Successive power increases from newer Merlin variants and improvements in the performance of the propellers fitted to later machines were to overcome these shortcomings. The idea of the universal wing able to accommodate a combination of 0.303-inch Brownings, cannon and the new Browning 0.5-inch calibre machine-guns was also floated in the design

of the Mk III.

Despite there being only two Mk III Spitfires built or, more accurately, modified from examples of other marks, many radical and innovative ideas were employed on the machines. They gave rise to a great many improvements in the usability of the Spitfire in operational service as well as laying the foundation for the continued improvement of the type over the coming years of the war. The first Mk III, a converted Mk I aircraft, N3297, underwent a vast array of tests before being allocated to Rolls-Royce at Hucknall where it was fitted with the Merlin 60 and 61 engines and further tested. It therefore became the prototype Mk IX Spitfire. The second Mk III was a converted Mk V machine, W3237, which had started life with a Merlin 45. It was converted by strengthening the fuselage, replacing the Merlin 45 with the XX and fitting the Rotol constant-speed propeller. It was this aircraft which was to be used to develop the ideas of the universal wing, which eventually found its way into operational service with the later Mk Vc Spitfires. Development of the Mk V Spitfire overtook the Mk III at about this point. Although W3237 was used for a variety of other handling tests, no further development of the airframe was carried out beyond this stage.

The mark had proved its worth in providing the basis for two future, and arguably the most successful, marks of Spitfire – the Mk V and the Mk IX. The Air Ministry had been so impressed by what they had seen of the Mk III that they had placed an initial order for 1000 of the machines, then backed this up with an order for a further 120. This enthusiasm was not wasted, however, as it was simply diverted into the production of Mk Vs instead. As a counter to the Messerschmitt Bf 109F, the Mk III had proved the perfect springboard for the later marks of Spitfire. Only two examples of the variant had existed but they had had a profound effect on the direction of the development of the type and had grabbed the attention of the Air Ministry at a most crucial time.

The Mk IV – not to be confused with the P.R. IV

The Mk IV Spitfire was a watershed in Spitfire development despite the programme never getting beyond the experimental stage and the construction of only two examples, DP845 and DP851. In fact, so impressed were the Air Ministry with the results of the tests on the two Mk IV aircraft, that they placed an order for 750 of the machines. Their faith was well founded if a little premature: the Mk IV was the first Griffon-engined Spitfire.

The Rolls-Royce Griffon IIB engine had to undergo considerable alterations in order to be fitted into the streamlined Spitfire front end but eventually a frontal area of 7.9 sq ft was achieved to compare with the Merlin's 7.5 sq ft and an adequate fit was achieved. With its greater capacity, the Griffon offered 1485 hp to the new Spitfire, although its greater length and weight caused a major rethink about the shape and styling of the engine cowlings and the length of the machine's nose. It also highlighted the need to alter the propeller, as the increase in power was considered to be too great for the existing three-bladed device to cope with. Thus the four-bladed propeller graced the front end of a Spitfire for the first time since the demise of the Speed Spitfire, the Rotol constant-speed unit being fitted. The wings of the Mk IV, DP845, were later modified to take a fit of six 20mm Hispano cannon, although this arrangement progressed no further than the experimental stage.

While the aircraft was able to sustain 433 mph at 23,500 ft and climb to 15,000 ft in 4.5 minutes, its development was curtailed before sufficient progress could be made by the arrival of the Focke-Wulf 190 in the skies of Europe. The Mk IV programme was effectively ended in order that effort could be concentrated into the Merlin 61-engined Mk IX. The two Griffon-engined examples were not lost however. DP845 was to become the prototype Mk XII and DP851 was used extensively to develop the Mk

20 and 21. The Ministry's order for the 750 Mk IVs was cancelled and the serials which had been allocated to the order were redistributed amongst the Mk V aircraft then in full production.

Now it's the P.R. IV

In fact, to use the designation P.R. IV is almost as much of a cheat as it was to adopt the Mk IV designation for the Griffon Spitfires. The photo-reconnaissance Mk IV Spitfires were actually converted Mk V Spitfires with the 'D' arrangement of specialist equipment, 229 of the type eventually being produced. Therefore, the Mk Vs preceded the P.R. IVs. The designation was simply adopted when it was realised that the Griffon Spitfire was not going to make it into production and the mark number IV was therefore spare. Before this, the fifteen existing Mk Vs which were converted to the P.R. role were known as P.R. V Spitfires but the remaining aircraft were built as P.R. machines directly from the Mk V production line.

While the standard engines for the P.R. IV became either a Merlin 45 or 46, it was not unusual to find the Merlin 50, 50A, 55 or 56 fitted, depending from where in the Mk V production lines the machines had been taken. Use of the Rotol constant-speed three-bladed propeller was universal, however, as was the removal of the armament from the wings. In each wing leading edge, an extra internal fuel tank was fitted, offering a further 66 gallons per tank and thus taking the capacity of the aircraft to very nearly 220 gallons. The machines were delivered directly to Photo-Reconnaissance Units both at home and abroad, and Mk V type tropical conversion kits were supplied with the aircraft when they were needed.

The cameras fitted internally to these aircraft came in three main variations. Two F.8 cameras with 20-inch lenses could be accommodated in the rear fuselage but only one of either the F.24 14-inch focal length device or the F.52 36-inch camera. The pair of F.8s were offset from one another very slightly so that the pilot could cover more of the ground with each pass and therefore reduce the amount of time he needed to spend over the target. The P.R. aircraft were also modified to carry a dinghy for the pilot in the event of a ditching into the sea and over a gallon of drinking water to aid his survival in such a situation. The last P.R. IV was withdrawn from active duty as late as February 1945.

The Ubiquitous Mk V

Of all the Spitfires ever produced, it was the much loved Mk V that was built in the largest numbers. In total, 6479 examples of the mark made their way off the three production lines at Castle Bromwich, where 4477 were accounted for, at Supermarine which added 1367 to the overall total and at Westland where 635 were built. Very few Mk Vas with the four-machine gun wings were built compared to totals for the mark, and the ninety-four examples that were constructed all came from Supermarine. The most numerous variant was the Vb, Castle Bromwich alone manufacturing over 3000 examples, although the Vc was also produced at a significant rate later in the production run.

It was down to the Germans that the Mk V, in the form described in detail elsewhere in this book, was produced at all. It was intended that the Mk Is and IIs, which had fought so hard in the Battle of Britain, were to be replaced by the Mk III Spitfire which was at that time entering into its design stage. The Luftwaffe, however, introduced the much improved Bf 109F to the skies over Britain during the month that followed the end of the Battle. The R.A.F. found that it was very hard pressed to contain these high-flying, and comparatively very fast, intruders. In fact, the front-line Hurricanes were unable to compete with the new German machines at anything above 20,000 ft, and the Mk I and II Spitfires found they had lost the edge they had enjoyed over the Bf 109E and were actually being outmanoeuvred by the enemy above 25,000ft.

The Mk III Spitfire was a long way from being ready and the decision was therefore taken to mate the Merlin XX engine, which powered the Mk III, to the available airframes at Mk I and Mk II standard although extensive modifications were to be made to both. The supercharger on the Merlin XX was designed and built to operate best at lower altitudes, which made the engine essentially unsuitable to chase intruding Bf 109Fs above 25,000 ft. It was also extremely difficult to manufacture in any great numbers, and the decision was therefore taken by Rolls-Royce that the engine should be built with a blower more suited to the altitudes expected in combat. The engine, designated the Merlin 45, was rated at 16,000 ft and it was to add 2000 ft to the Spitfire's ceiling, take the top speed to just under 370 mph and offer an increase of power to 1470 hp.

The most promising feature of the new engine as far as the Air Ministry were concerned, however, was that large numbers could be produced in a very short period – 500 being projected by 1 April 1941 by Rolls-Royce without disturbing production of the Merlin XX. Rather than having to wait for the new engines to be produced, the Air Ministry was relieved to be offered Merlin III engines, converted to the Merlin 45 specification by Rolls-Royce. With the use of a small number of Mk I aircraft to evaluate the performance of the new combination, larger numbers of Mk I aircraft were simultaneously fitted with the converted Merlin IIIs by the Civilian Repair Organisation (C.R.O.). The reports from the trials conducted on the Merlin 45 and Spitfire I combination delighted the Ministry which cancelled its huge order for the Mk III machines which could not be produced in the time they had specified and instead put their faith in what they termed the Mk V.

To cope with the increase in power delivered by the new Merlins, the airframe of the Mk I had to be beefed up, the forward sections of the main longerons being thickened and strengthened and vertical stiffeners were fitted between frames 15 and 19. The capacity of the radiator was increased to manage the higher demands for cooling. The very early examples of the mark took the A wing but these were soon, by June 1941, to be replaced by the cannon-armed Vbs on the production lines. Most of the initial conversions from the Mk I had been made from Mk Ib aircraft and the Ministry very quickly had to amend its order to include large numbers of these variants.

The attention of the Supermarine design team was very quickly directed to the problem of cooling the oil in the new engines. Increasing the radiator capacity had not been successful enough to prevent the oil temperature from soaring – in recorded cases, as high as 150°C.

The new Mk V was also having problems with its propeller. The oil in the constant-speed unit was prone to freeze at very high altitudes and therefore allow the engine to overspeed and do itself damage, sometimes terminal. Experiments with different propeller combinations were made before, in June of 1941, a metal-bladed Rotol unit not only showed itself capable of remaining unfrozen at altitudes but also raised the ceiling of the aircraft to very nearly 40,000 ft and added 5 mph to the speed of the aircraft above 20,000 ft. However, these propellers were directed away from the Mk V Spitfires as there was a more pressing need for their limited numbers in other aircraft.

Control of the aircraft at high speeds was recognised as being problematic in the Mk I and II Spitfires. It was decided in November 1940 that all Spitfire ailerons should henceforth be covered with a metal skin and not the canvas which tended to dimple as the air pressure built up causing the reduction in control. Seven months later, the metal units were fitted to the production airframes for the first time, a delay which did not escape the notice of the Air Ministry. The Ministry was even less pleased to be told that ailerons could be retrofitted to existing aircraft only at the rate of ten pairs a week.

Further modifications made at this point included the fitting of a controversial metal bulkhead between the lower fuel tank and the cockpit. The bulkhead was needed to give pilots extra time to remove themselves from the aircraft in the event of a fire. Self-sealing was not an option for the lower tank as it was too snug in its location to be able to fit the extra covering. The modification, as with the ailerons, took months to reach the production lines and the cost of retrofitting aircraft was in the region of 40 man-hours, making it a very expensive proposition.

Further controversy followed with the requirement to fit a bob-weight forward in the elevator control system. The Squadrons really did not like it and complained bitterly when asked to fly Mk Vs with the weights fitted. The bob was intended to make the elevators easier and smoother to operate with the aircraft under load but tended to make things more difficult when the load was light. The bob also compensated for the additional weight carried by the Mk Vs with cannon wings and wearing the Merlin 45 and 46 engines.

The Merlin 46s had been developed by further refining the XX engines and were able to offer a higher-rated altitude, although they lost a little power in the process. The new engines had been introduced in October 1941 and were fitted in the standard Mk Vs. A much lower rated engine – the Merlin 45M which had its supercharger impeller blades shortened – had been fitted to L.F. Mk V aircraft for low-altitude duty.

The range of the Spitfire had never caused any concern during the early stages of the war. The Battle of Britain had been fought over home territory and pilots running short of fuel were likely to find a warm welcome and an appropriate fuel bowser on whichever airfield they cared to park on. The war over Europe was a different matter, however. The Germans had earlier found that the Channel was a disconcerting final hurdle following a lengthy sortie, and now it was the turn of the R.A.F. to make this same jump after flying fighter sweeps and ground-attack sorties over France and the Low Countries. Attention was therefore turned towards providing the Spitfire forces with adequate external tanks to allow them to complete both the outward and return legs of their sorties.

The slipper tank, which fitted beneath the fuselage slightly forward of the wing leading edge in the case of the huge 170-gallon tank, came in a number of sizes from 30 gallons upwards. Low-speed handling with the tanks fitted was a mixture of entertainment and anxiety, although above 155 mph, in the case of the largest tank, the aircraft settled a bit and became rather more stable. The tanks could be jettisoned from the aeroplane if the need arose, although the pilot first had to ensure that his fuel cocks were set appropriately or the contents of his main tanks would pour from the open fuel feed of the auxiliary tank. The absolute range of the Spitfire could be increased to as much as 1450 miles using the largest tanks and this range was used to the full in the transfer of Mk V Spitfires from the U.K. to Malta via Gibraltar. It is interesting to note the effect on this figure of the extensive changes made by the Israelis when ferrying their Mk IXs from Czechoslovakia (see the history of TE566 elsewhere in this book).

The first Mk Vc aircraft were anticipated to be in service as early as October 1941 and deliveries were scheduled to begin that month. The Mk Vc sported either the Merlin 45 or 46 engine but introduced the C wing into service. The C wing contained four Hispano 20mm cannon in each pair of wings but also allowed the armament fit to be changed to suit the pilot, local conditions and the general availability of the weapons. In Malta, for instance, lack of 20mm ammunition meant that the rounds had to be rationed, with the result that the Spitfire Vs on the island were restricted to two cannon per aircraft. Pilots reported no significant loss of firepower but that rates of climb were much improved with this arrangement!

Performance of the new Mk Vcs was shown to be slightly inferior to the converted Mk Ib aircraft that had acted as the initial prototype. This was

attributed to the extra cannon blisters and muzzles on the wings, and it was calculated that some 5 mph was lost due to the increased drag from these items. Extra weight was also added by the second pair of cannon of course and these items took the all-up weight of the Mk Vc to around 6970 lb, close to a 500 lb jump from the 6499 lb of the Mk Va aircraft.

The Mk Vc mainly saw service in theatres other than the European war. Large numbers made their way to Russia, others to Australia and many to the African deserts where the problems of sand and grit ingestion by the engines made the work of the support engineers much more difficult by increasing the frequency of the engine overhauls. To counter the effects of sand ingestion, the Vokes filter was adopted despite its bulk and noticeable detrimental effects on top speed. It was, however, the only filter available which could cope with the sandy conditions. Large numbers of Vcs were produced already wearing the filter in preparation for their trip to North Africa.

In order to get large numbers of aircraft to Africa and the Mediterranean theatre, large distances had to be flown from bases such as Gibraltar and Takoradi, which could be reached easily by sea. With the armament removed and with a 170-gallon slipper tank completely full and with a further 29 gallons carried in the rear fuselage tank, the Spitfires were taking off weighing some 8000 lb with the prospect of a 1500-mile trip ahead of them.

Upwards of twenty-five modifications were required to allow Va or Vb aircraft to operate in the tropical conditions which the Mk Vcs were designed for. They included increased oil tankage, replacement of the air intake fairing and installation of the necessary fittings for all three types of overload fuel tanks. The tropicalised Mk Vc aircraft became known by the designation Mk Vc(T) effectively becoming a separate subtype of the mark. Successive local modifications to reduce the drag effects of the Vokes filter were made across North Africa. The most successful of them became known as the Aboukir filter as it had been devised by 103 M.U. at Aboukir. The filter was effectively compressed into a smaller unit, although it still offered improved air-cleaning qualities, which caused much less drag than the Vokes. The unit went on to form the basis for further filters which were to grace the Mk IX aircraft. Other modifications carried out in the field included fitting a pair of 250 lb bombs under the wings of the Mk Vc Spitfires and a 500 lb bomb under the fuselage.

A high-altitude Vc was also created, again at Aboukir, to counter the German P.R. flights by Ju 86P aircraft at 37,000 ft plus. The Spitfire's equipment was stripped to bare essentials. The cannon were removed leaving the two innermost machine-guns as the safe armament. The compression ratio of the standard Merlin 46 was increased by hand and a four-bladed de Havilland propeller was fitted, giving the machine the greatest power absorption. The Aboukir filter was further modified to house the 9.5-gallon oil tank and a pair of specially extended wing-tips, again made by hand at Aboukir, were fitted to the aircraft. No performance data is available for the aircraft but the Germans must have been more than a little surprised to have a Spitfire on their tail at an altitude they had thought to be completely safe for them.

The testing of Mk V Spitfires was to have pronounced benefits on all later marks of the aircraft. The selection of the slipper fuel tank was as a result of tests on the early Spitfires and benefited the machine in all theatres of the war. Tests were to continue into a variety of Spitfire characteristics and equipment add-ons well beyond the Mk V. The mark was at least responsible for trials of external fuel tanks (both slipper and torpedo type), bomb-carrying, jettisoning the cockpit canopy, de-icing the windscreen in flight, pioneering water-based operations with the three float-planes. The Mk V introduced the all-metal aileron, clipped wings, universal wings and extended wings and began work on the use of dive-brakes.

Successful trials were also undertaken at squadron level which involved Spitfires towing gliders loaded with the materials necessary for establishing a temporary base away from a main airfield. Over 5 tons of equipment were moved in this way on a number of occasions, although whether this method of transport was ever used in an operational situation is not recorded.

Production of the Mk V continued until October 1943 when Westland completed the last machine. Castle Bromwich had completed its last Mk V during August of the same year, but the machines were not declared obsolete until September 1945 and it was not until March 1948 that all of the many examples still being stored finally met the scrap man. Thankfully, an increasing number are now finding their way into workshops in various locations around the world. Australia particularly, having taken large numbers of the Mk Vc, has an ever-increasing number of the type under restoration and one can only wonder at the treasures yet to be discovered in the former Soviet Union and scattered across the North African desert!

The High-flying Mk VI

Once the need for high-flying fighters to combat the nuisance of enemy photo-reconnaissance aircraft had been realised, considerable effort was put into producing a Spitfire which could not only get itself to heights of around 40,000 ft but which could also offer its pilot some degree of consideration with regard to the cold and the obvious reduction in air pressure at that altitude. The aircraft was based wholly on the Mk V, although extensive modifications were required as the aircraft were to be built with a completely airtight cockpit area to allow the cabin to be pressurised. Two bulkheads were built into the cockpit area, one forward of the pilot, the other aft. All the control linkages had to be made airtight through these bulkheads and a specially designed Perspex canopy was arranged to be fitted to the machine once the pilot was on board. Thus the canopy rails and the pilot's door were deleted from the aeroplane and rubber seals were fitted around the rim of the canopy in order that an airtight seal could be maintained. The pilot did not have the ability to lose the canopy in flight if it became necessary for him to leave the aircraft. All metal-to-metal joints were sealed with the use of a substance not unlike bitumen, although the sealing process was far from easy in some of the trickier nooks and crannies.

Having arranged that the cockpit area could be sealed, the next step was to pressurise it. The Merlin 46 engine was modified to operate at the high altitudes then being reached by the enemy's reconnaissance aircraft by cropping the impeller blades in the supercharger. The result of this work, and a number of other modifications, was the Merlin 47, and it was this engine which was to power the Mk VI Spitfires. Attached to the engine on the starboard side was a small cabin air-blower which took in the outside air at atmospheric pressure, filtered it then compressed it. This caused the temperature of the air to rise. When the compressed air was fed back through a non-return valve into the cockpit, it was sufficient to maintain an internal pressure equivalent to 28,000 ft when the aircraft was flying at 40,000 ft. Delivered at 60 °C, the air was also warm enough to maintain a cabin temperature of slightly less than 10°C when the outside air was at –55°C! The fuel tanks also had to be pressurised at the high altitudes intended for the Mk VI, to prevent the fuel from vapourising in the tanks. The other feature noticeable on the service Mk VIs was the extensions to the wing-tips. The lift generated from these tips could account for as much as an extra 600 ft on the absolute ceiling of the aircraft and, as such, were a necessity.

An existing order for Mk I Spitfires, which were eventually produced as Mk Vs, was modified to include 100 of the new pressurised machines, the first of which was completed in early December 1941 and delivered to Worthy Down for weighing and assessment of the centre of gravity. The all-up weight was 6768 lb on an aircraft which sported a three-bladed propeller, the first of the four-bladed units not being delivered on a Mk VI until late April of the following year. Top speed was only 364 mph at 21,500 ft from an engine which was rated at 1415 hp, although a useful 264 mph was still attainable at 40,000 ft.

Further work was undertaken into the possibilities of a sliding hood which would allow cabin pressure to be maintained. Pilots were wary of the devices which had to be locked down before flight and only opened from the outside once the aircraft was on the ground and stationary. A double-glazed version of the sliding hood was developed and adopted. Although it was still prone to misting at altitude, it was received with some relief by the squadrons. A small number of the mark were dispatched to the Middle East to counter the reconnaissance threat but as these enemy machines were capable of 50,000 ft the Spitfire VIs were actually less effective than the locally-modified Spitfire Vs which were doing the job already. The last Mk VI left the production line at Supermarine in November 1942 and many of the mark were to spend their latter days after withdrawal from service as training aircraft sans pressurisation equipment and with the extended wing-tips replaced with standard units.

More Height and Power, the Mk VII

The lessons learnt from the Mk VI in terms of pressurised, high-altitude airframes was combined with a sudden leap forward in Merlin engine development and created a new, and very effective, mark of Spitfire, the Mk VII which was intended to be a dramatic improvement on its immediate predecessor. The new engine came about as a result of a great deal of work during 1941, when Rolls-Royce adopted and developed the idea of a two-stage, two-speed intercooled supercharger arrangement coupled with a modified Merlin 46. The first of the two supercharging stages was taken from a Rolls-Royce Vulture engine and slightly modified. The output from this stage was coupled to a charger from a standard Merlin 46 engine, and the results were a dramatic 300 hp improvement in power delivery at altitude when compared with a standard Merlin 46.

There was, of course, a drawback with this arrangement. The charge became heated to around 200°C during this two-stage compression and was very liable to premature detonation in the cylinders. The charge thus had to be cooled in order to reduce the pinking effects and to make it denser and thus get more of it into the cylinders. Cooling the charge, for reasons of space within the engine cowlings, had to be achieved with a water jacket around the supercharger structure rather than by diverting the airflow. This meant that the radiator capacity of the aircraft would have to be increased to house the cooling intercooler radiator and that there would therefore be an increase in drag due to the larger radiator area.

It was also obvious that the single radiator of the Mk VI Spitfire was not going to be capable of cooling the new 1565 hp engine and so the Mk VII Spitfire was the first member of the family to have two radiators, one under each wing, to cope with the combined cooling requirements of the oil system, the engine and the supercharger intercooler. The port housing was arranged to contain the oil cooler alongside the first engine radiator while the starboard side housed the second engine radiator and the intercooler radiator.

The first Mk VII was ready in July 1942 and it went straight to Rolls-Royce to undergo numerous flight and ground tests. The machine was based on the standard Mk V airframe with a pressurised cockpit area, the normal fin and rudder, and it was fitted with the universal C wing with a pair of extended tips. It was then modified to incorporate a retractable tail-wheel and a four-bladed Rotol propeller and, of course, it was fitted with the new Merlin 61 engine which lengthened the nose of the aircraft. This meant that reinforcement around the engine bay and the construction of a completely new set of engine cowlings and other fitments were needed. Later production aircraft were to have fuel cells, originally of the bag type but later metal, built into the wing leading edges. Several machines were also fitted with the taller broad-chord rudders and tail units to offer the increased tail areas necessary to provide adequate lateral control with the Merlin 61s.

Engine development was to continue throughout the production of the Mk VII. The Merlin 61 gave way to the much more powerful but numerically limited Merlin 64, the production version of the 61 which was named the Merlin 66 and which went on to prove very successful when mated with the Mk IX airframe, and the Merlin 71 which was loosely based on the 66 but which offered the ability to pressurise the cockpit. The Merlin 71s, of which only sixteen were built, were used on the H.F. Mk VII, a high-altitude version of what was generally intended to be a high-altitude mark of the aircraft. In all, 140 Mk VII Spitfires were built before being superseded, very quickly, by the Mk VIII and Mk IX aircraft which were unpressurised but continued with the Merlin 60 series of engines.

Some machines were adapted for meteorological duties after their service careers ended, and many were still in Air Force hands as the war drew to a close. Many were declared to be non-effective in 1946 and none saw further service beyond 1947. Only one example survives to this day. Spitfire EN474 was shipped to New York during 1943 for evaluation and is on display in the National Air and Space Museum, Washington DC, as the sole representative of her mark anywhere in the world.

The Best Merlin Spit, the Mk VIII

While the development work was underway on the Mk VII Spitfire, the R.A.F. and the Air Ministry began to realise that the superiority in the air over Europe, which they had enjoyed with the timely production of the Mk V, had all but been wrested from them again. A new radial-engined German fighter had appeared in the sky over France, and it was proving to be too much of a handful for the Mk Vs to cope with. The Focke-Wulf 190 had arrived, and was reported by the squadrons as early as September 1941. As instructions not to tangle unnecessarily with the new German fighters were passed to the front line, the Ministry began to take stock of what it had available to counter the new enemy weapon.

In about April 1941, about five months before the arrival of the FW 190, in the development of the two-stage, two-speed supercharged Merlin engines, a Merlin 60 engine had been fitted to the old Mk III prototype Spitfire, N3297, and the aircraft tested. Further work on the Merlin 60 had led to the development of the Merlin 61 – the 60 had really been produced with the high-altitude Wellington VIs in mind, and the 61 had eventually been fitted to the Mk III airframe. Coincidentally, this aircraft had flown with the new engine within a week or so of the FW 190 being noted and the Ministry was not slow to pick up on the significance of this flight. Neither did they miss the recorded top speed of 414 mph at a little over 27,000 ft.

The Mk VIII Spitfire was thus based on the Mk VII, although it was to be unpressurised and to incorporate the modifications suggested by the trials with N3297. Thus, the fuselage was further strengthened to absorb the heavier handling of operational and combat duties, was fitted with a retractable tailwheel and was produced with the universal C wing, although the tip design on the Mk VIIIs was to range from fully clipped, a field modification to meet the needs in the Middle East theatre, to fully extended on the H.F. versions. The engines were to differ greatly within the mark too – testament to the work of Rolls-Royce which was pursuing the two-stage, two-speed supercharger with some gusto. Three designations were to apply to the Mk VIII and were related solely to the engine fitted to the aircraft and were not a reflection of the type of wing-tip at all. The F. Mk VIII

aircraft, 273 of which were built, were fitted with a Merlin 61, 63 or 63A, each being a modification of its predecessor. The 1225 L.F. Mk VIIIs produced were intended for operations at lower altitudes and sported the Merlin 66 engines, while the 160 high-flying H.F. Mk VIIIs were fitted with the Merlin 70. Later examples of the mark were fitted with the broad-chord rudders which had been introduced with the Mk VIIs.

Because of the time taken to put the Mk VIIs and the Mk VIIIs into production, the opportunities for the new aircraft were limited by the success of the Mk IX which actually got into service well before the first Mk VIII. This did not stop those squadrons that were issued with the Mk VIII feeding back performance reports and suggestions for modifications. Not least among the latter were requests for the bubble-style of canopy to replace the standard hood which, it was felt, rather restricted the pilot's field of view in an area where most risk was likely to develop, i.e. behind him. A Mk VIII was suitably modified to demonstrate the new arrangement and the enthusiastic response which it engendered was not lost on Supermarine. The design was incorporated in mid-and late-production Mk IXs and Mk XVIs and in most other subsequent marks.

Mk VIIIs also contributed to the development of the species at this time, with further trials of the Griffon engine, and a restyled wing. The engine trials were to lead to the Mk XIV, and the wing developments were incorporated into the 20 series Spitfires. After the Ministry had noted that American aircraft were flying in a bare-metal finish they requested that trials were undertaken regarding the weight of the paint carried on the aircraft and the effect that its removal was likely to have on performance. Measurements were taken on a single Mk VIII with and without its paintwork and the difference calculated to be a mere 15 lb.

Mk VIII Spitfires never really saw action in the role that had been intended for them as the Mk IX machines were very effectively dealing with the Focke-Wulf 190s by the time that the Mk VIIIs made it into service. While the Air Ministry was impressed by the aircraft – the squadrons issued with them swore by them – it was largely in the overseas theatres that the Mk VIIIs were to serve. Australia took large numbers of them to complement and replace the Mk Vs which had equipped the R.A.A.F for so long. The Indian Air Force via S.E.A.C. took six, one of which is maintained in Delhi today. The U.S.A.A.F. took a number and even the Russians got in on the act by taking three. The machines in Australia were transferred from R.A.F. charge to the R.A.A.F. in 1946 at no charge and the mark was replaced in R.A.F. service at home by the Mk XIV in late 1944 and eventually withdrawn completely for scrapping in 1947.

However, the tale of the Mk VIII Spitfire would not be complete without at least a mention of the two-seater Spitfire MT818. The idea of a two-seater had first been mooted as early as 1941 but, despite a conversion by No. 261 Squadron in Sicily and at least one other by the Russians during the war, such a machine had never been designed by the Supermarine team. Revived by Vickers in 1946, the conversion of an existing airframe was thought to be preferable to starting afresh with a new design. Vickers acquired MT818 early in 1946 and the converted aircraft flew for the first time in August of the same year. The original cockpit had to be moved forward by 13.5 inches to accommodate the rear cockpit which was stepped up so that the instructor could see forward over and around the first canopy.

Conditions were cramped in both cockpits and the curvature of the screen in the rear meant that gunnery practice was not possible from the rear. The landing view was also somewhat distorted. Moreover, the take-off and landing attitude was likely to be excessively tail high when the aircraft was flown from the rear cockpit as the rear pilot tried to see over the canopy in front. Regrettably, the R.A.F. were not convinced that it needed a two-seat trainer and the idea was shelved until both the Indian

Air Force and the Irish Air Corps recognised a need some years later.

And so to the Mk IX

Two very sobering facts were made clear to the Air Ministry shortly after the first of the new Focke-Wulf 190s were reported from the squadrons. Firstly, as a result of tests on one of the new German aircraft which had luckily been flown to Wales by a disoriented Luftwaffe pilot, it was abundantly apparent that the existing Spitfires and Hurricanes were no match for the German machine. Secondly, waiting for the start of the full production run of the proposed Mk VIII Spitfire would give the Germans a clear year of air superiority in the skies over Europe. As it was, Mk V Spitfires were being lost in fights with the 190 and it was necessary to instruct R.A.F. pilots not to tangle with the Focke-Wulf unless the odds were weighted on the British side. An interim solution was needed and quickly.

The trials with the new Merlin 60, and subsequently the 61, in the Mk III Spitfire N3297 were to further not only the development work on the Mk VIII, as has already been related, but also to start a new programme whereby the engines were fitted to strengthened Mk V airframes which were in full production already. In the same way that the Mk V had come into being as an interim solution to counter a specific threat, so the Mk IX was devised as an amalgam of existing airframe and developing engine to meet the threat posed by the Focke-Wulf. As it was based on the Mk V, indeed early examples were production line conversions of Mk V airframes and many more Mk V machines were to be converted to the new standard, the Mk IX had a fixed tailwheel and standard rudder shape. The tail end of the fuselage was strengthened, as was the area around the 1565 hp Merlin 61 engine which was to wear a four-bladed propeller to dissipate the increased power to the surrounding air.

In all, 5665 Mk IX Spitfires were produced, a total second only to the Mk Vs which they replaced, and the list of variations on the basic Mk IX theme is extraordinarily long. The first Mk IX made it into service with No. 64 Squadron at R.A.F. Hornchurch in July 1942, some nine months before the first production Mk VIII entered service. One hundred converted Mk Vcs had been ordered in mid-April 1942, the Air Ministry having been convinced of the performance of the new fighter at that point, and deliveries to the squadrons commenced within four months of the receipt of the order – no mean feat.

With the thirstier Merlins, the range of the fighter with the standard tankage became even more limited. Extending the fuel capacity became something of a necessity and a variety of methods were found to enable the Spitfire to carry more fuel. More orthodox approaches involved including tanks, either bag type or metal, in the wings of the aircraft with the obvious penalty of reduction in armament, or in the rear fuselage. Tanks of various sizes were fitted behind the pilot but care had to be taken with this arrangement, not least because the pilot was now completely surrounded with fuel. Moreover, the extra fuel affected the centre of gravity of the aircraft.

The positioning of the centre of gravity was fundamental to the stability of the Spitfire. Additional weight behind the established centre of gravity could make the aircraft's handling rather entertaining at times, longitudinal stability suffering noticeably at speeds above 140 mph, getting progressively worse as the speed increased. At fast cruise, the control column had to be continually used to damp out the pitching effects as the aircraft just could not be trimmed. Further, during the flight, the centre of gravity would shift forwards altering the handling characteristics again although this time for the better. The machine stabilised when the rear tank was about half empty but could not reasonably be operated in combat with the rear fuselage tank more than one-fifth full and it was preferable that the fuel in this tank was completely used before combat. The Americans became involved in their own trials with externally carried drop tanks of

the type used by Mustangs, although this was supplemented with reduced rear fuselage tankage. The slipper tanks were found to still offer the best performance for weight of fuel carried. They came in 30-gallon, 45-gallon, 90-gallon and the massive 170-gallon variants to suit all occasions.

Even as the conversion of the Mk V airframes to F. Mk IX standards was getting underway in April 1942, so thoughts were beginning to turn to what needed to be done to produce a high-altitude variation on what was seen to be a very promising fighter. Using an R.A.E. report, which in turn was partly based on experiences with the prototype Mk VIII aircraft, a number of criteria were established for good high-altitude performance. In July 1942, a Merlin 77 which was based on the 76 but with a cabin blower, was installed in a Mk V airframe which had already been converted to Mk IX standard. Modifications were made to the tail fin and rudder, and unusually, a contra-rotating propeller was fitted to the aircraft. Trials were promising, and timely, for Britain was being subjected to nuisance raiders – Ju 86P aircraft which were bombing localised areas from altitudes in excess of 40,000 ft. The H.F. Mk IX was not in production at the time so a very small number of conversions were made to existing Mk IXs, including the removal of all armour-plating, the use of wooden propeller blades and the removal of all armament other than the two 20mm cannon. One of the converted fighters put the wind up a Ju 86P at over 45,000 ft while it was based with the Special Service Flight at Northolt, and damage was actually inflicted on one of the raiders the following day. The high-altitude raids were to end soon after. Production H.F. variants were fitted with the 1475 hp Merlin 70s which pulled the aircraft along at a respectable 416 mph at 27,000 ft.

The second major variant was the low-altitude fighter, the L.F. Mk IX. Fitted with the Merlin 66 engine, the L.F. variant was by far the most numerous of the all Mk IXs. The prototype was not prepared until May 1943 as a result of the C.-in-C. Air Forces in the Western Desert demanding large numbers of additional L.F. Mk Vs to supplement his existing squadrons. The Air Ministry did not see the sense in prolonging the Mk V production run while there was something better to offer the African campaign and so Merlin 66s were added to Mk IX airframes with revised tropical and temperate air intakes. Bomb-fitting was also made possible, with both fuselage- and wing-mounted bombs being made available.

Large numbers of these aircraft were sent all round the world, not just to North Africa, with Spitfire Mk IXs seeing service in Belgium, Czechoslovakia, France, Ireland as the two-seaters – Italy, Denmark, Egypt, Greece, Holland, Norway, Russia, South Africa, Turkey and the USA. A healthy secondary market grew up for these aircraft, with Israel not least among the purchasers for second-or third-hand aircraft. Mk IXs also served with civilian organisations, a Belgian firm operating a small number as target-tugs after the war and thereby preserving them for the warbird community today.

The Mk IXs had been developed with the power to do a great many things that the Mk Vs could not and they formed the pinnacle of what could be achieved with the Merlin engine. Derivations of the Mk IX were to include the P.R. version, which evolved into the P.R. XI, and the Mk XVI which was so close to being a Mk IX that the new designation was not really warranted.

Sixteen Examples of the Mk X

The service life of the sixteen Mk X Spitfires was a mere sixteen months. Introduced into service in May 1944 to fulfil a high-altitude photo-reconnaissance role, the aircraft was not deemed to be particularly successful and the two squadrons which operated the type made only limited use of their allotted machines. Born out of a Mk VII fuselage, but fitted with P.R. XI wings and a Merlin 64 engine, the Mk X was not sufficiently different or capable to make an impact. Despite removing armament and armour-plate, fitting a larger oil tank inside the chin cowling to give the P.R. XI style profile, and a pressurised cockpit area, the Mk X was conceived at a time when the race to beat the Focke-Wulfs was in full flow and the production lines were full of Mk IXs and their variants. It was withdrawn from service in September 1945.

The More Popular P.R. XI

The P.R. XI Spitfire was a development of the F. Mk IX, despite original intentions being to develop it from the P.R. version of the Mk VIII. No. 1 P.R.U. (Photo-Reconnaissance Unit) was to convert the first fifteen aircraft from Mk IX to P.R.XI by removing all armament and armour-plating and installing camera gear in the rear fuselage. The full specification for the P.R. XI also called for leading edge fuel tanks to be fitted in the same way that they had been on the P.R. IV. This was a specialist operation and definitely not the sort of thing to be carried out by the P.R.U. The other distinguishing feature of the P.R. XI was the oil tank, or more accurately, the shape of the cowling which fitted around the larger oil tank. Slung under the nose of the Merlin, the tank gave the machine a very definite chin.

Supermarine eventually installed the leading edge wing tanks into the aircraft modified by the P.R.U., and began to divert the aircraft from the established Mk IX production lines. These aircraft were normal Mk IXs with Merlin 61, 63 and 63A engines, a fixed tailwheel and the early type of rudder. Some armament and armour was removed from the aircraft, however. The full P.R. XI production aircraft offered a retractable tailwheel and a broad-chord rudder, and adopted the Merlin 70 engine as standard. Standard camera fit in the P.R. XIs was a pair of fanned F.52 cameras, each having a 36-inch focal length, in the rear fuselage. Two further 5-inch focal length cameras could also be carried in specialised blisters in each wing.

The P.R. XI served with the Danish and Norwegian air forces and examples also serviced the U.S.A.A.F. It was adopted by Coastal Command during 1943 and 1944, and was finally withdrawn from service as late as February 1948. Supermarine built 471 Spitfire P.R. XIs, many of which were tropicalised for service overseas. Two were used by civilians after the war, one making an epic flight down to Buenos Aires from the U.K. to engage in map-making work, and the second being converted to carry mail.

Time for a Griffon – the Mk XII

The Focke-Wulf 190, instrumental in precipitating the postponement of the Mk VIII programme in favour of the Mk IX, was to have another say in the development of the Spitfire. Small numbers of enemy aircraft, in which modified Focke-Wulfs were prominent, were harassing targets on the English south coast in so-called tip-and-run attacks. The Air Ministry wanted a machine which was fast at low level and which packed a noticeable punch to fend off these raiders. By casting about in the pots of Mk V, Mk VIII and Mk IX airframes under construction at that point, they came up with an interim solution to their problem which was to provide an impetus to the whole development programme of Griffon engines mated to Spitfire airframes.

Six Mk VIII airframes had been allocated to the Griffon test programme, which had begun with the two Spitfire Mk IV aircraft, DP845 and DP851. However, before the Mk VIII airframes could be actively used in the programme, the need to counter the tip-and-run raiding of the derated FW 190s became urgent and so DP845, now designated a Mk XX after having undergone further modifications, was pressed into service as a ready-made test bed for the Griffons. Both the Griffon IIB and the Griffon III were tested, with heat dissipation from the more powerful engine being the most critical factor in terms of conventional and oil cooling. Further performance trials with the Griffon IV and five-bladed propellers were not initially encouraging when compared to the results from previous tests, and production of the Mk XII was begun in mid-1942 with Griffon III engines and the Rotol propeller with four Dural blades fitted. The most obvious difference to the Merlin-engined Spitfires discovered by the few squadrons which took the new machines was its increased tendency to swing on take-off. This was nothing new on a Spitfire but with the Griffon engine the Spitfire would swing to the right and thus need bootfuls of left rudder to keep it straight on take-off and on power-on landings, whereas the Merlin's opposite rotation swung the aircraft to the left and therefore needed right rudder to stay aligned. It is easy to spot the obvious confusion which many pilots suffered on their transition between the types as many a machine attempted to take off in a big circle.

In the summer of 1942, the Mk XII airframes were being culled from both the Mk IX and Mk VIII production lines, which meant that the earlier versions of the mark, based on the Mk IX, had fixed tailwheels and standard Mk V type rudders. Later versions, diverted from the Mk VIII lines, featured retractable tailwheels and the broad-chord rudder. Both sets of airframes needed modifications up front with strengthening of the fittings and considerable reshaping of the cowls to contain the larger engine while not overly increasing the frontal area of the aircraft. The shape of the cowls was sufficiently noteworthy that the description was passed to the Air Transport Auxiliary who were told that the aircraft 'could be recognised by the humps on either side of the engine cowling'.

The speed of the aircraft was a respectable 393 mph straight and level at 18,000 ft while, at sea level, the machine was capable of 346 mph – a significant improvement over even the Mk IX which could manage only 312 mph among the daisies.

As the Griffon VI stabilised in both its design and performance, so the engine was fitted to the available airframes, although all Mk XIIs wore the four-bladed Rotol propellers. Internal tankage was limited to the 85 gallons carried in the two forward fuselage tanks, although overload external tanks could be carried under the fuselage when extra range was required. Internal tanks gave 329 miles useful range which was adequate for the short-haul defensive role the aircraft was to fulfil, although the thirst of the Griffon and the limited capacity for fuel on the Spitfire was to prove more difficult to balance on future Griffon models. The aircraft was fitted with two 20mm cannon and four Browning 0.303-inch machine-guns, and could also carry a single 250 lb or 500 lb bomb slung beneath the fuselage.

Nos 41 and 91 Squadrons were issued with the Mk XII, although the machines also saw service with other units during the three and a half years of its R.A.F. career. Never moved away from the U.K. mainland, the surviving Mk XIIs were struck off charge in February 1946 and scrapped. As a test bed for the continued development of the Griffon engine, the Mk XII had proved to be extremely useful. As a front-line fighting machine it left a little to be desired, especially when compared to the next stage in the Mk VIII airframe and Griffon engine marriage – the Mk XIV.

Another Modified Mk V – P.R. XIII

Only eighteen P.R. XIII aircraft were built specifically to fill the low-level photo-reconnaissance role. The airframes were standard Mk V but the engine was a low-altitude Merlin, the Merlin 32. The engine offered improved take-off power and improved low-level output when compared to the Merlin 45s and 46s which were then being fitted into the Mk V airframes. At 1645 hp, the engine was worth taking some note of, especially as it was fitted with a negative g carburettor but it was to power only the Seafire IIs and IIIs and the P.R. XIII Spitfire. Conversion of the Mk V airframes was commenced in December 1942 and completed by the following May. The airscrew was a standard three-bladed de Havilland unit which was capable of pulling the aircraft through the air at 348 mph. Camera fit on the P.R. XIII was a single vertically-mounted F.24 camera with a 5-inch lens and two F.24s with 24-inch lenses mounted vertically and obliquely in the rear fuselage. The eighteen aircraft representing the mark which never really existed, were withdrawn from R.A.F. service in March 1945.

In Lieu of the 'Super Spitfire' – the Mk XIV

Both the Air Ministry and Supermarine had their eyes on the distant horizon, pursuing what they chose to call the 'Super Spitfire' at the time that the Mk XIV was envisaged. Despite it being the first production Griffon-engined Spitfire, having a production run of some 975 aircraft and equipping thirty-seven R.A.F. squadrons at various times, it was never really considered as anything other than an interim aircraft. Again, the Mk VIII airframe was to provide the basis of the aircraft, and with the addition of the Griffon 61 engine producing 2035 hp, the aeroplane was going to be no slouch. In the same way that the Merlin had had a two-stage, two-speed supercharger added to provide a much needed power boost, so the same approach on the Griffon produced a similar result. It also added more than 2 ft to the overall length of the Spitfire, specifically forward of the cockpit which made visibility over the nose almost negligible, and increased the weight forward of the centre of gravity by such an extent that about 150 lb of ballast had to be fitted in the tail. The additional weight of the five-bladed propeller cannot have helped a great deal in this respect either.

Early comparison trials were flown in July 1943 when a Mk VIII Spitfire was flown against a converted Mk VIII with the new Griffon engine. It was found that between 10,000 ft and 15,000 ft the Mk VIII had a speed advantage over the new XIV but the latter machine could easily outpace the former above 30,000 ft where it also climbed and handled significantly better than the VIII. It was also found that when the two machines stayed with each other through identical test flights, the Griffon was using 10 to 15 gallons of fuel an hour more than the Merlin. The trials of the two aircraft showed the Mk VIII to be a very potent performer up to 25,000 ft, having an edge over the Griffon-engined machine in all aspects of its performance except turns. It was found to be easier to fly and much lighter on the controls. The Mk XIV was, however, significantly better above 25,000 ft and it was felt that the heaviness of the controls and the need for constant trim adjustments would become accepted by pilots as they became familiar with the machine.

The official description of the early versions of the mark termed the Mk XIV as being a standard Mk VIII fuselage from frame 5 backwards, although this frame was adapted to the Mk 21 engine equipment, incorporating a Mk 21 engine mounting (these Griffons came already wrapped up in a mounting as an integral part of the engine), and specially strengthened longerons and a modified tail end. The wings were described as standard Mk VIII with adapted cooling and standard wing-tips. The cooling adaptations were the same as those carried out on the Mk IX aircraft – the jump in engine power needed a similar jump in cooling capacity and the Mk XIV was the first Griffon-powered Spitfire to need twin radiators; the Mk XII had only a single unit under the starboard wing. It was also deemed necessary to strengthen the wing in certain areas but the undercarriage was standard Mk VIII.

Just after production of the F. Mk XIV began in October 1943, the specification for an F.R. Mk XIV was issued which called for camera fitments into the standard rear fuselage, along with 31 extra gallons of fuel in internal fuselage tanks. The extra weight of the internal fuel and camera gear meant that the wing spars needed to be strengthened and the oleo legs replaced with stronger units. The weight of the Spitfire also caused Supermarine to fit the clipped wing-tips to all aircraft when pilots began to

report skin wrinkles around the wing attachment points. Despite Supermarine not considering the wrinkling to be serious, the R.A.F. decided the wing area was to be reduced by removing the normal tips and all Mk XIV aircraft were retrospectively fitted with the clipped tips.

Such skin wrinkling was never completely eliminated from the mark, although further strengthening work was carried out later in the development of the Mk XIV and the R.A.F. were persuaded to live with the small amount of wrinkling which did occur. The E-type wings were fitted to aircraft alongside the C-types, effectively introducing F. Mk XIVe and F.R. Mk XIVe designations to the ever growing list. The E wings contained a Browning 0.5-inch machine-gun alongside, and just inboard of, the 20mm Hispano cannon thereby forming an extremely potent combination.

In the same way that the low-back, bubble-canopied Mk IX Spitfires had been much sought after by the R.A.F. pilots, so the same request was made regarding the Mk XIV and later models were produced with the cut-down rear fuselage. A few aircraft even had Griffon 85 engines installed in them which allowed a contra-rotating propeller to be fitted, so removing the problems of torque swing on take-off and landing. The tail units of the Mk XIVs were produced along the lines that the F.21 was to adopt. They were taller and deeper than the Mk VIII units which, it was considered after trials, were not of sufficient area to adequately control the lateral stability of the aircraft. The effect of the longer nose, the bubble canopy and cut-down rear fuselage with this extended tail was to produce a very sleek-looking aeroplane which packed a real punch. It was capable of 439 mph and could reach 43,000 ft and had a normal range of some 610 miles.

The Mk XIV was superseded by the Mk XVIII, despite being built in greater quantities. The mark proved itself time and again in the air defence of Great Britain, particularly against the German V-1 'doodle bugs', but it also saw solid service in the 2nd Tactical Air Force in Europe and, in the closing stages of the war, in the Far East. Many aircraft were sold abroad as the hostilities in Europe ended, Belgium particularly benefiting from large numbers of the aircraft, although Indian and Thai air forces were also on the list of beneficiaries. Mk XIVs were also the mainstay of the Royal Auxiliary Air Force squadrons after the war, and were not completely removed from service until 1951. They had proved themselves in combat and more than proved the worth of progressing with the Spitfire–Griffon combination for future marks.

Packard Merlin Plus Mk IX Equals Mk XVI

As early as mid-1940, the British government, through the Air Ministry, realised that production of the Merlin engines necessary to power the numbers of fighter and bomber aircraft that were envisaged, was going to be beyond the powers of Rolls-Royce alone, mighty though it was. Henry Ford was initially approached to build Merlins under licence but he declined and so the deal was done with Packard. An initial order for 1500 of the engines was placed with the American company, with options being taken out on a further 10,000 to be agreed in two stages of 5000 each. By the time that production ceased in the Packard factories, some 55,000 Merlin engines had been produced, 25,000 of which had found their way to Britain. The early engines began to arrive in 1942 and these were allotted to Lancasters, Canadian-built Hurricanes, and Mk II Kittyhawks to replace the Allison engines the Mk I Kittyhawks had been fitted with. It was to be 1944, when the American version of the Merlin 66 was under production, before Spitfires were to benefit from the American investment.

The engines were designated Merlin 266 and were slightly different to the Rolls-Royce Merlin 66 engines in that they had electro-hydraulically-operated supercharger gear. The British engine had an electro-pneumatic system to do the same job. Further, the header tank for the intercooler was built on the American engine and oil piping was to run in a slightly different way to that required by the engines built by Rolls-Royce. The only reason for redesignating the aircraft was to enable spares ordering for the engine to be simpler. It was easier to direct a request for Merlin 266 spares to American stocks and for British stocks to provide Merlin 66 spares if the mark of the aircraft was completely different.

The early Mk XVIs had the C wing with the mix of 20mm Hispanos and 0.303-inch Browning machine-guns but the later variants were fitted with the E wing containing 0.5-inch Brownings instead of the smaller calibre. Most Mk XVIs had clipped wing-tips to complement their role as low-level fighters.

Internal fuel capacity and distribution depended on the type of fuselage of the particular aircraft. Those with cut-down fuselages had rear fuselage tanks of 66 gallons while the high-backs were able to carry 76 gallons in the slighter greater volume available. Even with a full 66-gallon tank, the aircraft was unstable in pitch and it was deemed necessary to burn fuel from this tank before any ideas regarding combat should be allowed to enter the pilot's head. All Mk XVIs carried 47 gallons in the lower forward fuselage tank, as opposed to the 37 gallons available in the same tank in the Mk IX aircraft.

In total, 1054 Mk XVIs were built, many with the now standard bubble canopy and cut-down rear fuselage and many saw service abroad – particularly in Greece. Many more became maintenance airframes but a surprising number stayed in service with the U.K.-based Royal Auxiliary Air Force until well in to the 1950s. A proportionately high number are still in existence today, proving to be both reliable and relatively uncomplicated to operate in a civilian organisation. They are adapted to either Rolls-Royce or Packard engines and, of course, Mk IX airframe spares as the parts become available.

The Super Spitfire – the Mk XVIII

The years of war in Europe had dramatically accelerated the understanding and appreciation of aerodynamics as an applicable science, with new ideas being formed on both sides of the Atlantic at an unprecedented rate. Further, because every advantage could mean a real difference to air superiority during hostilities, money was made available to support and develop these new ideas to the point where they were either adopted or proved to be unworkable.

One such idea was the introduction of the laminar-flow wing, a wing which was shaped and formed so as to prevent airflow break-away over its surface and encourage the highly mobile air to 'stick' to its upper skin in layers. The lift advantages of such wings were considerable and adoption of the principles of laminar flow was seen to be mandatory in late-war aircraft, just to keep up with the opposition.

Power increases from the late Merlin, and especially the Griffon, engines meant that the tail shapes of the aircraft they were fitted to had to be substantially altered to counteract the large amounts of torque produced by the huge propellers. It was realised by the British authorities and the aircraft manufacturers that either a new aircraft had to be developed around these principles or the Spitfire had to be modified yet again to incorporate them. The latter course was chosen in late 1943 and the Spitfire Mk XIVs then entering service were to become the interim version of the so-called 'Super Spitfire' which turned out in practice to be called the Mk XVIII.

The first production model F.R. Mk XVIII, SM843, began tests at High Post aerodrome on 8 June 1945 and initial reports on its handling above 400 mph were poor. It was also judged to have excessive propeller vibration towards the top end of its performance envelope. On investigation of the propeller, the vibration was attributed to damage which had been caused during its delivery flight and was soon sorted out. Other handling characteristics also came in for criticism but, as the R.A.F. had been taking

delivery of the aircraft to the Middle East since the middle of May 1945, it was seen to be a little late in the day for making fine adjustments to the trim of the aircraft.

There was a two-to-one split in the variants of the 300 Mk XVIII aircraft produced, with 201 F.R. variants being produced. The rest were F. machines. The F.R. was fitted with two F.24 cameras, one with a 20-inch and the other with a 14-inch focal length lens, mounted in the rear fuselage along with a reduced fuel tank of 31 gallons. The space saved with the employment of the smaller tank enabled an obliquely mounted camera to be fitted. This was the third of the three cameras carried by the F.R. Mk XVIII. The oblique camera could be easily spotted by the adoption of a small 'window' high in the port side fuselage. In contrast, the F. Mk XVIII was able to carry a full 66 gallons in the rear fuselage and consequently managed a fuel load of 175 gallons before external overload tanks needed to be considered. The fuel load in both types of XVIII was helped by the adaptation of the E-wing to carry 12.5 extra gallons on each side, this additional 25 gallons approximating to 15 minutes' flying time.

The wing had also been modified to carry 500 lb bombs or the rocket projectiles which were later to prove so useful in the jungles of Malaya. In addition, the wing had been strengthened further to more easily accept the external armament being carried – internal armament remained the standard E configuration – and the undercarriage oleos were also much heavier duty units for the same reason. The Griffon 65s and 67s which powered the F. and F.R. Mk XVIIIs were capable of 2035 hp and 2375 hp respectively, although the 67 produced its highest power readings at very low altitude – around 1200 ft and this was translated into 437 mph at around 25,000 ft for a take-off weight of some 8860 lb for what was probably the most aggressive of Spitfires.

Production of the aircraft continued from mid-1945 through to early in 1946 but many of the machines were destined to see service abroad, very few finding their way into the skies of Europe once hostilities ceased. The Royal Indian Air Force, then an extension of the R.A.F. services abroad, took a large number of the machines on charge and many of these were transferred directly to the Indian Air Force itself when it became independent of the R.A.F. in January 1946. The Burmese also took three of the type. The machine remained in service with the R.A.F. in various locations around the world from Kai Tak to Singapore after the war but, like the Mk XIV, was withdrawn from use having been declared obsolete in May 1955.

The Last P.R. Variant– the PR XIX

The operating altitudes for home-based P.R. XI aircraft had been increasing steadily in an effort to avoid the German interceptors which had begun to include jet aircraft. The Merlin 61 and 63 engines were not capable of pulling the P.R. XIs up to the required heights and, although Merlin 70 engines had been fitted to a small number of aircraft, it was soon realised that only the Griffon engines would enable the P.R. operations to continue above 40,000 ft. Use of the Griffon introduced the usual raft of fuel capacity issues which, for a P.R. aircraft were more critical than they may otherwise have been for a fighter. The initial solution to this problem was to adopt a variation of the Mk Vc wing – dubbed the 'bowser' wing – in which a 66-gallon fuel tank had been built into the leading edge. As the P.R. machines were not going to carry any kind of armament, more space was available to use for fuel cells and so more modified wings with another 19 gallons in each were later produced, but not until twenty-five of the original bowser wings had been mated to Mk VIII fuselages with Mk XIV tails.

These first twenty-five aircraft were fitted with the readily available Griffon 65 engine but were unpressurised and untropicalised, despite sixteen of their number being sent overseas. The main order for the

P.R. XIX aircraft followed very shortly after the initial conversion work, and the remaining 200 were completed by the end of June 1944. The specification of these aircraft called for Mk XIV fuselages with pressure cabins and the double-skinned Lobelle canopy hood, use of the Griffon 66 engine with the cabin blower, and five-bladed Rotol propeller, P.R. XI wings with the Mk XIV undercarriage arrangement and the extra 20 gallons of fuel tank capacity, and the Mk XIV tail with provision for adjusting the ballast should this prove to be necessary. The port side access hatch door was removed from these later models and a small but lengthy air intake for the cabin blower was fitted on the port engine cowling underneath the exhaust stacks on all but the last few examples which were not pressurised. The camera installation was two fanned vertical F.52 cameras with 20-inch or 36-inch lenses; two vertical F.8 cameras with 20-inch lenses or two vertical F.24 cameras with 14-inch lenses with an oblique port-facing F.24 with 8-inch or 14-inch lens.

The fuel tanks on these aircraft were arranged two in the forward fuselage with a combined capacity of 82 gallons and two in each wing with a combined capacity of 87 gallons per wing, giving an overall total of 256 gallons which was enough to take the aircraft over 1000 miles on internal fuel alone. Another 500 miles could be achieved if the external fuel tanks were used. Stability in the air was a problem with the massive 170-gallon external tanks, and fairly entertaining with the 90-gallon tanks, but the Spitfires would calm down as the external fuel and wing fuel was used and become a lot more manageable on the ground after a flight once the wing tanks were empty than ever they were with full tanks.

The P.R. XIXs were devised as much for service overseas as they were for duties over Europe. In the event, they saw action in the Middle East and Far East and were used by the Royal Indian Air Force. At home, they saw service with Bomber Command, supporting bombing raids by photographing the damage caused after the event and searching out likely targets before raids were decided. After the war ended, the Swedish Air Force ordered seventy of the mark but later reduced this to fifty. All fifty were eventually scrapped after they too had been replaced by jet aircraft. Some years later, the Swedes were lucky enough to be able to acquire the fifty-first P.R. XIX aircraft to commemorate the type in Swedish service.

This machine is one of a healthy number of P.R. XIXs which still exist in various locations around the world today, the most famous arguably being those still flown by the R.A.F. in the Battle of Britain Memorial Flight. The three P.R. XIX aircraft which originally formed the basis of the Flight, spent the postwar years up until 1957 carrying out meteorological measurements. Three of the type found their way to the Royal Thai Air Force after the war and two were acquired by the U.S.A.A.F., while a further twelve were transferred to the newly independent Indian Air Force.

Should it still be a Spitfire? The F.21

As early as February 1942, a major redesign of the Spitfire was begun. Development of the Mk III Spitfire had been halted in its tracks by the need to concentrate on Mk V Spitfires to counter the much improved Bf 109F. For much the same reason, the Mk XIII development was diluted by the production of the Mk IX needed to oppose the new Focke-Wulf 190s. A vast amount of information, both operational and theoretical, had been amassed about the characteristics of the Spitfire in a wide variety of situations, and its shortcomings were well known and understood.

The first area to come in for some serious Supermarine attention was the wing, first designed by Mitchell around the leading edge torsion box and main spar. Supermarine kept this device as it offered a great deal of strength to the wing but they supplemented this inherent stability with additional torsion boxes and load-bearing joints. Larger area ailerons were thought to be necessary and were added after a period of digesting wing perfor-

mance data from a modified Mk VIII airframe. Further theoretical work into laminar-flow wings was incorporated into the design which was eventually built and tested on the former Mk IV aircraft, DP851. This aircraft, which was powered by a Griffon 61 engine and five-bladed Rotol propeller, began test flights in October 1942.

Interestingly, because the undercarriage of the new wing had been extended as part of the initial design – and moved outwards to cure the famous Spitfire dig-in syndrome – a propeller of larger diameter could be used. The new blades on the Rotol unit were of 11 ft diameter instead of the 10 ft 5 in propeller of the Mk XIV. The wheels of the machine, when retracted, were contained fully within a two door arrangement for the first time on a Spitfire. Flight testing on DP851 was to continue until 13 May 1943 when an undercarriage failure on landing caused the aircraft to be written off.

At this point, the main wing spar was redesigned, moving away from the concentric square box-sections which had served so well in the early marks of Spitfire, to a single extruded tube which had walls of tapering thickness as well as an overall root to tip taper. It was decided that this arrangement would offer greater overall strength than the original unit and be lighter, provided it could be made. Specialist manufacturers maintained that it could and that first deliveries could be made in the early months of 1944.

At the same time, the decision to eliminate the Browning machine-guns from the wing and to concentrate solely on the 20mm Hispano cannon led to a four cannon wing being devised. Up to 325 cannon rounds per wing could be contained, making the fire-power from these new Spitfires something to be reckoned with. Two fuel tanks holding a total of 18 gallons of fuel were incorporated in the wing. They were fitted between the torsion box braces in the wing leading edge.

To cope with the additional wing weight, and the power from the Griffon engines, the high-back fuselage was further strengthened, with the four main longerons now being made from stainless steel. Propeller trials on Rotol and de Havilland units, including six- and even eight-bladed contra-rotating devices, were undertaken in an effort to establish the best combination for the new machine. The first few F.21 Spitfires delivered to the R.A.F. adopted the six-bladed contra propellers and therefore used the Griffon 85 engines capable of a little over 2000 hp, while the majority of the 122 F.21s built were to operate with the standard five-bladed Rotol units and the Griffon 61 engine.

The performance of the new fighter was in line with the improvements which were being made by modifying and converting existing marks to higher specifications. The top straight and level speed of a Spitfire reached 450 mph for the first time, while the maximum allowed dive speed was extended by the F.21 to 520 mph. The ceiling of the new aircraft was found to be a very healthy 43,000 ft which must have been extremely uncomfortable for the pilots in the unpressurised cockpits. The F.21 went into service in late 1945 and, as much because of their late arrival as anything else, were soon to find themselves relegated to the Auxiliary squadrons where they were to survive into the mid-1950s, although they were little used beyond about 1952.

The Low-cut F.22

The F.22 Spitfire was devised and produced alongside the F.21. The differences between the two marks are very few. The electrical systems on the F.22 were all produced at 24 volts but this is hardly a reason for the mark change, as the late production F.21s had a similarly rated electrical system. The F.22 had fuel tanks located in the rear fuselage, whereas the F.21 had not. The F.22s were effectively barred from making use of this extra tankage for reasons of stability and it was not until modifications approaching the F.24 specification were made that the tanks were made available for squadron use. The main difference between the two marks was the use of the cut-down rear fuselage and the bubble canopy, and the F.22 did not sport a rear-view mirror above the cockpit screen. Its all-round view canopy made it unnecessary. The Mk IX and Mk XVI aircraft had proved that these changes alone were not sufficient to warrant a change in designation. Whatever the reason for the use of the F.22 designation, it cannot have had a great deal to do with the differences between the types.

Late-production F.22s were fitted with the much larger, and very distinctive, Spiteful type of tail unit which gave the aircraft a very rear-heavy look. The performance of the standard elevators from the Mk XIV type of tail had given some problems during testing on the aircraft. Distortion and revised balances had indicated that the units were approaching the top end of their performance envelopes. With the Spiteful type of units suddenly becoming available, and having been designed to take the flight stresses with the Griffon engines and increased all-up weight of the machines, their adoption was a logical choice.

Air Ministry requirements for front-line fighter aircraft were reducing drastically with the cessation of hostilities in Europe and the orders for F.22 and F.24 Spitfires reflected this general trend. Castle Bromwich Aircraft Factory closed in September 1945 and production of the remaining orders transferred to Supermarine at South Marston. The final order for 800 aircraft, which included Mk IX aircraft, was reduced to 627 on 9 October 1945, then to 287 aircraft the following month. In the end, 278 F.22s were delivered, but there is some argument between the Air Force and Vickers as to whether this included part of the F.24 production or not.

The F.22 was issued to R.A.F. squadrons as a front-line aircraft; the majority were used by the Auxiliary Air Force. They were little used by 1952 when eighty machines were stored and sixty-three were sold by Vickers to other Air Forces. In 1955 they were declared obsolete to R.A.F. requirements and stocks held in this country were scrapped. Twenty F.22s made their way to the Egyptian Air Force in 1950, the deal costing the Egyptians £239,000. Twenty-two were bought by the Southern Rhodesian Air Force in two batches of eleven each. A further ten were acquired by the Syrians.

Last of the breed – the F.24

If the designation change from F.21 to F.22 was contentious, then the jump from F.22 to F.24 was even more so. The last twenty-seven F.22 airframes on the Castle Bromwich production line were completed as F.24s

before the factory finally closed. There were fifty-four incomplete airframes left in the factory and these were transported to the Vickers Supermarine South Marston factory where they were to be completed as F.24s over a two-year period – a far cry from the heady days of rapid production. The early F.24s had the long-barrelled Mk II Hispano cannon but the later versions had the newer Mk V and the machines equipped with the Mk II were then upgraded to take the Mk V. Two 33-gallon fuel tanks were fitted into the rear fuselage to give a total internal tankage of 275 gallons. Top speed of the machine, which was fitted with the Griffon 61, 64 or 85 contra-prop engines, was 454 mph straight and level at 26,000 ft. It had a normal take-off weight of 10,102 lb.

F.24 aircraft were mainly reserved for U.K. use but sixteen which entered service at home in November 1946, were sent to No.80 Squadron in Hong Kong in 1950. Twenty were put into long-term storage in the U.K. in 1952 but were condemned for scrap by 1956. The last six F.24s to be retained in Hong Kong with the Royal Auxiliary Hong Kong Air Force were ordered to be scrapped at about the same time. The Squadron boss had other ideas, however, and one machine was hidden behind a hangar while the other five were reduced to small pieces. Six piles of these pieces, plus sundry spares, were duly signed off as being the earthly remains of six F.24 Spitfires and were disposed of. Some considerable time later, the survivor, VN485, was released from her hiding place and used to guard the gate at the R.H.K.A.F. station at Kai Tak. The machine is now displayed at the Imperial War Museum base at Duxford in the U.K.

And so a long line of aircraft was ended. From the Mk I through to the F.24, the Spitfire had never been very far from the leading edge of technology and performance. The machines had fought in every conceivable theatre of conflict – from the frozen wastes of Northern Russia to the baking sands of Africa, and then still further south through India to Australia. Of the 20,334 Spitfires which were built in just a few short and war-pressured years, only about one per cent remain in existence today and that must be the ultimate testament to the fighter which was originally devised as a short-term expedient to defend the shores of the United Kingdom against a vastly superior aggressor. The Spitfire still lives.

6
Test-Flying the Spitfire

(ABOVE): *Flying two aircraft in one day can be a little exhausting! Here Charlie Brown unwinds after flight testing Mk XVI RW382 and, earlier, the Mk IX TE566.*

What is it like in layman's terms to actually fly and test a new Spitfire? Clearly, from a personal point of view it is extremely exciting. It evokes the sort of mental pictures that I would imagine occurred at Castle Bromwich – the Spitfire, prepared for flight, standing ready by the side of the grass aerodrome with both pilot and groundcrew eagerly waiting for the early morning mist to clear. From a professional point of view, it is challenging. Challenging in terms of the technical preparation – which must be thorough and also the routine operational preparation – Notices to Airmen(NOTAMs), weather, diversion aerodromes and numerous other factors and 'what ifs' that should have been thought of and addressed. So the personal and professional preparation is complete – not quite, there are always a couple of last minute questions to ask either Tim or Chief Engineer Peter.

Now strapping in, I feel at one with the aircraft. The familiar start up and taxi and already I am beginning to get the feel of the aircraft. Now the testing – engine checks and pre-flight checks . . . I allow myself to remember that this is the first time that this aircraft has flown for fifty years but this is countered by my trust and faith in our engineers. I line up on the runway, look through the nose of the aircraft and take a mental picture of the aircraft's attitude on the runway. It is, of course, exactly the attitude I will need to pull off a perfect three-point landing. Opening the throttle smoothly, keeping it straight with rudder and wings level with ailerons, a quick look inside to check that air speed is increasing and engine instruments read normal and the aircraft flies itself off the ground, climbing away safely, I check instruments, raise the undercarriage, reduce the boost and rpm and check the all-important engine temperatures and pressures are within the limits.

All being well, I climb to a safe height – within gliding distance of Duxford, and carry out clean and approach configuration states to establish circuit and threshold speeds. Up to cruise speed and I look at the lateral trim – will the aircraft fly wings level at cruise speed hands off? If not, I level the wings and record the rate of roll for subsequent rectification. Now I have been airborne for around 15 minutes – quite long enough for a first flight. If the aircraft is a Merlin-engined Spitfire, I will probably land back at Audley End, wind permitting. If it is a Griffon-engined aircraft I land at Duxford.

Meanwhile, Tim, Peter and our friends at Audley End have been observing my flying with a critical eye and have probably been in contact

(ABOVE AND NEXT PAGE TOP LEFT): *Undoubtedly the most delightful of all to fly is the Mk V Spitfire (Mk Vb EP120).*

(ABOVE): Merlin-engined variant TE566 emits a puff of smoke as the engine bursts into life. This is a high-back Mk IX with a pointed rudder. Testing the aircraft on this crisp autumnal day is Historic Flying's test pilot Charlie Brown.

(BELOW): Flight Lieutenant Charlie Brown warms up the engine prior to taking Mk XVI RW382 aloft.

(ABOVE): *Charlie Brown takes a quick mental picture of the aircraft's attitude on the ground.*

(BELOW): *Mk XVIe low-back starts up prior to first flight.*

(ABOVE): Elliptical wing, high-back Mk IX ready to roll.

(BELOW): Time for a final pre take off check .

(ABOVE): Getting airborne.

(BELOW): Sir John Allison seconds before lifting TD248 into the air for the first time in over fifty years.

10. Climb

Flight conditions   VMC in non turbulent air
Normal climb configuration

Altimeter   1013 mb (29.92 in Hg)

Fuel contents _____ Weight _____

Flap setting _____ Engine cowls _____

Comment, if applicable, on power setting selected for climb _____

_____

Time (min)	Altitude (ft) (1013 mb)	IAS (knots/mph)	OAT (°C)
0			
½			
1			
1½			
2			
2½			
3			
3½			
4			
4½			
5			

Note: If no Outside Air Temperature gauge is fitted, obtain the temperature at the climb altitude for the local area from the Meteorological Office. State whether the figure quoted is forecast (F) or indicated (I).

Towards the end of the climb record:-

Manifold pressure	
RPM	
Oil pressure	
Oil temperature	

Fuel Pressure	
Cylinder head temperature	

Trimmer positions:-

Elevator/Stabilator	

Rudder	

If there is any difficulty in recording these figures during the timed climb, maintain the climb speed and power, and record them at the end of the climb.

6

(LEFT): In flight test results are recorded with China clay pencil on Charlie Brown's kneepad.

(ABOVE AND BELOW): Leaving Duxford behind, Peter Kynsey sets course for Audley End airfield.

(*ABOVE AND BELOW*): *Over Audley End airfield. Peter Kynsey completes a circuit of the airfield prior to landing.*

(ABOVE): Looking for the perfect three-pointer!

on the wireless. Today, it is a Merlin-engined aircraft, a Mk Vb. It flies beautifully and the wind is such that I will land at Audley. Flying at 220 mph at low level down the strip, I throttle back (not too much so as to prevent the engine from popping back) and enter the downwind leg at 130 mph. Pre-landing checks and I am flying at 100 mph at the end of the downwind leg, hood back, door half-cocked. Flaps down, I taper the speed from 90 mph to 80 mph aiming for my threshold speed of 75 mph. Trimmed out and curving all the way to touchdown, I aim to have a trickle of power on.

I remember the picture before take-off and close the throttle. I am rewarded with a very presentable three-pointer. I keep concentrating to keep the aircraft straight as she rolls out. A kiss or two of the brake and the

aircraft stops. I taxi back to the hangar. As I complete the shut-down checks, I start to smile and the trouble is I can't stop. I receive a barrage of questions, all of which I try to answer. Basically, I am delighted with the aircraft's first flight. Tim, Peter and I decide that once we have checked for leaks the aircraft should fly again today.

At the end of the day, I have time to reflect as I drive home up the A1. I am tired but elated and fulfilled.

A Blow-by-Blow Walk-Around

Approaching the aircraft, I check its general condition, the availability of fire extinguishers and chocks, and where the tail is pointing. Standing on the wing walkway, I check that the ignition switches are off, the undercarriage lever is in the down position and in the gate, and the contents gauge of emergency undercarriage blow-down bottle. After checking that all elec-

trical switches are off, I switch on the battery, check the undercarriage down indicator lights, voltmeter, low fuel pressure warning light and the fuel contents. Off goes the battery and I turn my attention to checking the outside of the aircraft, starting with the canopy and the cockpit door.

When doing the walk-around I try not to be distracted by detail – the danger is that you will miss something more fundamental. It is often said that people can look but do not see, and it is important to systematically scan the exterior of the aircraft from known vantage points where a loose panel or any form of damage will be most easily seen. This often involves getting on my knees to get a good view underneath. With the Spitfire in particular, there are panels which

are retained by a very large number of screws; my trick for checking whether they are tight is to tap the panel with my fingers and if there is a rattle a screw is loose and normally it is easy to hear which screw it is. I move through the full range of the flying controls and check for freedom of movement and any free play in the control runs.

Having started at the port wing trailing edge, the walk-around proceeds in a clockwise direction round the aircraft and finishes where I started. Now strap in and we're off.

Comparison of Different Variants

I have had the privilege and pleasure to fly, in numerical order, Mk V, Mk IX, Mk XIV, Mk XVI, and Mk XVIII Spitfires. Personally, I would split them into three groups based on the power of their engines: single-stage supercharged Merlin (Mk V), twin-stage supercharged Merlin (Mk IX, Mk XVI), and Griffon (Mk XIV, Mk XVIII). Before comparing the three groups, I should also cover the clipped as opposed to elliptical wing-tip option that, in my opinion, has the same effect upon all the marks of Spitfire that I have flown.

Clipped versus Elliptical Wing-tips

Clipped wing-tips have the following effects:
• Cruise speed increases by approximately 15 mph
• Rate of roll is markedly increased

(ABOVE): Clipped wing low-back Mk XVI.

- Slight increase in stall speed (3–5 mph)
- Noticeable increase in drag during manoeuvre – elliptical wing-tips really do minimise drag during manoeuvre

The aircraft is easier to land because in the three-point attitude the aircraft has stopped flying very shortly after touchdown – elliptical tips require the aircraft to be 'flown' on the ground for a considerable period after touchdown and where any bumps will make the aircraft bounce around like a spring lamb.

Comparison of the Three Groups

I shall start with the Mk V, as the standard against which the other two groups will be compared. The Mk V is undoubtedly the most delightful, capable and yet utterly benign aircraft that I have ever flown. All Spitfires speak to you through the controls but none more than this aircraft. It is utterly predictable in its handling and positively inspires me with confidence. Even the take-off and landing are easy when compared to other aircraft of the same configuration, power and weight. To put the feel of the aircraft in perspective for the reader, I should perhaps compare it with the de Havilland Chipmunk, a relatively accessible aircraft and one which is often quoted as

(BELOW): Amidst a beautifully scenic backdrop is Mk V AR614.

having the ideal control harmonisation (or feel). Those that have been lucky enough to experience the joy of the Chipmunk will know exactly what I mean.

The Mk IX and Mk XVI are both twin-stage supercharged Merlin-powered aircraft. The difference is that the Mk IX has a Rolls-Royce-built Merlin whereas the Mk XVI has a Packard-built Merlin. I am sorry, but having flown behind both types of motor I cannot tell the difference between them. Those motors deliver approximately 1700 bhp. The nose of these aircraft is longer than that of the Mk V and the aircraft are heavier than the Mk V. The extra power provides a useful increase in climb rate, cruise speed and high-altitude performance. The aircraft feel marginally heavier on the controls than the Mk V but the airframe is still very capable of controlling all the power that the engines will deliver.

The Mk XIV and Mk XVIII: now we are playing quite a different ballgame. These Griffon engines will produce a maximum of around 2250 bhp. The nose of these aircraft is longer still and the basic Spitfire airframe has been quite heavily modified, most significantly the fin and rudder. The area of both has been substantially increased and the rudder is fitted with an anti-balance tab. This is arranged so that it moves in the same direction as the rudder to provide an aerodynamic force that opposes the pilot's inputs to the rudder (it fights the pilot's attempts to move the rudder). It was fitted to enhance directional stability during high-speed dives. Nowadays, it means that it gives your legs a real work-out during an aerobatic display sequence. Of course, the engine rotates in the opposite direction too. Just as well to get the rudder trim-setting correct for take-off! In the case of these aircraft, the airframe cannot control all the power the Griffon can deliver. For example, less than 110 kt at the top of a loop and your loop becomes a torque roll off the top despite full aileron to oppose the roll! The aircraft also feels substantially heavier in pitch and roll rates are reduced.

In summary, the Griffon-engined Spitfire is a fire-breathing brute of an aircraft, very different in character to the Mk V, but if you can afford the fuel and you want to cruise at high speed, the Griffon is for you. At comparable percentage power settings the Mk V will cruise at 210 mph, the Mk IX at 225 mph and the Mk XIV at 280 mph.

(ABOVE): A belch of smoke as the Griffon bursts into life (Mk XIV SM832).

(BELOW): Mk XVIe TD248.

(ABOVE): *Full bore engine runs underway.*

(BELOW): *Whilst the Merlin has a crackling growl, the Griffon howls like a demented beast – different but equally glorious.*

(ABOVE): The massive five-bladed propeller dominates the rest of the airframe.

How I Became Involved with Historic Flying/Warbirds

It all started in 1983. I had just been awarded my wings at R.A.F. Valley. I had some leave and then a number of weeks holding prior to going to the Tactics and Weapons Unit at Chivenor. During this period, I decided to try and obtain a P.P.L. and learn to fly tail-dragger aircraft that were aerobatic.

A chance encounter with an acquaintance of Len Gruber led to a telephone call and a Chipmunk (G-BDIM) check-out the very next day. The Chipmunk was owned jointly by Len Gruber and Terry Mattocks and Len converted me to the Chipmunk. I was smitten and spent as much of my spare time as I could at Goodwood flying the Chipmunk. Len and Terry were very encouraging and generous and I owe them a great deal for what they taught me. They also owned a Stampe (G-ASHS) which I converted to in due course. Then the Chipmunk and Stampe moved to Rochester where I continued to fly with 3 Point Flying, which is what Len and Terry called themselves.

Meanwhile, I continued my fast-jet training with the R.A.F. and having been posted to the Tornado GR.1 I arrived at R.A.F. Cottesmore. It was here that one weekend I decided to go to the Cambridge Flying Group in order to try and get checked out on their Tiger Moths. It was here that I met Tim Routsis who was then a Private Pilot's Licence member of the Group and keen to progress his aerobatic and formation flying. We flew

together for a fair amount of time and our friendship developed from there. This was all happening in 1984 which is when Tim developed the itch for a Spitfire.

Tim had the inspiration for the 'Gate Guardians' deal which he was able to set up with the M.o.D. The deal took from 1984 to 1989 to complete. Having got not one but five Spitfires, Tim then started to look at how to restore them to flying condition. He formed his own company and Historic Flying was born out of Vintage Fabrics (which was based at Rayne in Essex and run by Clive Denney – Clive became a senior director of Historic Flying) and after a short time retired from being a fireman with the Essex Fire Service. Historic Flying outgrew their premises at Rayne and moved to their current premises at Audley End in 1990. By this time, our first aircraft to be restored, RW382, a low-back clipped Mk XVIe, was well on its way to being completed.

Tim asked John Allison to join Historic Flying as Chief Pilot. John was a serving senior R.A.F. officer who had the necessary provenance and who was already acquainted with Tim. I had always kept in contact with Tim and as often as possible had been both to Rayne and Audley to work on RW382. Tim had long since acquired his Chipmunk (G-BDIM) from 3 Point Flying and we continued to fly together – all three of us: Tim, myself and G-BDIM. Clive, of course, was a P.P.L. holder as well and had learnt to fly on the Tiger Moths at Cambridge Flying Group. He also flew G-BDIM

At last, in 1991, RW382 was test-flown by John. John then checked out Tim, Clive and me in a borrowed Harvard and in one day, within a few hours, all of us first soloed in RW382. I had already been doing some display flying in the Chipmunk and, under John's watchful eye, I soon upgraded to the Spitfire. John introduced me to the flight testing of the company aircraft. I might add that, by now, I was instructing at Cranwell on Tucanos and my primary duty was as a Unit Test Pilot – nothing fancy, just a trusted pair of hands and a fertile interest in the technical and engineering aspects of the Unit's Tucanos.

So five years down the line (1996) and I had around 200 hours on Spitfires, about 30 hours on the Bf 109 Black 6 and a handful of hours on aircraft such as the Mustang, Kittyhawk, King Cobra, Yak-11, Harvard, and the like. As a Qualified Flying Instructor I have also converted five people to the Spitfire which has been a great challenge and a source of delight in itself.

I have often been asked how you get to fly in a Spitfire. The answer is that you can be either very rich or very lucky. Clearly, I have been very lucky, having

been in the right place at the right time and having the good fortune to meet the right people – 3 Point Flying, the Cambridge Flying Group, Tim Routsis and Clive Denney who formed Historic Flying, and Sir John Allison, our Chief Pilot, because without his help and encouragement I would not have had the chance to fly Spitfires or to gain the experience on other types of warbird.

(RIGHT): Proving that any flight in a Spitfire is a special moment, Tim Routsis and Clive Denney pose beside Mk IX TE566 at Duxford airfield. Tim flew the aircraft over from Audley End after which Clive air tested it.

119

First Flight - Clive Denney

(ABOVE): Clive Denney poses with Mk IX TE566.

8 August 1991 is a day that will stay with me for the rest of my life. Having finished the rebuild of Spitfire XVI RW382, and with its Permit to Fly in place, we were in a position to fly the aircraft. Sir John Allison had checked us out on 2 July, in Richard Parker's Harvard IIB (G-BAFM) from the rear seat, carrying out stalls and practice Spitfire circuits ready for the real thing. After 45 minutes John cleared me to fly the Spitfire. It would be nearly 5 weeks before we got our hands on the Spitfire but I managed to fly Chipmunks, a T-6, the Tiger Moth and Stampe up to the Spitfire flight, so tail wheel currency was on-going.

On the day, Tim Routsis and Sir John Allison flew to Duxford in the Chipmunk to check the conditions and found them to be satisfactory, good visibility and around 10 kts on the nose. We duly drove to Duxford and John flew the Spitfire over. It was decided that Tim would go first followed by Charlie (Flt Lt Charlie Brown) and myself last. Each flight was briefed to last around 20 to 25 minutes, with some stalling with the gear up, gear down and gear and flaps down, some practice circuits at around 2,500ft, a little fun and then rejoin to land.

Both Tim and Charlie flew their sorties successfully and my time was now getting close. At the start of the day I was about to fulfil the most exciting of all boyhood dreams but at 15:00 hrs as I was strapping myself into the cockpit, I was thinking God I really don't want to do this, but then I thought well they would not let me fly this if they thought I couldn't do it safely; so get on with it. Because I was the last to go, I was aware the temperatures were fairly high so I would not have a lot of time on the ground before she started to boil. I had prepared myself (I thought) mentally having carried out several flights in the hanger, in the bath, in bed – but always just walking away, now this was it for real. The next time I walked, I would have flown a Spitfire.

Time to go. External and internal checks carried out, notes safely stowed in my flying suit pockets now let's see if I can start the still hot engine. It needed two shots of primer and she was settling down to around 1200 rpm and with that warm smell and exciting music, that only a Merlin can produce, I called for taxi clearance, waved the chocks away and taxied out. The tower had cleared me to the hold for runway 06 (Easterly) grass. By now temperatures were starting to creep up. 115 degrees was shut down point and I was now at 90 degrees; I needed to get a move on. Engine checks to do, 1800 rpm, check the mags, then prop and supercharger, check the temperatures and pressures – "all satisfactory". Temperature now 100 degrees, pre flight checks to carry out. Trims set, throttle friction tight (I do not want the throttle closing after take off when I change hands to get the gear up). Fuel on, fuel pump on DI, set hatches, harness tight, let's go. "Spitfire India Alpha ready for departure". Lining up on the 06 runway the pangs of anxiety have now gone. Gently opening up the throttle the Spitfire starts to move, at an alarming rate, full right rudder and full right

aileron are needed to keep it straight. Gradually increasing the power to +4lb boost and gradually backing off the right aileron then increasing to +7lb boost. The noise is incredible, you can almost feel the fuselage trying to twist due to the torque from the now roaring Merlin.

A skip on the famous 06 bump and she's airborne (my God) a touch of brake to stop the wheels rotating. A change of hands from throttle to control column to allow the right hand to raise the gear. Please keep level, no porpoising, I know I'm being watched, thud, thud as the gear locks in the wheel wells and the lights go to red up. Reducing the power after take off to +4lb and 2,600 rpm she climbs away at 170 mph, with radiator flaps to auto, "Boy this is brilliant" (where the hell am I?). A gentle turn to port to establish myself just north of Duxford. Power back to +2lb and 2,000 rpm and she settles down to the cruise. As Victor Meldrew would say "I don't believe it" here I am actually flying a Spitfire, not in the bath, in bed, or in my dreams, but for real – a real dream. Settle down now, you have a job to do.

Firstly I climb up to about 3,500 ft, no power change, just let it cruise on up, level up and think about the stall. As described, the stall was very gentle, slight left wing drop and an absolutely normal recovery, this was carried both clean and dirty configuration (gear up and down). After the stall, I would try, as briefed, the practice circuit. I picked the A10 running north past Bassingbourne as my runway and joined down wind to establish at around 140 mph. Carry out downwind checks, brakes off, undercarriage down and locked (light to green down) pitch to fully fine, fuel on, fuel pump on, hatches and harness checked. At the end of the practice downwind leg reduce the speed to 120 mph and drop the flaps, a marked nose down pitch, retrim and start the turn to finals, speed back to 100 mph and keep the turn going lining up on the runway (A10). That was fine, now let's try it for real. As much as I wanted to I couldn't stay up here all day, but first some simple fun. A gentle turn left and right following by some wing overs. I was surprised how heavy the ailerons were in roll but how responsive, the elevator as described, was over sensitive. Now time to return to Duxford and the landing.

"Duxford Spitfire India Alpha" (I'd always wanted to say that) "Request rejoin". I was cleared to rejoin for right-hand downwind for runway 06 grass. This was it, the first landing 600ft circuits were quite low but that was the briefed height. At the end of the downwind leg I started the turn for finals. All the checks carried out, I was cleared to land. With the speed falling to 90 mph and with the turn still going it was fairly easy to keep the runway in sight, until short finals, when the runway disappeared under the wings. Now on rabbit vision and the aircraft in the flare, close the throttle, the runway is there and just let it settle. It touches down and to my surprise just runs on straight as a die. With no surprises in the landing roll, I just let it run out to a virtual standstill. At the end of the landing roll I raise the flaps and open the radiator flap door (to keep the temperature down). Turning off at the end 06 there is just a short taxi back to the base of the Duxford Tower . The last hiss of the brakes as the Spitfire comes to a halt, marks the end of my first Spitfire sortie, just a dead cut to check on the mags, the temperatures have stabilised and all is satisfactory with 1200 rpm set. I pull the idle cut-off and the engine dies, the large prop now at a standstill. The gentle ticking of the engine as she cools is the only sound I can hear, oblivious of the people around me offering warm congratulations, I had done it. I'd flown the most famous aeroplane ever built, I didn't know whether to laugh or cry, I did neither, I just grinned. Seven years on I'm still grinning!

Appendix 1: Surviving Spitfires.

The pages that follow contain brief service details for all the Spitfires that can reasonably be said to exist today. It is always difficult to define what a Spitfire looks like now – despite the detail of the preceding chapters, because what may appear to be nothing more than tangled, corroded, metal to one man may be only five years away from a post restoration flight to another. It is certain that machines other than those listed here can be identified from data plates, or fuselage markings of some description, on collections of metalwork which exist in a number of workshops around the world, but their general content, shape and state of health does not currently reasonably allow their inclusion into a list of living Spitfire aircraft. The machines that have been included in the list are known to be either stored, under restoration, on display in a museum somewhere in the world – or are capable of taking to the element for which they were designed. I have no doubt that if this list were to be repeated in even a matter of months time, there would be new entries to be included.

Long may that state of affairs be allowed to continue.

Serial No.	Type	Mark	Construction No.	Aircraft Military History
N3200	F	I		441st Spitfire built. 29-11-39: First flight. 2-12-39: 8 MU. 19-4-40: 19 Sqn. 27-5-40: Did not return from ops.
K9942	F	Ia	6S/30225	155th Spitfire built. 21-4-38: First flight from Eastleigh. 24-4-39: 72 Sqn at Church Fenton. 6 MU Brize Norton 17-8-40: 57 OTU at Eshoff. 27-9-42: 33 MU Lyneham. 10-4-43: 53 OTU at Kirton in Lindsey. 26-8-44: 52 MU Cardiff in store for museum use.
P9306	F	Ia		508th Spitfire built. 19-1-40: First flight. 24-1-40: 24 MU. 6-7-40: 74 (Tiger) Sqn at Hornchurch. 17-7-41: 54 MU. July 41: 131 Sqn. October 41: 52 OTU. 4-5-43: 61 OTU (Cat B damaged). Nov 44: Loaned to Chicago Museum of Science & Industry. Credited with 5 enemy aircraft destroyed.
P9374	F	Ia		557th Spitfire built. 23-2-40: First flight from Eastleigh. 2-3-40: 9 MU Cosford. 6-3-40: 92 Sqn. 24-5-40: Failed to return from Ops.
P9444	F	Ia	6S/30613	607th Spitfire Built. 2-4-40: First flight from Eastleigh. 23-5-40: RAF

Serial No.	Type	Mark	Construction No.	Aircraft Military History
				Farnborough for trials. 23-5-40: 6 MU Brize Norton. 4-6-40: 72 Sqn. 3-7-41: 58 OTU. 18-6-42: 12 MU. 5-8-42: 61 OTU. 4-2-43: AST Hamble. 30-3-43: 12 MU. 12-5-43: 53 OTU at Kirton in Lindsey. 28-11-43: 39 MU Colerne. 11-5-44: Into long term storage at 83 MU.
R6915	F	Ia	6S/80914	874th Spitfire built. 11-7-40: first flight from Eastleigh. 11-7-40: 6 MU Brize Norton. 21-7-40: 609 Sqn. Battle damaged. January 41: 602 Sqn. July 41: 61 OTU. Credited with 4 enemy aircraft destroyed.
X4590	F	Ia	6S/81254	1198th Spitfire built. 30-9-40: first flight from Eastleigh. October 40: A Flt 609 Sqn. 24-2-41: 66 Sqn at Exeter. 7-4-41: 57 OTU at Hawarden, Chester. 18-7-41: 303 (Polish) Sqn at Speke. 14-2-42: 53 OTU at Llandow. 3 accidents. 4-10-43: 33 MU at Lyneham. 16-5-44: 82 MU at Lichfield. 28-8-44: 52 MU Cardiff for museum purposes.
AR213	F	Ia	WASP/20/2	Built by Westland Aircraft. 24-7-41: 12 MU 31-7-41: 57 OTU, Hawarden.

Serial No.	Type	Mark	Construction No.	Aircraft Military History	Serial No.	Type	Mark	Construction No.	Aircraft Military History
P7350	F	IIa	CBAF-14	Built at Castle Bromwich. 13-8-40: 6 MU Brize Norton. 6-9-40: 266 (Rhodesia) Sqn at Wittering. 17-10-40: 603 Sqn. 10-4-41: 616 Sqn. 27-4-42: Central Gunnery School, Sutton Bridge 4-2-43: AST, following accident. 24-7-44: 39 MU Colerne					140 Sqn. 26-8-42: Instrument failure in cloud – aircraft abandoned, crashed in Sussex Cat E. 31-8-42: Struck Off Charge.
P7540	F	IIa		Built at Castle Bromwich. 20-10-40: 6 MU Brize Norton. 29-10-40: 66 Sqn at West Malling. 24-2-41: 609 Sqn at Biggin Hill. 14-6-41: 266 Sqn at Wittering. 6-7-41: 312 Sqn at Martlesham Heath. 25-10-41: Crashed into Loch Doon.	BL370	F	V		23-11-41: 37 MU. 8-12-41: 130 Sqn. 28-4-42: 224 Sqn. 31-12-42: 130 Sqn. 20-2-43: 610 Sqn. 27-3-43: 350 Sqn. 11-5-43: Scottish Aviation Ltd for repair. 3-8-43: 118 Sqn. 25-9-43: 64 Sqn. 11-8-44: 53 OTU. 30-9-44: Written off.
P7973	F	IIa	CBAF-492	Built at Castle Bromwich. 4-2-41: 6 MU Brize Norton. 452 (RAAF) Sqn, Hornchurch & Kenley. 313 Sqn 23-2-45: Despatched to Australia by sea. July 45: stored by RAAF.	AD540	LF	Va		22-10-41: 24 MU at Tern Hill. 15-11-41: 122 Sqn at Scorton and Hornchurch. 23-4-42: 242 Sqn at Ayr. 23-5-42: crashed near Carsphairn.
P8208	F	IIa		26-3-41: 12 MU. 12-5-41: 303 Sqn. 24-12-41: 1 CACF. 9-10-42: 52 OTU. 26-1-43: Mid air collision with P8207 during gunnery practice over the Severn estuary.	AB910	LF	Vb	CBAF-1061	Built at Castle Bromwich. 22-8-41: 222 Sqn North Weald. 30-9-41: 37 MU at Burtonwood. December 41: 130 Sqn at Perranporth. 8-4-42: 6 MU at Brize Norton. 13-6-42: 133 (Eagle) Sqn at Biggin Hill. 2-9-42: 242 Sqn at Digby. 12-11-42: 12 MU Kirkbride for storage. 8-6-43: 33 MU Lyneham. 2-7-43: 416 Sqn (RCAF). 17-7-43: 402 Sqn (RCAF) at Digby. 20-4-44: 53 OTU Kirton in Lindsey.
P8332	F	IIb	CBAF-711	Built at Castle Bromwich. 29-4-41: 45 MU Kinloss. 25-5-41: 222 Sqn. 7-12-41: 82 MU Lichfield. 1-4-42: Transferred to RCAF. 13-4-42: Shipped to Canada, to No 1 Training Command, Mountain View, Ontario.	BL614	F	Vb	CBAF-1646	4-1-42: 8 MU at Little Rissington. 7-2-42: 611 Sqn at Drem. 2-6-42: 242 Sqn at Drem. 11-8-42: 222 Sqn at Drem. 31-3-43: 64 Sqn at Ayr. 25-9-43: 118 Sqn at Petershead. 6-12-43: 6 SoTT at Hednesford.
AB130	PR	IV		Supermarine built at dispersal units. 22-11-41: First flight from Eastleigh. 23-11-10: 8 MU. 26-1-42: 1 PRU.	BL628	F	Vb	CBAF-1660	Built at Castle Bromwich. 25-1-42: 12 MU.

Serial No.	Type	Mark	Construction No.	Aircraft Military History	Serial No.	Type	Mark	Construction No.	Aircraft Military History
				1-4-42: 401 Sqn. 5-8-42: 308 Sqn. 12-8-42: 167 Sqn. 14-10-42: 610 Sqn. 19-6-43: Cunliffe Owen Aircraft Ltd. 17-8-43: 33 MU at Lyneham. 16-1-44: Royal Naval Disposal Account. 30-1-44: Royal Naval Air Station, Belfast. Summer 44: 719 Sqn St Merryn.	BR108	F	Vc		7-3-42: First flight from High Post aerodrome. 8-3-42: 8 MU. 23-3-42: 47 MU. 8-6-42: Arrived in Malta. Allocated to 603 Sqn. 8-7-42: Shot down into Marsalform Bay by Bf 109.
BL655	F	Vb	CBAF-	Built at Castle Bromwich. 4-2-42: 9 MU Cosford. 24-3-42: 416 Sqn. 15-7-42: 602 Sqn. 11-9-42: 164 Sqn. 3-2-43: 341 Sqn. 30-5-43: 129 Sqn. 11-6-43: 416 Sqn. 1-7-43: Crashed near Digby while on training flight.	]BR545	F	Vc	CBAF-3155	11-7-42: First Flight from High Post Aerodrome 13-7-42: 45 MU Kinloss 29-7-42: 47 MU 4-8-42: Despatched to Australia, SS *Hoperidge* 23-10-42: Arrived Australia as A58-51 Force landed near Derby – Prince Regent River tidal flats due to fuel shortage 24-12-43.
BM597	F	Vb	CBAF-2461	24-4-42: 37 MU Burtonwood. 7-5-42: 315 Sqn. 26-6-43: Vickers for modifications. 4-1-44: 222 MU. 2-4-45: 58 OTU.	BS164	F	Vc	CBAF-3074	21-6-42: First Flight from Chattis Hill.22-6-42: 8 MU. 19-7-42: 215 MU 4-8-42: Despatched to Australia aboard the SS *Hoperidge*. 23-10-42: Arrived in Australia as A58-63 Served with 54 Sqn (RAF) as 'K'. Mid air collision, crashed near Straus Strip, New Territorics.
EP120	LF	Vb	CBAF-2403	3-5-42: 45 MU Kinloss. 4-6-42: 501 Sqn at Tangmere. 9-9-42: 19 Sqn at Perranporth. 22-4-43: 402 Sqn (RCAF) at Digby. 8-6-44: 33 MU Lyneham. 12-10-44: 53 OTU at Kirton in Lindsey. Credited with seven enemy aircraft destroyed.	BS199	F	Vc	6S/199407	26-7-42: First Flew from Chattis Hill 29-7-42: 39 MU . 5-8-42: 215 MU. 17-8-42: Despatched to Australia aboard the SS *Teakoelei*. Numbered A58-81. 11-11-42: Arrived in Australia. May 43: Crashed during combat near Millingimbi, New Territories.
AR501	LF	Vc	WASP/20/223	22-6-42: 8 MU. 19-7-42: 310 Sqn. 18-8-43: 504 Sqn. 16-10-43: 312 Sqn. 27-2-44: 422 Sqn. 30-3-44: 55 OTU. 24-4-45: Central Gunnery School.	BS231	F	Vc		26-7-42: First flight from High Post aerodrome. 28-7-42: 6 MU Brize Norton. 12-8-42: 215 MU. 17-8-42: Despatched to Australia aboard the SS *Teakoelei*. Numbered A58-92. 11-11-42: Arrived in Australia. Assigned to 452 Sqn. 15-3-43: Shot down over Darwin. CO Sqn Ldr Thorold-Smith killed.
AR614	F	Vc	WASP/20/228	24-8-42: 39 MU. 11-9-42: 312 Sqn. 20-11-43: 610 Sqn. 30-1-44: 130 Sqn. 16-2-44: 222 Sqn. 2-9-44: 53 OTU Kirton in Lindsey.					

Serial No.	Type	Mark	Construction No.	Aircraft Military History	Serial No.	Type	Mark	Construction No.	Aircraft Military History
EE606	F	Vc	WWA-2822	14-9-42: 6 MU. 23-9-42: 215 MU. 9-10-42: despatched to Australia aboard the *Port Wyndham*, numbered A58-102. 21-11-42: Arrived in Australia.					215 MU. 14-9-43: Sent to Australia on the *Hororata*. 21-10-43: Arrived in Australia as A58-246. Allocated to 54 Sqn, Darwin. 452 Sqn. Central Gunnery School.
EE853	F	Vc	WASP/20/484	23-1-43: 8MU. 8-2-43: 215MU 9-3-43: Despatched to Australia aboard the *Sussex* 16-4-43: Arrived in Australia as A58-146 79 Sqn Royal Australian AF. Lost on ops after being abandoned near Goodenough Island in the Solomons. 19-3-44: Struck off charge	EN474	F	VIIc	6S/171652	First flown from Eastleigh. 13-3-43: 47 MU. 10-4-43: Sent to USA aboard the *Glenapp*. 2-5-43: Arrived in New York USA. 6-1-44: Issued to US Army HQ on transfer. Freeman Field, Indiana 1946 as FE-400.
EF545	F	Vc	WWA-3832	15-2-43: 6 MU Brize Norton. 24-2-43: 215 MU. 5-3-43: Despatched to Australia aboard the *Asphalian*. 17-5-43: Arrived Australia as A58-149. Crashed on the Trobriand Islands.	JF294	F	VIII	6S/238666	19-1-43: Eastleigh First flight. 33 MU Lyneham. 4-8-42: 82 MU Lichfield for packing. 1-9-42: Arrived in Casablanca for MEAF. 3-3-44: Flew non-stop from Cairo to Cape Town. To the South African Air Force as 5501, for exhibition flights, the only Mk VIII to travel to the SAAF.
JG891	F	Vc		2-1-43: 39 MU. 21-1-43: 215 MU. 4-2-43: Despatched to Australia aboard the *Tijuga*. 13-4-43: Arrived in Australia as A58-178 1-44: Went missing on ferry flight.	JF620	LF	VIII		First flight from High Post Aerodrome. 13-8-43: 9 MU Cosford. 31-8-43: 215 MU. 14-9-43: Sent to Australia on the *Hororata* 21-10-43: Arrived in Australia as A58-300.
JK448	F	Vc	CBAF-4690	7-2-43: 46 MU. 1-3-43: 215 MU. 25-3-43: Despatched to Gibraltar aboard SS672. 12-4-43: Gibraltar. 30-4-43: North West Africa. 1-7-43: Malta. 1-9-43: Middle East. 30-11-44: Struck off charge. To Yugoslav Air Force.	JG267	LF	VIII	6S/399579	First flight from Eastleigh. 9-10-43: 6 MU 19-10-43: 215 MU 1-12-43: Sent to Australia on the *Tekoa* 21-1-44: Arrived in Australia as A58-377 and allocated to 452 Sqn, Darwin. 2-11-44: Crash-landed in to shallow water during practice dive-bombing and gunnery attacks. Flt Sgt B O'Connor was killed.
MA353	F	Vc		30-5-43: 9 MU. 8-6-43: 215 MU. 26-6-43: Sent to Australia aboard the SSLS627. 2-8-43: Arrived in Australia as A58-232. Allocated to 452 Sqn. 24/4/44: Went missing on high altitude air test from Straus Strip, Darwin, after collision with another Spitfire. Sgt Dunning killed.	JG355	LF	VIII	6S/445748	First Flight from Chattis Hill. 17-10-43: 9 MU Cosford. 29-10-43: 215 MU. 11-12-43: Sent to Australia on the *Fort Philip*.
MA863	F	Vc		8-8-43: 6 MU. 16-8-43:					

Serial No.	Type	Mark	Construction No.	Aircraft Military History	Serial No.	Type	Mark	Construction No.	Aircraft Military History
				16-1-44: Arrived in Australia as A58-359.	MV154	HF	VIIIc	6S/583793	First flight from Southampton in 1944. 15-9-44: 6 MU Brize Norton. 27-9-44: 82 MU Lichfield for packing. 15-10-44: Sent to Australia on the SS *Port Fairey*. 24-11-44: Arrived in Australia as A58-671.
JG484	LF	VIII	HAI/6S/196330	First Flight from Chattis Hill. 1-12-43: 6 MU Brize Norton. 15-12-43: 215 MU. 5-1-44: Sent to Australia on the *Sussex*. 29-2-44: Arrived in Australia as A58-408.					
MV321	HF	VIII		First flight from Southampton. 15-9-44: 6 MU. 26-9-44: 82 MU Lichfield. 15-10-44: Sent to Australia on the *Hororata*. 30-11-44: Arrived in Australia as A58-642. 5-46: Authorised for write off.	MV239	HF	VIIIc	6S/581740	Crashed on test flight 20-3-45: 6 MU 8-5-45: Despatched to Australia on the SS *Rangitana*. 19-6-45: Arrived in Australia as A58-758 Stored at Richmond, NSW.
					NH631	LF	VIIIc	6S/326987	First flew from Keevil.16-12-44: 6 MU. 5-1-45: 222 MU High Ercall. 22-1-45: Sent to India aboard the SS *Mahadive*. 19-2-45: Arrived in India and allocated to No 12 CMU in Bombay. 9 Sqn RIAF. 31-12-47: Sold to the Indian AF.
MD228	LF	VIIIc	HAI/6S/196387	1-12-43: First flight from Chattis Hill. 25-12-43: 82 MU Lichfield. 6-2-44: Sent to Australia on the *Hindustan*. 18-4-44: Arrived in Australia as A58-445.					
MD338	LF	VIIIc		30-1-44: 6MU. 11-2-43: 82 MU Lichfield. 26-2-44: Sent to Australia on the *Elenafaire*. 9-5-44: Arrived in Australia as A58-467.	BR601	F	IX	GAL/R/6S/160931	16-6-42: First flight from Eastleigh. 17-6-42: 45 MU Kinloss. 10-7-42: 64 Sqn at Hornchurch. 2-4-43: 454 Sqn at Hornchurch. 16-4-43: Air Service Training for mods, 17-7-43: 129 Sqn at Hornchurch, 28-8-43: 316 Sqn at Northolt, 28-9-43: 165 Sqn at Culmhead, 1-3-45: Vickers-Armstrong for mods 22-8-45: 33 MU Lyneham in store. 27-1-49: Despatched to South Africa aboard the *Clan MacKellar*. 13-3-49: with the SAAF as 5631.
MT719	LF	VIIIc	6S/479770, although the code 6S/442296 has also been quoted for this aircraft.	First flight from Southampton. 21-6-44: 9 MU Cosford. 10-7-44: 215 MU Dumfries. 28-7-44: Despatched to India aboard the SS *Turkestan*. 5-9-44: Arrived in India. 29-12-47: Transferred to the Indian AF.					
MT818	LF	VIIIc	6S/729058	First flight from Southampton. 13-6-44: Allocated to the Controller of Research & Development at High Post and then Farnborough. 21-6-47: Sold to Vickers-Armstrong and converted to type 502 – 2-seat trainer B-condition, and serialled N32. Civil Reg G-AIDN.	LZ842	F	IX	CBAF-5056	24-4-48: 232 Sqn SAAF til early '50 when it ended service life at the wrong end of a firing range.
					MH603	F	IX	CBAF-5589	15-10-43: 39 MU 25-10-43: 405 ARF Croydon

Serial No.	Type	Mark	Construction No.	Aircraft Military History	Serial No.	Type	Mark	Construction No.	Aircraft Military History
				3-1-44: 331 Sqn 2-6-44: 274 Sqn 21-8-44: Flight Leaders School, Millfield Central Fighter Establishment (CFE) Tangmere 1-6-45: FACB – AST Hamble for repair. 10-3-49: South African AF.					Casablanca. 16-1-47: 253 Sqn collision with TA808 landing at Treviso, Italy. 26-6-47: Transferred to Italian AF as MM4014. 5-12-49: Sold Vickers-Armstrong. Transferred to Israel – serial unknown. Later transferred to Burma.
MJ627	T	IX	CBAF-7722	4-12-43: 9 MU 18-8-44: to General Aircraft Ltd 28-9-44: 441 Sqn 9-3-45: Flying Accident Cat E 11-9-45: Brought back on charge recat B Air Service Training for repair 19-7-50: Sold Vickers-Armstrong as Non-effective aircraft. Became G-15-171. 5-6-51: Converted to type 509 (2-seat T9) for the Irish Air Corps as 158.	RK858	F	IX	CBAF-9746	2-10-44: 33 MU Lyneham. 11-10-44: 52 MU Cardiff – prepared for Russia. 4-11-44: Shipped to Russia on the *Empire Stalwart*. 8-12-44: Arrived in Hapmat for Russian service. Very heavy forced landing.
MJ772	T	IX	CBAF-7369	20-12-43: 33 MU Lyneham 20-1-44: 341 Sqn 18-6-44: Category AC ops 22-6-44: 340 Sqn 19-8-44: 33 MU Lyneham 27-9-44: 83 GSU 25-1-45: 49 MU 19-7-45: Heston Aircraft Ltd 19-7-50: Sold Vickers-Armstrong as Non-effective aircraft. Vickers test serial G-15-172. 31-5-51: Converted to 2-seat training T9 for the Irish Air Corps as 159.	SM520	HF	IX	CBAF-10164	23-11-44: 33 MU Lyneham. 21-6-48: Transferred to the South African AF.
					SM639		IX		2-12-44: 33 MU Lyneham. 10-1-45: 82 MU Lichfield prepared for transit to Russia. 28-1-45: transported to Russia. 13-2-45: Arrived Hapmat and Russian service.
MK805	LF	IX	CBAF-IX-1780	11-3-44: 33 MU Lyneham 8-6-44: 312 Sqn 29-9-44: 64 Sqn 16-10-44: Repair on site de Havilland 13-4-45: 3 APU 16-5-45: Mediterranean Allied Air Force, 145 Sqn 27-6-46: Transferred to Italian Air Force as MM4084.	TA805	LF	IX	CBAF-10372	3-1-45: 39 MU. 24-6-45: 183 Sqn. 2-8-45: 234 Sqn. 2-4-49: Transferred to the South African AF.
					TD314	F	IX		30-3-45: 33 MU Lyneham. 24-6-45: 183 Sqn. 26-7-45: 234 Sqn. 12-5-48: Transferred to the South African AF.
					TE294	HF	IX		7-6-45: 39 MU. 10-4-45: 122 Sqn. 24-9-45: Flying Accident – Repair on site. 7-8-47: Transferred to South African AF.
PV270	F	IX	CBAF-IX-3128	28-9-44: 9 MU. 18-10-44: 82 MU. 21-10-44: Shipped to Middle East AF on SSLS2135 3-11-44: Arrived at	TE566	LF	IX	CBAF-171363	15-6-45: 33 MU Lyneham. 3-8-45: 312 Sqn. 30-8-45: Transferred to

Serial No.	Type	Mark	Construction No.	Aircraft Military History	Serial No.	Type	Mark	Construction No.	Aircraft Military History
				the Czech AF. Transferred to the Air Force Academy and in '48/'49 sold to the Israelis. IDFAF (Israeli) 20-32 or '32 of 101 Sqn.					Training Exeter. 18-12-46: White Waltham for export to Turkey.
MH415	LF	IXb	CBAF-IX-533	8-43: 129 Sqn at Hornchurch. 10-43: 222 Sqn at Hornchurch. 2-1-44: AFDU at Wittering. 9-44: 126 Sqn Bradwell Bay. 5-47: Transferred to Royal Netherlands AF as H-108, later H-65. 4-53: Transferred to the Belgian AF as SM40. 6-56: Sold off as a target tug with COGEA, serialled OO-ARD.	MJ271	LF	IXc	CBAF-IX-970	2-10-43: 33 MU Lyneham. 411 ARF 132 Sqn Air Service Training 23-11-44: 401 Sqn. 14-12-44: Category AC Ops. 21-12-44: 410 RSU 23-2-45: 29 MU in storage. 25-11-46: Transferred to the Royal Netherlands AF as H-8. Also 3W-8 (in 1951 the H regs changed to 3W) based at Twente. From 1950 it served with 322 Sqn.
MH434	LF	IXb	CBAF-IX-552	8-43: First flight Alex Henshaw 13-8-43: 222 Sqn. 15-6-44: 84 GSU 27-7-46: 76 MU for disposal. 19-2-47: Transferred to the Royal Netherlands AF as H-105, serving with 332 Sqn as H-68, later to become H-105. 9-10-53: Belgian Air Force as SM-41. 26-3-56: Sold to COGEA as a target tug, serialled OO-ARA.	MJ755	LF	IXc	CBAF-IX-1285	10-1-44: 33MU Lyneham. Feb 44: Despatched to Casablanca. 1947: Transferred to the Royal Hellenic Air Force.
					MJ783	LF	IXc	CBAF-IX-1301	27-4-44: 83GSU. 15-6-44: 132 Sqn. 27-7-44: 403 Sqn. 5-8-44: Cat E damage on Ops. Feb 48: Delivered from 29MU High Ercall to the Belgian AF as SM15 – flew until '51 with AFS. 7-1-52: Delivered to the Royal Army Museum.
MJ143	LF	IXc	CBAF-IX-907	16-10-43: 33MU 26-10-43: 486 Sqn. 19-5-44: 66 Sqn, suffered Category AC damage. 10-12-44: 33 MU 3-12-44: Air Service Training. 31-5-45: 39 MU. 17-6-46: Flown to Holland and the Royal Netherlands AF as H-1.	MK356	LF	IXc	CBAF-IX-1561	4-2-44: 9MU. 11-3-44: 443 Sqn. 13-6-44: Wheels up landing with 443 Sqn. 6-8-44: 83GSU. 2-10-45: to 5690M RAF Halton.
MJ147	LF	IXc		16-10-43: 33 MU Lyneham. 29-10-43: 403 ARF. 602 Sqn. 6-7-44: 421 Sqn. 24-3-44: 401 Sqn. 31-8-44: 411 Sqn. 10-9-44: 126 Wing. 5-10-44: 132 Wing. 10-2-45: Air Service	MK732	LF	IXc	CBAF-IX-1732	8-3-44: 39 MU. 25-4-44: 485 Sqn. 11-7-44: Damaged in a flying accident, repaired by 41 RSU, it suffered further damage in an air battle on 2 Sept needing major repair at No 1 Civilian Repair Unit at Cowley. Dec 44: 39 MU for storage. 28-6-48: allocated to the Royal Netherlands AF and despatched to Holland as H-25.

Serial No.	Type	Mark	Construction No.	Aircraft Military History	Serial No.	Type	Mark	Construction No.	Aircraft Military History
				19-4-51: Fighter School at Twente after storage. 322 Sqn at Soesterberg with 3W-17. 4-6-54: Written off charge, it moved to Eindhoven for decoy use on 1 July.					25-9-46: Royal Netherlands AF, as H-15. 4-48: 322 Sqn. 4-6-54: Struck off charge.
MK912	LF	IXc	CBAF-IX-1875	24-3-44: 8 MU at Little Rissington. 17-5-44: 84 Group Support Unit at RAF Aston Down. 8-6-44: 312 Sqn at Appledram coded DU-?. 22-6-44: returned to No 84 GSU. 30-11-44: Air Service Training, Exeter for repairs/mods. 18-4-45 33 MU Lyneham. 26-7-46: Sold to Royal Netherlands AF, moved to RAF Wroughton. 29-9-46: 47 MU RAF Sealand for packing. 19-5-47: to Dutch East Indies on SS *Rotti*. 47&48 stored at 2VB Andir. 17-3-48: 322 Sqn at Kalidjati as H-119, later H-59. 31-4-52: Bought by Belgian AF as SM-29. 11-6-52: To Ecole de Pilotage Advance at Brustem. Then to the Ecole de Chasse at Coxyde. 30-4-54: Withdrawn from service, stored at Brustem.	ML255	HF	IXc	CBAF-8342	19-4-44: 6 MU. 5-5-44: 127 Sqn. 8-7-44: 313 Sqn. 15-7-44: 118 Sqn. 3-2-45: 441 Sqn. 5-4-45: 313 Sqn. 2-8-45: Westland A/C Ltd. 16-11-48: Transferred to the South African AF as 5563.
					ML411	LF	IXc		26-4-44: 8 MU. 27-7-44: 403 Sqn. 24-8-44: Cat AC damage on ops. 31-8-44: 127 Wing. 7-12-44: 421 Sqn. 18-1-45: 302 Sqn. 8-2-45: 317 Sqn. 14-10-47: Sold to Turkey.
					ML417	LF	IXc	6S/730116	28-4-44: 6 MU Brize Norton. 22-6-44: 443 Sqn. 10-8-44: 127 Wg HQ. 29-9-44: 443 Sqn. 12-10-44: 401 Sqn. 5-4-45: 411 Sqn. 12-4-45: 412 Sqn 31-10-46: Sold Vickers-Armstrong at Eastleigh. 29-9-48: Converted to 2-seat trainer as G-15-11 Jan 49: transferred to the Indian AF as HS543.
MK923	LF	IXc	CBAF-	24-3-44: 9 MU Cosford. 10-5-44: 126 Sqn. 11-5-45: 39 MU. 19-5-47: Royal Netherlands AF as H-61 later H-104 Feb 53: Belgian Air Force as target tug SM-37. Sold to COGEA as target tug OO-ARF	ML427	LF	IXc	CBAF-IX-2131	29-4-44: 9 MU. 16-5-44: 350 ISU. 7-6-44: Rolls-Royce Hucknall for new engine. 27-8-45: 29 MU. 31-10-46: Vickers-Armstrong – South Marston as 6457M 15-10-47: 4 SoTT – School of Technical Training.
MK959	LF	IXc	CBAF-8125	15-4-44: 39 MU at Colerne. 3-5-44: 302 Sqn at Chailey 15-6-44: 329 Sqn coded 5A-K based at Merston. 30-8-44: 163 Sqn coded SK-M. 6-2-45: Scottish Aviation Ltd. 13-4-45: 29 MU High Ercall.	NH188	LF	IXc	CBAF-IX-2161	1-5-44: 6 MU. 18-5-44: Air Service Training. 15-6-44: 308 Sqn. 30-11-44: 416 Sqn. 17-9-45: 47 MU. 17-5-47: Sold to Royal Netherlands AF as H-64, later H-109 Served with 322 Sqn in Java

Serial No.	Type	Mark	Construction No.	Aircraft Military History	Serial No.	Type	Mark	Construction No.	Aircraft Military History
				3-53: Sold to Belgian Air Force as SM-39 Sold to COGEA as OO-ARC					Flight 6-12-42: 39MU at Colerne 14-12-42: 47MU 23-12-42: Sent to Gibraltar on the *Empire Tower*. 13-1-43: Arrived in Gibraltar. 28-2-43: Despatched to North West Africa. 26-4-45: Taken on strength of Mediterranean Air Force. 26-6-47: Transferred to the Italian Air Force as 4116. Sold later to the Israeli Air Force.
NH417	HF	IXc		20-5-44: 33 MU Lyneham. Served with 127, 313, 118, 441 & 329 Sqns 24-5-45: 58 OTU. 1-8-45: Westland Aircraft for overhaul. 22-12-45: 29 MU High Ercall 11-1-49: Flown to the Royal Danish Air Force as 41-401. Damaged on arrival. 13-4-51: Struck off charge RDAF.					
PV202	T	IXc	CBAF-IX-9590	18-9-44: 33 MU Lyneham. 9-10-44: 84 GSU. 19-10-44: 33 Sqn at Merville. 15-12-44: 84 GSU. 20-1-45: 83 GSU. 25-1-45: 412 Sqn RCAF, served with 2nd TAF in Holland and Germany. Credited with 3 kills (2x190s and 1x109) in 76 sorties. 29-7-45: 29 MU High Ercall. 19-7-50: Sold to Vickers-Armstrong and converted to type 509 – 2-seat trainer. 29-6-51: Sold to the Irish Air Corps as 161.	EN199	F	IXe		28-11-42: First flew from Eastleigh. 1-12-42: 12 MU. 9-12-42: 47 MU. 20-12-42: Despatched to Gibraltar aboard the *Marsalform*. 13-1-43: Arrived in Gibraltar 28-2-43: Sent to North West Africa. 1-8-43: Arrived in Sicily. 31-10-43: North African Allied Strategic Command. 23-12-43: Ground Accident Cat E – Blown away in a gale at Luqa, Malta when with 73 Sqn. 30-1-47: Struck off charge.
RR232	HF	IXc		14-10-44: 45MU. 26-10-44: Flying Accident Cat AC, repair on site. 6-45: involved in trials to test handling with rear fuselage fuel tanks. 17-3-45: ECFS. 21-4-48: Sold to the South African AF as 5632.	MA793	HF	IXe		19-7-43: 6 MU 27-7-43: 47 MU 5-8-43: Sent to North Africa on shipment SS732. 18-8-43: Arrived in Casablanca. 1-10-43: Sent to North West Africa. 31-5-44: Returned to UK 23-5-45: Air Service Training for refurb 9-2-48: 47 MU for storage. 30-9-48: Sold to the South African AF as 5601. Despatched on the *Clan Campbell*. 14-10-49: Struck off charge.
TE308	T	IXc	CBAF-IX-4497	9-6-45: 39 MU at Colerne. Jan 50: 29 MU High Ercall. July 50: Sold to Vickers-Armstrong. Converted to type 509 – two-seat trainer. 30-7-51: Irish Air Corps as IAC 163.	MH350	LF	IXe	CBAF-IX-490	7-8-43: 485 (New Zealand) Sqn at Hornchurch. 15-6-44: 84 GSU.
EN145	F	IXe	6S/240837	5-12-42: Chattis Hill, First					

Serial No.	Type	Mark	Construction No.	Aircraft Military History	Serial No.	Type	Mark	Construction No.	Aircraft Military History
				29-9-44: 64 Sqn – damaged on delivery. 14-4-45: 33 MU Lyneham. 10-5-45: 332 (Norwegian) Sqn, to Gardermoen. 13-12-50: 331 Sqn RNoAF. Placed in storage.					19-7-50: Sold to Vickers-Armstrong as Non-effective aircraft. VA Serial G-15-175. 1951: Converted to type 509 2-seat trainer. Sold to the Irish Air Corps as 162. Struck off charge July 1960.
MJ730	LF	IXe	CBAF-78883	12-12-43: 33MU Lyneham. 24-12-43: 222MU. 21-1-44: Sent to North Africa aboard the *Leeds City*. 17-2-44: Arrived in Casablanca. 30-11-44: Moved to the Middle East. 31-5-45: taken on strength Mediterranean Allied Air Forces. 27-6-46: Transferred to the Italian Air Force as MM4094 Sold to the Israeli AF as No 20-66, IDFAF56 & IDFAF66, although it also carried the Israeli ferry serial 0606.	NH238	HF	IXe	CBAF-IX-2200 and CBAF-8563	6-5-44: 6 MU Brize Norton. 30-8-44: 84 GSU. 9-6-45: 9 MU Cosford for long term storage. 29-7-46 : 76 MU Wroughton, prepared for sale to Royal Netherlands AF. 29-9-46: 47 MU Sealand for packing. 13-6-47: Despatched to RNAF aboard SS *Rotti*. 30-5-47: taken on charge RNAF and serialled H-60. Allocated to 322 Sqn. Jan 53: Sold to the Belgian Air Force as SM-36 and then to COGEA as OO-ARE.
ML119	LF	IXe	CBAF-IX-1892 or CBAF-8208	24-3-44: 9MU. 4-4-44: 1 Sqn. 6-12-46: Sold to the Czech AF. Sold on to the Israeli AF as 20-20. Passed to the Burmese AF as UB441.	PL344	LF	IXe		1-3-44: 8MU 24-8-44: 602 Sqn 28-9-44: 442 Sqn 26-12-44: Flying Accident Cat B 19-4-45: 401 Sqn 16-9-45: 130 Sqn. 6-5-46: 129 Sqn at Church Fenton 5-9-46: 151 RU – Repair Unit 10-12-46: Recat E.
ML196	HF	IXe		26-4-44: 8 MU. 22-5-44: 127 Sqn. 8-7-4: 313 Sqn. 15-7-44: 118 Sqn. 15-2-45: 441 Sqn. 5-4-45: 313 Sqn. 2-8-45: Westland Aircraft Ltd. 6-2-48: 47 MU. 10-8-48: delivered to South African AF, but crash-landed on delivery and not taken on charge.	PT462	HF	IXe		21-7-44: 39 MU 31-7-44: 215 MU 9-8-44: depatched to North Africa on the *Silver Sandal* 23-8-44: Arrived at Casablanca. 26-6-47: Sold to the Italian Air Force as MM4100 Sold on to Israel as 2067.
ML407	T	IXe	CBAF-8463	23-4-44: 33 MU Lyneham. 30-4-44: 485 Sqn. 12-10-44: Category AC Ops. 4-1-45: 341 Sqn. 11-1-45: 308 Sqn 8-2-45: 349 Sqn 22-3-45: 345 Sqn 19-4-45: 332 Sqn	PT601	HF	IXe	CBAF-IX-2716	22-7-44: 33 MU 7-8-44: 504 Sqn 23-4-45: 30 MU 23-6-45: 183 Sqn 9-8-45: 234 Sqn 5-8-48: Sold to the South African AF as 5573.

Serial No.	Type	Mark	Construction No.	Aircraft Military History	Serial No.	Type	Mark	Construction No.	Aircraft Military History
TE213	F	IXe	CBAF-11274	15-5-45: 33 MU Lyneham and stored. 1-7-47: To RAF Pershore for preparation for sale. 24-7-47: Flown to RAF Fayid, Egypt and thence to South Africa. 30-7-47: Taken on charge with the SAAF as 5518.	PL965	PR	XI	6S/504719	1944: Built at Aldermaston. 2-10-44: 9 MU Cosford. 18-1-45: 169 Sqn. 11-10-45: 151 Repair Unit. Then into storage. 8-7-47: Sold and ferried to Holland for ground instructional training at Deelen. 1952: Retired from training role.
TE517	LF	IXe	SH/ CBAF-IX-558	2-6-45: 33 MU Lyneham. 25-7-45: 313 (Czech) Sqn, to be transferred to Czech Air Force. 30-8-45: Taken on charge with Czech AF. Later sold to Israel as 2046.	PL983	PR	XI	6S/583723	31-10-44: 6 MU Brize Norton. 24-11-44: No 1 Pilots Pool (PR HQ). 22-2-45: 4 Sqn. 6-9-45: 2 Sqn. 12-1-46: 6 MU Brize Norton. 15-7-46: 39 MU Colerne. 33 MU Lyneham for storage.
TE554	LF	IXe	17-1351	26-5-45: 33 MU Lyneham 1-8-45: 310 (Czech) Sqn, to be transferred to the Czech AF. 30-8-45: Transferred to the Czech AF as KR-6 and A-708 July 52: Sold to the Israeli AF as 57. Call sign was 4X-FOG.	PL979	PR	XI	6S/583719	17-10-44: 9 MU Cosford. 18-1-46: 4 Sqn. 3-5-45: 151 Repair Unit. 6-9-45: 2 Sqn 31-1-46: 6 MU Brize Norton into storage. 15-7-47: Pershore for preparation to sell to RNoAF. 31-7-47: Ferried to Gardermoen, Norway.
TE565	LF	IXe	CBAF-	7-6-45: 33 MU Lyneham 30-7-45: 310 (Czech) Sqn, in preparation for transfer to the Czech AF. 30-8-45: Transferred to the Czech AF.					
TE5**	LF	IXe	SH/ CBAF-IX-550	Serial cannot be established.	EN244	F	XII	6S/197707	First flight from High Post Aerodrome.15-12-42: Allocated to Controller Research & Development, Farnborough for handling trials. 13-2-43: Air Service training – Hamble 15-5-44: 41 Sqn 27-6-44: Flying Accident Cat AC 15-12-44: Air Service Training Westland Aircraft Ltd for modifications. 14-5-45: 585 Sqn 4-7-46: Installed at the College of Aeronautics, Cranfield.
TE5**	LF	IXe	CBAF-IX-558	Serial cannot be established.					
'UB424'	LF	IXe							
PA908	PR	XI	6S/417723	Late 43: Built at Chattis Hill. 30-1-44: Taken on charge at RAF Benson. 4-3-44: 1 OADU – Overseas Aircraft Dispatch Unit. 17-3-44: Arrived with Air Command South East Asia. 5- & 6-44: 681 Sqn at Alipore, coded 'E'. 9-5-46: Struck off charge beyond economic repair, but probably stayed in India as ground instructional airframe. Transferred to the Indian AF as instructional airframe, serialled M342.	NH799	FR	XIV	6S/	Built at Aldermaston.16-2-45: 9 MU Cosford. 22-5-45: 215 MU, despatch to India. 2-7-45: Departed for India aboard the *Samsturdy*. 28-7-45: Arrived in India 9-8-45: taken on

Serial No.	Type	Mark	Construction No.	Aircraft Military History	Serial No.	Type	Mark	Construction No.	Aircraft Military History
				charge with Air Command South East Asia. 27-2-47: 49 Sqn, Flying Accident Cat CE. 29-12-47: Sold to the Indian AF.					2-12-45: Cat B damage on Ops – repaired at Air Service Training Hamble. 4-11-46: 610 Sqn 2-5-49: 6 MU Brize Norton. 1-2-50: Declared Non-effective aircraft. 14-11-50: Sold to Vickers-Armstrong. 4-51: Sold to the Belgian Air Force as SG-108. As IQ-V, she served with the Ecole de Chasse at Coxyde.
RM694	F	XIV	6S/432268	July 44: 33 MU Lyneham. 18-7-44: 91 (Nigeria) Sqn. 402 Sqn. 27-10-44: Air Service Training for repairs. 13-5-45: 6 MU Brize Norton. 13-7-45: CFE West Raynham Feb 49: 5 SoTT at Locking May '50: On display at Hornchurch. 60 MU Dishforth on the dump.	RM921	FR	XIVc	6S/432331	11-44: 30 MU 10-12-44: 33 MU Lyneham. Jan 45: 84 GSU Jan 45: 2 Sqn Aug 45: 414 Sqn Sep 45: 33 MU Lyneham. Aug 48: Sold to Belgian AF as SG-57 No 2 Wing de Chasse, Florennes.
RM873	F	XIV	6S/432296	8-10-44: 39 MU 25-10-44: 402 Sqn 8-11-44: Cat B damaged on Ops - Air Service Training for repair. 1-3-45: 130 Sqn – Category AC Ops 409 RSU for repair.10-5-45: 410 Sqn 26-7-45: 411 Sqn. 10-5-50: Sold to Vickers-Armstrong. 4-11-50: Sold to the Thai AF as U14-6/93.	SM832	F	XIVc	6S/663452	Built at Chattis Hill. Sold to the Indian AF
					MT847	FR	XIVe	6S/643779	Built at Keevil. 4-4-44: Production prototype for the introduction of thicker skin at tailplane root. 24-2-45: 6 MU Brize Norton 15-12-45: Issued to A&AEE, Boscombe Down for tests. 18-2-46: 29 MU High Ercall 14-11-50: 226 OCU at Stradishall, coded UU-A 2-8-51: 33 MU Lyneham 9-2-52: declared Non-effective aircraft 26-2-52: to 33 MU from NEA/rep to NEA/serviced and transfer from Cat 4RE to Cat 5. 30-4-52: Transferred to 90 MU Warton and displayed on the gate.
MV246	F	XIVc	6S/649170	23-11-44: first flight from Aldermaston 29-11-44: 9 MU Cosford 24-8-48: Sold to the Belgian Air Force as SG-55 Served with No. 1 Wing, 349 Sqn as GE-R. Written off 11-10-48 at Opvelp following crash.					
MV370	FR	XIVc		Built at Keevil. 10-2-45: 39 MU. 30-8-45: 83 MU – preparation for transfer to India. 4-9-45: Despatched to India aboard the *Ocean Gallent* 14-10-45: Arrived in India and registered as T.44. 29-11-45: Air Command South East Asia. 31-12-47: Sold to the Indian AF.	MV262	FR	XIVe	6S/649186	Built at Southampton 8-3-45: 9 MU Cosford 13-4-45: Despatched to India under SSLS2861. 21-5-45: Arrived in India. 31-12-47: Sold to the Indian AF.
NH904	FR	XIVc	6S/648206	Built at Aldermaston. 26-3-45: 6 MU Brize Norton 15-4-45: 414 Sqn	MV293	FR	XIVe	6S/649205	Built at Keevil 25-7-44: Production prototype for

Serial No.	Type	Mark	Construction No.	Aircraft Military History	Serial No.	Type	Mark	Construction No.	Aircraft Military History
				aileron mods 1-3-45: 33 MU Lyneham 20-8-45: 215 MU – preparation for despatch to India. 6-9-45: sailed for India aboard the SS *Deelank* 14-10-45: Arrived in India. 31-12-47: Sold to the Indian AF. Served as instructional airframe at Jalahalli Technical College- reg T.20.					Sept 45: 61 OTU. Dec 45: 9 MU Cosford for storage. June 47: 612 Sqn RAuxAF at Dyce. 27-10-49: 6 MU Brize Norton for storage. May 50: Sold to Vickers-Armstrong. Sold to the Thai Air Force as U14-1/93.
NH749	FR	XIVe	6S/583887	Built at Aldermaston. 23-2-45: 33 MU Lyneham. 20-5-45: 215 MU – preparation for India. 2-7-45: Despatched to India aboard the *Samsturdy*. 28-7-45: Arrived in India as T.3.9-8-45: Air Command South East Asia.29-12-47: Sold to the Indian AF.	TZ138	FR	XIVe	6S/676505	Built at Aldermaston. July 45: delivered to the Controller of Research and Development at Rolls-Royce Hucknall. 47 MU Sealand for despatch to Canada for winterisation trials. Nov 45: Arrived in New-foundland aboard the SS *Alda Park*. Completed a large number of trials before being sold off.
RM797	F	XIVe	6S/534585	Built at Southampton. Sep 44: 33 MU Lyneham. 15-9-44: 41 Sqn at Lympne. 22-10-45: 29 MU High Ercall into storage. May 50: Sold to Vickers-Armstrong. Sold on to Thailand as U14 16/93.	RR263	LF	XVIe	CBAF-IX-3310	Oct 44: Built at Castle Bromwich. 19-10-44: 45 GSU at Kinloss. 23-11-44: 66 Sqn at Grimbergen. 21-6-45: 416 (RCAF) Sqn. 22-10-45: 29 MU High Ercall. 28 4 49: 6 MU Brize Norton. 31-8-51: 4 CAACU at Llandow as a target tug. 31-7-54: 9 MU Cosford for storage.
RM927	FR	XIVe	6S/381758	21-11-44: 30 MU Sealand 2-12-44: 39 MU Colerne. 6-1-45: 83 GSU. 25-1-45: 403 (RCAF) Sqn. 4-5-45: Air Service Training Hamble for repair. 1-11-45: 29 MU High Ercall in storage. 14-11-47: Sold to the Belgian AF as SG-25.	RW382	LF	XVIe	CBAF-IX-4640	20-7-45: 6 MU Brize Norton. 1-4-47: 604 RAuxAF Sqn. 14-4-50: 33 MU Lyneham. 11-6-51: 3 CAACU at Exeter. 17-10-51: Control & Reporting School, Middle Wallop. 14-7-53: 45 MU at Kinloss. 28-7-53: 29 MU High Ercall 14-12-54: Declared non-effective.
RN201	F	XIVe	6S/663417	Built at Keevil. 22-2-45: 9 MU Cosford. July 45: 83 GSU. Dec 45: 350 (Belgian) Sqn at Fassberg. May 46: 29 MU High Ercall. Feb 48: Sold to the Belgian AF as SG-31.					
SM914	FR	XIVe	6S/662808	Built at Keevil. 31-5-45: 29 MU High Ercall.	RW386	LF	XVIe	CBAF-	2-8-45: 6 MU Brize Norton 25-3-47: 604 RAuxAF Sqn

Serial No.	Type	Mark	Construction No.	Aircraft Military History
				as NG-D. 24-1-52: 58 MU Skellingthorpe as 6944M 30-8-57: 1 SoTT at Halton.
RW388	LF	XVIe	CBAF-IX-4646	18-7-45: 6 MU Brize Norton 2-8-45: 667 Sqn. 9-5-46: 29 MU High Ercall. 12-1-49: 6 MU Brize Norton 2-6-49: 5 Sqn. 1-4-51: 612 Sqn 4-7-51: Fighter Command Control & Reporting School, Middle Wallop. 1-1-52: Colerne as 6946M.
RW393	LF	XVIe	CBAF-IX-4651	20-7-45: 6 MU Brize Norton. 3-11-47: 203 Advanced Flying School. 22-1-48: Fighter Command Control & Reporting School, Middle Wallop. Personal Aircraft of AOC Fighter Command – in the charge of 31 Sqn. 28-10-53: 3 CAACU at Exeter. 6-7-54: 45 MU Kinloss. 13-12-54: declared non-effective.
SL542	LF	XVIe	CBAF-IX-4656	Built at Castle Bromwich in 1945. 18-7-45: 9 MU Cosford. 30-8-45: 595 Sqn. Cat 3 Flying accident 3-7-45. Repaired at 34 MU Stoke Heath by 24-11-45 and returned to Sqn. 28-7-48: 695 Sqn coded 4M-N. 7-12-50: 1 CAACU at Hornchurch. 11-6-51: 29 MU High Ercall. 1-3-54: 2 CAACU at Little Snoring. 1-4-55: Stn Flt Duxford. 31-1-57: 58 MU. 31-5-57: Reclassified Cat 5 by 5 MU at Kemble. 8390M.
SL574	LF	XVIe	CBAF-IX-4688	14-8-45: 6 MU Brize Norton. 28-10-48: Flying Accident Cat AC.

Serial No.	Type	Mark	Construction No.	Aircraft Military History
				19-7-49: Central Gunnery School Sept 49: 3 CAACU at Exeter 8391M Joined the Battle of Britain Flight, Biggin Hill. 20-9-59 Force-landed on the Oxo cricket ground Bromley in Kent.
SL611	LF	XVIe		20-8-45: 33 MU Lyneham. 27-9-45: 111 OTU. 3-1-46: 29 MU High Ercall. 19-2-47: 603 Sqn. 20-11-47: hit mountain on ferry flight from Hawarden to Turnhouse.
SL674	LF	XVIe	CBAF-IX-4701	Built CBAF in 1945. 26-7-45: 29MU High Ercall. 1-4-46: 17 OTU. 23-10-46: 6 MU Brize Norton. 7-8-47: 501 Sqn as RAB-R. 29-4-49: 612 Sqn. 17-7-51: Moved to 9 MU Cosford for storage. To 8392M. 11-9-54: Flown to Biggin Hill for display next to the Chapel.
SL721	LF	XVIe	CBAF-IX-4756	27-8-45: 6 MU Brize Norton. 10-10-46: Fighter Command Comms Sqn North. 5-2-48: Met Com Sqn. 17-7-48: Flying Accident Cat A To Vickers-Armstrong – 135 South Marston Special finish, gun bays removed, converted to luggage compartment. 17-12-48: Delivered by M Lithgow to RAF Bovington for use of AOC Fighter Command. Was known as the 5 Star Spitfire, although Robb was only entitled to four.
SM411	LF	XVIe	CBAF-IX-3495	Nov 45: 45 MU Kinloss. No 83 Group Support Unit. 421 (RCAF) Sqn. July 45: No 83 Group Support Unit at Dunsfold. Apr 51: 102 FRS - Flight

Serial No.	Type	Mark	Construction No.	Aircraft Military History	Serial No.	Type	Mark	Construction No.	Aircraft Military History
				Refresher School. 30-6-51: 103 FRS – Flight Refresher School at Full Sutton. Oct 51: 9 MU Cosford. Oct 53: 3 CAACU at Exeter. May 54: 9 MU Cosford. Dec 54: declared non-effective.					24-3-45: 453 Sqn, 2nd TAF, at Matlaske. 21-6-45: 183 (Gold Coast) Sqn.5-7-45: 567 Sqn. 20-6-46: 691 Sqn at Chivenor. 15-3-51: 3 CAACU at Exeter. 17-7-51: Cat 5 damage sustained. 28-9-51: Struck off charge.
TB252	LF	XVIe	CBAF-IX-3807	6-1-45: 9 MU Cosford. 1-3-45: 329 (Free French) Sqn (les Cicoques) at Turnhouse. 15-3-45: 341 (Free French) Sqn. 15-1-46: 350 Sqn (of No 146 Wing) at Fassberg. 15-10-46: 151 RU. 29-5-47: 61 OTU at Keevil. Stayed there when the Unit became 203 Advanced Flying School. 18-1-49: Old Sarum. 27-2-53: 33 MU Lyneham as 7257M. 12-9-55: Odiham for ground instruction use.	TB885	LF	XVIe		Feb 45: 322 (RNAF) Sqn in France & Germany. 28-6-55: Struck off RAF charge at 9 MU Cosford. RAF Kenley for fire fighting practice.
					TD135	LF	XVIe	CBAF-IX-4218	March 45: 6 MU Brize Norton. May 45: AFDS at Tangmere. March 47: 604 RAuxAF Sqn at Hendon. 11-11-50: Cat 5 damaged. 23-11-50: relegated to 6798M.
TB382	LF	XVIe		Built at Castle Bromwich in late 1944. 19-1-45: 6 MU Brize Norton. 21-2-45: 602 RAuxAF Sqn at Ludham. 22-7-45: 29 MU High Ercall. 16-12-54: Declared non-effective.	TD248	LF	XVIe	CBAF-IX-4262	16-5-45: 6 MU Brize Norton. 695 Sqn. 31-8-51: 2 CAACU at Little Snoring. 27-5-54: 9 MU Cosford. 14-12-54: Declared non-effective.
TB752	LF	XVIe	CBAF-IX-4113	21-2-45: 33 MU Lyneham. 66 Sqn at Linton-on-Ouse and then into Holland. 19-4-45: 403 (RCAF) Sqn at Diepholtz. Accounted for four enemy aircraft with 403 Sqn. 2-8-45: 29 MU High Ercall. 19-4-51: 102 FRS – Flight refresher school. May 51: 103 FRS. 24-8-53: 29 MU High Ercall. 23-11-53: 5 CAACU at Llanbedr. 24-11-54: 33 MU Lyneham. Dec 54: Declared non-effective.	TE184	LF	XVIe	CBAF-IX-4394	30-5-45: 9 MU Cosford. 12-10-45: 20 MU at Aston Down. 16-9-46: 6 MU Brize Norton. 7-9-48: 203 Advanced Flying School. 27-2-50: 607 RAuxAF Sqn at Ouston. 13-6-50: 33 MU Lyneham. 9-11-50: Central Gunnery School at Leconfield. 27-2-51: relegated to 6850M after Cat 5 damage sustained.
TB863	LF	XVIe	CBAF-10895	27-2-45: 19 MU St Athan.	TE214	LF	XVIe	CBAF-IX-4424	April 45: Built at Castle Bromwich. April 45: 9 MU Cosford. 11-7-45: Central Gunnery School, Leconfield. 8-3-50: Struck off charge from CGS after Cat 5 damage.

Serial No.	Type	Mark	Construction No.	Aircraft Military History	Serial No.	Type	Mark	Construction No.	Aircraft Military History
TE288	LF	XVIe	CBAF-11414	1-6-45: 9 MU Cosford. 61 OTU at Keevil 9-5-45: 9 MU Cosford after accident. 14-11-48: 501 RAuxAF at Filton. March 49: 6 MU Brize Norton. April 51: 102 Flight refresher School at North Luffenham. Oct 51: 33 MU Lyneham for storage.13-1254: Declared non-effective.					501 Sqn at Filton. March 49: 612 RAuxAF Sqn at Dyce. July 51: Repaired at Gatwick by AST. 3-7-52: Cat 4R damage sustained. 9 MU Cosford. Aug 54: 20 MU Aston Down. 20-9-54: 9 MU Cosford. Dec 54: Declared non-effective.
TE311	LF	XVIe	CBAF-IX-4497	16-6-45: 39 MU Colerne. 5-10-45: Empire Central Flying School at Hullavington. 17-2-46: 33 MU Lyneham for storage. 31-5-51: 1689 FPT. 31-7-52: Flying Training Command. 9-4-53: Ferry Training Unit at Benson. 23-9-53: 33 MU Lyneham. 12-1-54: 2 CAACU at Langham. 23-2-54: 33 MU Lyneham. 13-12-54: Declared non-effective.	TE392	LF	XVIe	CBAF-IX-4551	15-6-45: 9 MU Cosford. 11-2-46: Heston Aircraft Ltd. 8-3-46: 126 Sqn, and the 65 Sqn at Hethel. 29-8-46: 164 Sqn at Middle Wallop. Dec 47: 63 Sqn at Thorney Island. May 48: 595 Sqn. 29-7-48: 695 Sqn. 31-8-51: 2 CAACU at Little Snoring. 1-9-52: Cat 5 damaged and relegated to 7000M.
TE330	LF	XVIe	CBAF-11446	14-6-45: 9 MU Cosford. Feb 47: 601 RAuxAF Sqn at Hendon. March 50: 6 MU Brize Norton. Sept 51: 9 MU Cosford. Jan 54: 2 CAACU at Langham. April 55: 29 MU High Ercall. May 56: 20 MU Aston Down. 16-6-56: 5 MU Kemble. 16-7-57: Declared non-effective.	TE456	LF	XVIe	CBAF-IX-4590 or CBAF-23682	3-8-45: 6 MU Brize Norton into storage. 21-3-46: 501 RAuxAF Sqn at Filton. 12-5-49: 612 RAuxAF Sqn at Dyce. 15-7-51: 9 MU Cosford. 17-8-53: 33 MU Lyneham. 29-9-53: 3 CAACU at Exeter. August 55: 33 MU Lyneham. Included in film *Reach for the Sky*. 16-7-56: 47 MU Sealand. 30-9-56: Despatched to Domain War Museum, Auckland Institute.
TE356	LF	XVIe	CBAF-11470	23-6-45: 29 MU High Ercall. 11-7-45: 695 Sqn. 14-2-49: 34 Sqn. 20-8-51: 2 CAACU at Little Snoring. 1-9-52: became ground instructional airframe.	TE462	LF	XVIe	CBAF-IX-4596	26-6-45: 39 MU Colerne. 22-2-50: 33 MU Lyneham. 11-10-50: Station Flight at Finningley. 6-9-51: 101 Flying Refresher School. 29 MU High Ercall. 14-12-54: Declared non-effective.
TE384	LF	XVIe	CBAF-11485	3-8-45: 6 MU Brize Norton. May 47: 603 RAuxAF Sqn at Turnhouse.	TE476	LF	XVIe	CBAF-IX-4610	30-6-45: 39 MU Colerne into storage. 19-10-49: 33 MU

Serial No.	Type	Mark	Construction No.	Aircraft Military History	Serial No.	Type	Mark	Construction No.	Aircraft Military History
				Lyneham. 4-7-51: 1 CAACU at Hornchurch. 11-9-56: 5 MU Kemble. 17-1-57: Declared non-effective.					31-7-47: Returned to the UK. 31-12-47: Sold to the Indian Air Force as HS687.
					SM969	FR	XVIIIe	6S/663052	Built at Keevil. 30-8-45: 6 MU Brize Norton. 10-1-46: 76 MU Wroughton for packing. 19-1-46: despatched for Karachi aboard SS *Sampenn*. 28-2-46: Taken on charge with ACSEA. Stored. 2-6-47: Returned to the UK. 24-8-47: 47 MU Sealand. July 49: Sold to R&J Parkes, thence to Indian Air Force as HS877.
TP285	FR	XVIII	6S/672268	Built at Aldermaston. 2-7-45: 39 MU Colerne. 11-12-45: 76 MU Wroughton for packing. 18-1-46: Shipped from Glasgow aboard SS *Fort Saleesh*. 12-2-46: Arrived in Karachi. 28-2-46: Allocated to ACSEA and stored. 27-11-47: Brought back on charge in Mauripor. 31-12-47: Sold to the Indian Air Force as HS649.					
					SM986	F	XVIIIe	6S/64388/ or 6S/699526	Built at Southampton. 11-10-45: 33 MU Lyneham. 27-12-45: 76 MU Wroughton for packing. 19-1-46: despatched for Karachi aboard SS *Sampenn*. 18-2-46: 320 MU for storage. June 47: Returned to the UK. 47 MU Sealand for storage. 30-6-49: Sold to R&J Parkes, thence to Indian Air Force as HS986.
TP367	F	XVIII	HAI/6S/ 663145	Built at Aldermaston. 22-10-45: 33 MU Lyneham. 1-12-45: 76 MU Wroughton. 29-12-45: Shipped to India aboard the *Clan MacBrayne*. 31-1-46: Arrived in Karachi. 14-2-46: Allocated to ACSEA and stored. 31-12-47: Sold to the Indian Air Force as HS669.					
TZ219	F	XVIII	6S/676555	8-12-45: 33 MU Lyneham. 27-12-45: 47 MU Sealand. 19-1-46: despatched for Karachi aboard SS *Sampenn*. 11-2-46: Arrived at Karachi. 28-2-46: Taken on charge with ACSEA. Stored. 31-12-47: Sold to the Indian Air Force.	TP276	FR	XVIIIe	6S/676368	Built at Aldermaston. June 45: 33 MU Lyneham. 47 MU Sealand for despatch to Far East. 18-1-46: Shipped from Glasgow aboard SS *Fort Saleesh*. Feb 46: arrived Karachi and stored. Nov 47: Brought back on charge in Mauripor. 31-12-47: Sold to the Indian Air Force as HS653.
SM845	FR	XVIIIe	6S/672224	Built at Southampton. 28-5-45: 39 MU Colerne. 13-12-45: 76 MU Wroughton. 19-1-46: despatched for Karachi aboard SS *Sampenn*. 11-2-46: Arrived in Karachi. 28-2-46: On charge with ACSEA and stored.	TP280	FR	XVIIIe	6S/676372	June 45: 39 MU Colerne. Feb 46: 76 MU Wroughton for packing. Feb 46: Shipped from Birkenhead to Karachi aboard the SS *Farautia*. March 46: Arrived Karachi and stored.

Serial No.	Type	Mark	Construction No.	Aircraft Military History	Serial No.	Type	Mark	Construction No.	Aircraft Military History
				31-12-47: Sold to the Indian Air Force as HS654.					15-1-51: AGT Gatwick for refurbishment and storage. 15-3-54: THUM Flight at Woodvale. 14-4-54: Cat 4R damage caused. 16-7-54: Struck off charge.
PM627	PR	XIX	6S/683524 or 6S/725878	Built at Southampton. 6 MU Brize Norton in store. April 49: 2 Sqn, 2 TAF. 9-3-51: AGT Gatwick for refurbishment. 4-6-52: 9 MU Cosford for storage. Early 53: Purchased by AGT Gatwick for the Indian Air Force. Despatched to India as HS964.	PS836	PR	XIX	6S/637129	Built at Southampton. 4-1-45: No 1 Pilots Pool at Benson. May 45: 542 Sqn. Stored at 6 MU Brize Norton. 10-1-51: Air transported to Far East Air Force via Chivenor. Jan 51: 81 Sqn at Seletar Singapore. June 54: Transferred to the Royal Thai Air Force as U14-27/97.
PM630	PR	XIX	6S/683527	Built at Southampton. 26-11-45: A&AEE at Boscombe Down. 1-4-47: 6 MU Brize Norton for storage. 10-2-49: 541 Sqn. 1-3-50: Transfer to Bomber Command. 28-2-51: 237 OCU. 18-7-51: AGT Gatwick for repair. June 52: 9 MU Cosford for storage. Dec 52: 47 MU Sealand for packing. 18-1-53: Shipped to Seletar aboard the SS *Mentor*. 19-2-53: 390 MU Seletar. 7-8-54: Struck off charge having been transferred to the Royal Thai Air Force.	PS853	PR	XIX	6S/594677	Built at Southampton. 13-1-45: Central Photographic Reconn Unit at Benson. 1-3-45: 16 Sqn at Melsbroek. 268 Sqn 18-9-45: 16 Sqn. 18-4-46: 29 MU High Ercall for storage. 17-1-49: Cat B damage caused. 30-3-49: 6 MU Brize Norton. 13-7-49: 9 MU Cosford. THUM Flight at Woodvale.
PM631	PR	XIX	6S/683528	Built at Reading. 6-11-45: 6 MU Brize Norton. 6-5-49: 203 Advanced Flying School at Keevil. 13-1-50: 6 MU Brize Norton. 30-6-50: 9 MU Cosford. 15-1-51: Station Flight Buckeberg. 10-2-51: 9 MU Cosford. 2-7-51: THUM Flight at Hooton Park. 11-7-57: Historic Aircraft Flight at Biggin Hill.	PS890	PR	XIX	6S/585110	Built at Southampton. Early 45: 6 MU Brize Norton. 30-4-45: RAF Benson. June 45: 542 Sqn. Oct 45: 6 MU Brize Norton for storage. Dec 50: Allocated to the Far East Air Force. 10-1-51: Arrived Seletar via Chivenor. 81 Sqn Seletar June 55: Transferred to the Royal Thai Air Force as U14-26/97.
PM651	PR	XIX	6S/687107	Built at Reading. 27-11-45: Controller of Research and Development at White Waltham. 31-7-47: ML Aviation. 30-9-47: 6 MU Brize Norton.	PS915	PR	XIX	6S/585121	Built at Southampton. 17-4-45: 6 MU Brize Norton. 21-6-45: 541 Sqn. 20-12-45: No 1 Pilots Pool at Benson. 22-7-46: PR Development Unit at Benson. 8-7-48: 2 Sqn. 4-6-54: THUM Flight at

Serial No.	Type	Mark	Construction No.	Aircraft Military History	Serial No.	Type	Mark	Construction No.	Aircraft Military History
				Woodvale. 13-6-57: Historic Aircraft Flight at Biggin Hill.					24-2-49:611 RAuxAF Sqn coded RAR-D. June 51: AGT Gatwick for refurb. 45 MU Kinloss. 14-8-52: Loan to Ministry of Supply. May 53: Vickers for mods. 5 MU Kemble as non-effective aircraft.
LA198	F	21	SMAF-4338	Built at South Marston. 2-10-44: 33 MU Lyneham. 3-5-45: No1 Sqn at Manston coded JX-C. 4-10-45: 9 MU Cosford. 12-5-46: 602 RAuxAF Sqn coded RAI-G. 25-10-47: Cat A damage caused. 11-5-48: Repairs completed by 63 MU. 22-7-49: Cat B damage caused. 21-7-50: Repairs completed by Vickers. 27-7-50: 33 MU Lyneham. 19-9-51: 3 CAACU Exeter. 19-2-54: 187 Sqn ATC as 7118M.	PK624	F	22	CBAF-189	21-12-45: 33 MU Lyneham into store. 5-12-46: Vickers at South Marston for mods. 6-6-47: 6 MU Brize Norton into store. 26-8-48: 614 RAuxAF Sqn at Llandow. 31-10-50: 6 MU Brize Norton into store. 9 MU Cosford. Jan 51: AGT Gatwick for refurb. 26-7-52: 9 MU Cosford into store. 16-6-53: Declared non-effective. 14-2-54: Sold to Vickers-Armstrong.
LA226	F	21	SMAF-4371	Built at South Marston. 21-2-45: 33 MU Lyneham. 7-3-45: 91 (Nigerian) Sqn at West Malling. 17-4-46: 122 Sqn at Dalcross. 15-12-47: Declared non-effective at 9 MU Cosford. 28-11-49: 33 MU Lyneham. 3 CAACU Exeter 18-1-54: Retired as 7119M.	PK664	F	22	CBAF-217	5-12-45: 39 MU Colerne into store. 14-3-47: Vickers at South Marston for mods. 25-6-47: 33 MU Lyneham into store. 11-5-49: 615 RAuxAF Sqn at Biggin Hill. 14-12-50: 33 MU Lyneham into store. 2-2-51: AGT Gatwick for refurb. 2-7-51: 9 MU Cosford into store. 16-6-53: Declared non-effective. 4-2-54: Sold to Vickers.
LA255	F	21	SMAF-4388	Built at South Marston. 10-4-45: 39 MU Colerne. 29-6-45: No 1 Sqn. 13-11-47: Cat E damage caused. RAF Tangmere as 6490M.					
PK355	F	22	CBAF-	3-8-45: 39 MU Colerne. Oct 46: Vickers for mods. 16-11-47: 6 MU Brize Norton. Early 51: Sold to South Rhodesian AF. 14-3-51: Departed UK under own power. 28-3-51: Arrived Cranbourne, Rhodesia and serialled SR65.	PK683	F	24	CBAF-236	13-8-46: 33 MU Lyneham into store. 1950: 47 MU Sealand for packing. 10-8-50: Birkenhead Docks for despatch. 13-9-50: Arrived Singapore, No 30 Maintenance base. 31-7-51: Singapore Auxiliary AF. 29-2-52: Flying accident. 10-2-53: 390 MU Seletar. 15-4-54: Struck off charge as 7150M.
PK481	F	22	CBAF-70	3-9-45: 33 MU Lyneham into store. 11-12-47: Eastleigh for mods. June 48: 39 MU Colerne into store.					

Serial No.	Type	Mark	Construction No.	Aircraft Military History
PK724	F	24	CBAF-61255	30-10-46: 33 MU Lyneham into store. 9-2-50: 9 MU Cosford into store. 14-12-54: Declared non-effective as 7288M.
VN485	F	24	SMAF-21567	Built at Castle Bromwich – completed at Vickers South Marston. 29-8-47: 9 MU Cosford into store. 30-6-49: RNAS Renfrew for packing to Far East. 25-8-49: Arrived Seletar and stored. Sept 50: 80 Sqn Hong Kong. Jan 51: Take off accident. Oct 51: Back with 80 Sqn. Jan 52: Royal Hong Kong Aux AF at Kai Tak. 31-7-55: Stored at Kai Tak. 30-9-55: Struck off charge.

Appendix 2: Surviving Seafires.

The machines that appear in the following table are verified as existing and wholly recognisable Seafires – albeit in various states of repair. Many are being painstakingly restored to flying condition as both parts and the necessary funding allow and others are static exhibits in museums around the world. As with their land borne brethren, the numbers of Seafires in a state approaching 'live' have increased over recent years and – with the collection of three F.XV examples now under cover in Myanmar (formerly Burma), those that have been around for some time look set to be preserved for the foreseeable future.

Serial No.	Type	Mark	Construction No.	Aircraft Military History	Serial No.	Type	Mark	Construction No.	Aircraft Military History
MB293	LF	IIc	6S/65239292	Built by Supermarine as F.IIc, first flight 21-11-42. 8-11-42: Converted to LF.IIC at Air Service Training, Hamble. 29-11-49: 15 MU. 14-12-42: Boscombe Down for trials of smoke bomb and general purpose bombs. 879 Sqn aboard HMS *Attacker*.					Air Corps at 157. 27-10-53: Withdrawn from service.
					PP972	LF	IIIc		Built at Westlands in 1944. 1945: 809 Sqn. May 46: 767 Sqn at Easthaven and Lossiemouth. Early 1948: One of 65 LF.IIIc Seafires to be sold to France. Assigned to Flottille 1 and Flottille 12, and served in Vietnam.
RX168	LF	III		Built at Westlands in 1944. 20-1-45: Royal Naval Disposal Account. Before 12-9-47: With Vickers-Armstrong at South Marston for Refurbishment. 27-9-47: Delivered to Irish	PR376	F	XV	CO-9621	Built by Cunliffe Owen Aircraft Ltd. 30-6-45: Royal Naval Disposal Account. 805 Sqn at Machrihanish

Serial No.	Type	Mark	Construction No.	Aircraft Military History	Serial No.	Type	Mark	Construction No.	Aircraft Military History
				Sold to Vickers-Armstrong for refurbishment – test flying serial G-15-220. Sold to Burma as UB409.					5-2-46: First Line Reserve at Henstridge. 5-4-46: Moved to Fleetlands. 17-6-47: Moved to Westlands in Ilchester for mods. 26-8-47: Gosport for storage. 27-2-48: Moved to Fleetlands. 21-4-48: Receipt & Despatch Unit at Anthorn 18-6-51: 1831 Sqn Sqn Royal Naval Volunteer Reserve at Stretton. 6-11-51: 759 Sqn at Culdrose. 12-5-53: Stored at Stretton. 9-7-53: 764 Sqn at Yeovilton. 6-5-55: Struck off charge and stored for display purposes. 12-8-58: Brought back on charge for display.
PR422	F	XV	CO-9675	Built by Cunliffe Owen Aircraft Ltd. 6-9-45: Royal Naval Disposal Account. Sold to Vickers-Armstrong for refurbishment – test flying serial G-15-226. Sold to Burma as UB415.					
PR451	F	XV	CO-9673	Built by Cunliffe Owen Aircraft Ltd. 4-10-45: Royal Naval Disposal Account. 1-6-46: Sold to Royal Canadian Navy despatched aboard HMCS *Warrior*. 803 Sqn, part of 1st Training Group at Dartmouth, Nova Scotia. 25-5-49: Struck off charge.					
					SX300	F	XVII		Built at Westlands. Early service history not known. 28-2-46: Royal Navy Disposal Account. Sept 54: RNAS Bramcote for possible ground instructional use.
PR503	F	XV	COA-30621	Built by Cunliffe Owen Aircraft Ltd. 7-12-45: Royal Naval Disposal Account. 1-6-46: Sold to Royal Canadian Navy despatched aboard HMCS *Warrior*. 803 Sqn, part of 1st Training Group at Dartmouth, Nova Scotia.					
					SX336	F	XVII	FLWA/25488	Built at Westlands. Early service history not known. 30-4-46: Royal Navy Disposal Account. June 54: RNAS Bramcote for possible ground instructional use.
SR462	F	XV	WASE-14106	10-2-45: Royal Naval Disposal Account. 20-2-45: 33 MU Lyneham. Sold to Vickers-Armstrong for refurbishment – test flying serial G-15-225. Sold to Burma as UB414.					
					LA546	F	46	SMAF-19989	One of only 24 Mk.46 Seafires built. Built at Castle Bromwich 1945. Final assembly at South Marston. 25-3-46: RNAS Anthorn.
SW800	F	XV	WASP-4417	30-6-45: Royal Naval Disposal Account. 7-7-45: 33 MU Lyneham. 1831 Sqn Sqn Royal Naval Volunteer Reserve at Stretton. 6-55: Vickers-Armstrong, Worthy Down for spares.					
					LA564	F	46	SMAF-19985	Built at Castle Bromwich 1945. Final assembly at South Marston. 14-3-46: First flight. 2-5-46: Controller of Research & Development at High Post. 14-9-46: Aircraft & Armament Experimental
SX137	F	XVII	WASE-15325	Built by Westlands in 1945. 22-9-45: Receipt & Despatch Unit at Culham.					

Serial No.	Type	Mark	Construction No.	Aircraft Military History
				Establishment, handling trials with bomb loads – Jeffrey Quill pilot. 14-10-46: RNAS Fleet. March 47: 781 Training Sqn at Lee-on-Solent. 9-5-47: RNAS Gosport. July 47: 1832 Sqn Royal Naval Volunteer Reserve at Culham. Jan 49: Receipt & Despatch Unit at Anthorn April 50: 767 Sqn. July 50: 738 Sqn. 29-6-51: Struck off charge from RNAS Anthorn. Sold as scrap – Carlisle.
VP441	FR	47	6S/73229	Built by Supermarine in 1947. 29-11-47: Royal Navy Disposal Account. 30-11-47: to Supermarine South Marston. 15-12-47: RNAS Anthorn

Appendix 3: Spitfire Powerplants.

I have discussed at some length the two Rolls-Royce engines that powered the Spitfire exclusively throughout its R.A.F. career in this book. The development of the machine could not have taken place without a parallel development path for the engines – the Merlin and the Griffon. In this appendix, the association of the powerplants and the airframes is charted by listing which Spitfires made use of which engines.

Merlin engines: 12-cylinder, 60-degree V, liquid-cooled, 27 litres.

Engine	Type	Mark	Power (hp)	Weight (lb)	Notes
C	K5054	Prototype	1,045	1,370	K5054 only.
F	K5054	Prototype	1,045	1,410	K5054 engine tests.
II	F.	Mk I	1,030	1,440	K9787 to K9960 production.
III	F.	Mk I	1,030	1,440	K9961 onwards. Production.
IIIM	Speed Spitfire		2,160	1,400	Heavily modified engine using 100-octane fuel.
XII	F.	Mk IIa	1,150	1,450	Mk II production & specials.
XII	F.	Mk IIb	"	"	Mk II production & specials.
XII	LF.	Mk IIc	"	"	Mk II production & specials.
XX	LF.	Mk III	1,240	1,450	Experimental & trials.
32	PR.	XIII	1,470	1,385	Improved take-off power.
45	F.	Va	1,470	1,385	Converted Mk Is.
45	F.	Vb	"	"	Converted Mk Is.
45	F.	Vc	"	"	Converted Mk Is.
45	PR.	IV	"	"	Photo-recon Spitfires.
45M	LF.	Va	1,585	1,385	Converted Mk Is. Clipped wings.
45M	LF.	Vb	"	"	Converted Mk Is. Clipped wings.
45M	LF.	Vc	"	"	Converted Mk Is. Clipped wings.
46	F.	Va	1,415	1,385	Converted Mk Is.
46	F.	Vb	"	"	Converted Mk Is.
46	F.	Vc	"	"	Converted Mk Is.
46	PR.	IV	"	"	Photo-recon Spitfires.
47	HF.	VI	1,415	1,400	High flying Mk V.
50	F.	Va	1,470	1,390	Converted Mk Is.
50	F.	Vb	"	"	Converted Mk Is.
50	F.	Vc	"	"	Converted Mk Is.
50	PR.	IV	"	"	Photo-recon Spitfires.
50A	F.	Va	1,470	1,390	Converted Mk Is.
50A	F.	Vb	"	"	Converted Mk Is.
50A	F.	Vc	"	"	Converted Mk Is.
50A	PR.	IV	"	"	Photo-recon Spitfires.
50M	LF.	Va	"	"	Converted Mk Is. Clipped wings.
50M	LF.	Vb	"	"	Converted Mk Is. Clipped wings.
50M	LF.	Vc	1,585	1,385	Converted Mk Is. Clipped wings.
55	PR.	IV	1,470	1,400	Photo-recon Spitfires.
55M	LF.	Va	1,585	1,385	Converted Mk Is. Clipped wings.
56	F.	Va	1,470	1,400	Converted Mk Is.
56	F.	Vb	"	"	Converted Mk Is.
56	F.	Vc	"	"	Converted Mk Is.
56	PR.	IV	"	"	Photo-recon Spitfires.
60	LF.	III	1,565	1,630	Experimental & trials.
61	F.	IX	1,565	1,640	Strengthened Mk V.
61	F.	IXe	"	"	E wing fit.
61	F.	VII	"	"	Strengthened Mk VI.
61	F.	VIII	"	"	Strengthened Mk VII.
61	LF.	III	"	"	Experimental & trials.
61	PR.	XI	"	"	Photo-recon version.
63	F.	IX	1,650	1,645	Strengthened Mk V.
63	F.	IXe	"	"	E wing fit.
63	F.	VIII	"	"	Strengthened Mk VII.

Engine	Type	Mark	Power (hp)	Weight (lb)	Notes	Engine	Type	Mark	Power (hp)	Weight (lb)	Notes
63	PR.	XI	"	"	Photo-recon version.	266	F.	XVI	1,580	1,645	American-built Packard Merlins.
63A	F.	IX	1,710	1,645	Strengthened Mk V.	70	HF.	IX	1,475	1,640	High altitude variant.
63A	F.	IXe	"	"	E wing fit.	70	HF.	IXe	"	"	High altitude variant with E wing.
63A	F.	VIII	"	"	Strengthened Mk VII.	70	HF.	VIII	"	"	High altitude variant.
63A	PR.	XI	"	"	Photo-recon version.	70	PR.	XI	"	"	Photo-recon version.
64	F.	VII	1,710	1,665	Strengthened Mk VI.	71	HF.	VII	1,475	1,650	Strengthened Mk VI.
66	LF.	IX	1,580	1,645	Low altitude variant.	77	PR.	X	1,475	1,640	Pressurised Mk XI.
66	LF.	VIII	"	"	Low altitude optimisation.						

Griffon engines: 12-cylinder, 60-degree V, liquid-cooled, 36.7 litres.

Engine	Type	Mark	Power (hp)	Weight (lb)	Notes	Engine	Type	Mark	Power (hp)	Weight (lb)	Notes
IIB	–	IV	1,735	1,980	DP845 trials.	65	FR.	XIVe	"	"	Fuselage tanks & cameras.
III	F.	XII	"	"	Mk IX strengthened for Griffon.	65	FR.	XVIII	"	"	As F.XVIII but with cameras.
IV	F.	XII	"	"	Mk IX strengthened for Griffon.	65	PR.	XIX	"	"	Modified Mk XIV aircraft.
61	F.	21	2,035	2,090	Redesigned Spitfire.	66	PR.	XIX	2,035	2,090	Full PR spec.
61	F.	22	"	"	F.21 with tear-drop canopy.	67	F.	XIV	2,375	2,090	Mk VIII strengthened for Griffon.
61	F.	24	"	"	The last variant.	67	F.	XIVe	"	"	Mk VIII strengthened for Griffon.
64	F.	21	2,375	2,090	Redesigned Spitfire.	67	F.	XVIII	"	"	Mk XIVe plus new wing.
64	F.	22	"	"	F.21 with tear-drop canopy.	67	FR.	XIV	"	"	Fuselage tanks & cameras.
65	F.	XIV	2,035	2,090	Mk VIII strengthened for Griffon.	67	FR.	XIVe	"	"	Fuselage tanks & cameras.
65	F.	XIVc	"	"	Mk VIII strengthened for Griffon.	67	FR.	XVIII	"	"	As F.XVIII but with cameras.
65	F.	XVIII	"	"	Mk XIVe plus new wing.	85	F.	22	2,045	2,090	Contra-rotating prop.
65	FR.	XIV	"	"	Fuselage tanks & cameras.						

INDEX